45.95

The Speaker

The Speaker
Leadership in the
U.S. House of Representatives

Ronald M. Peters, Jr., *Editor*

The Carl Albert Congressional
Research and Studies Center
University of Oklahoma

Congressional Quarterly Inc.
Washington, D.C.

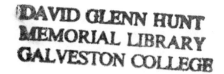

Copyright © 1994 Congressional Quarterly Inc.
1414 22nd Street, N.W., Washington, D.C. 20037

Printed and bound in the United States of America.

Cover design: Debra Naylor

Library of Congress Cataloging-in-Publication Data

The speaker : leadership in the U.S. House of Representatives /
Ronald M. Peters, Jr., editor
    p. cm.
Includes bibliographical references and index.
ISBN 0-87187-947-6
1. United States. Congress. House--Speaker. I. Peters, Ronald M.
JK1411.S64   1994
328.73'0762--dc20
94-44151
CIP

To Julian J. Rothbaum
and
Joel Jankowsky

Professors of Politics

Contents

Foreword

In 1994, I will complete thirty years of service in the House of Representatives, the last six as Speaker. I respect the institution of the House; I recognize its flaws; and I regard its role as central to American democracy. This book appears at a critical moment in the history of Congress. Public opinion and public policymaking alike offer challenges to the House greater than any it has faced in modern times.

The genius of the American political system throughout more than two centuries has been its ability to embrace change and continuously renew the structures of government. The brilliance of the constitutional design is its lack of rigidity, the fact that it is not brittle. There is room for evolution, for adjustment, amendment, and revitalization to meet new pressures and new realities.

As we again seek to improve our political institutions, we should be guided by principle and not merely party interest. In general, when reform of the House is considered, Democrats have argued for "efficiency" and Republicans have argued for "fairness." This is the natural vocabulary of the majority and minority parties. In fact, both values are important and to them we have to add a third one, accountability to the public. It is the challenge of the House to advance all three values through institutional change; it is the obligation of the Speaker to be guided by these values on a daily basis.

It is plain that the public is increasingly hostile toward government, skeptical of its leadership, and cynical about chances for genuine reform. But ours is a resilient system, one that will yield to responsible discussion, debate, and compromise. Essential to informed discussion is public education about Congress. This book offers rich insights into one of the most fundamental aspects of the House, the speakership.

The speakership that I inherited from my predecessors is a very different institution from the one that existed when I first came to Congress, perhaps as different as Congress itself is. When I arrived in Washington in 1965, there was a monopoly of power in the hands of a few senior members. Some of us thought that was wrong; eventually, through the Democratic Caucus, we sought a forum for junior members who were demanding a greater role.

Through the Caucus, we pressed for change and passed the Legislative Reorganization Act of 1970 and the Bolling-Hansen committee reforms of 1974. Committee votes were made public for the first time; the nomination process for choosing committee leadership became more often and democratic; the referral process was reformed; we established the congressional budget process; we limited individual membership on multiple committees and subcommittees, which opened up leadership positions; seniority was no longer the single, decisive factor in making assignments, and committee chairs became accountable to the majority; and every member was guaranteed an exclusive or major committee assignment. This extraordinary, unprecedented wave of reform transferred more power to individual members and enhanced virtually every member's potential impact on the legislative process.

Along the way, the speakership was changed in many respects, and strengthened in some. The most significant change was giving the Speaker greater authority in relation to the Rules Committee. The Speaker was also given the power of multiple referral of bills, providing control over legislation at both the beginning and end of the process. The budget process in effect empowered the Speaker, since it became normal for the Speaker's office to be heavily involved in the development of the budget resolutions. The right to make nominations for committee appointments was transferred to the Democratic Steering and Policy Committee, an arm of the leadership. Other techniques of leadership, such as the use of task forces, also expanded the Speaker's influence.

When I became Speaker in 1989 there was measurably more power at the disposal of the office than when I came to Congress in 1965, while the reforms for which I had fought had decentralized the House in other ways and had made members more independent. The House became more democratic, *and* the speakership became stronger.

Where does the office go from here? At times every Speaker wishes that the office had more institutional power. When a Speaker is burdened with public responsibility for events over which he has no direct line of authority, the natural reaction is to try to avoid the former or enhance the latter. But I think it would be unwise for the House to change its fundamental character in order to strengthen its central leadership. No one wants to return to the days of Cannonism described in this book. I do not believe that the Speaker in this time and circumstance ought to appoint committee chairs beyond those he presently appoints, or exercise the total authority over legislative affairs that exists in the speakerships of some state legislatures. We do not want government by fiat.

The legislative process is now more complex than in the past. Members of Congress today rightly expect that when they come to the House they will begin immediately to represent their constituencies without any diminution of their right to speak or act. While authority is still respected in the House, things are very different than under the slightly more diffuse but far more rigid tyranny of seniority that existed when I first came here as a new member.

Issues today are also more complex than was the case a generation ago. I do not mean to imply they are more significant, only that they are more difficult to deal with legislatively. This makes it hard to gather consensus. In the late 1960s, the federal government made a commitment to protect the environment, ushering in an entirely new and greatly complicated area of public policy. The civil rights questions of the 1960s went to fundamental principles— for instance, that all citizens should have the same access to public facilities and interstate travel and fully share in the right to vote. Those propositions are wholly unchallenged today. But we now face new challenges of providing opportunity and making the American experience real for people of every background and circumstance. Health care reform is just one example, and it illustrates the complexity of the challenges.

Thus, the legislative agenda inevitably reflects the complications of social and economic change as well as the shifting structures of our politics. These, in turn, are reflected in the ways we work and the character of the House as an institution.

Public disaffection for the institution of government is a result of very difficult problems that, in my view, are not a consequence of institutional failure. Our institutions need to be improved, but I do not believe that they are basically flawed. To the contrary, I find it remarkable that they have served us so well for so long.

Nor am I able to fault the character of today's members, as some do. We who are involved in the process have a sense that, despite our shortcomings, this institution and the intentions of those who serve here are much better than the public's perception of them seems to be. I am convinced that if most Americans could spend time—not just a casual visit, but real time—inside the House, going with members to committee meetings, spending the day with them, joining in the private consultations and meetings they have, Americans would come away with an enormously enhanced view of the work of the House.

Since most Americans will never have that chance, I hope that many of them will do the next best thing—read what those who closely study the Congress have written. In this book, the reader will find both in-depth history and insightful analysis of the speakership. The selection of Speakers; the Speaker's role as a party leader; the Speaker's relationship to the minority party, the budget process, foreign policy, the press, and reform—these are vital topics in understanding how the speakership, and hence the House, functions today.

I am especially pleased to recommend the chapters contributed by my three predecessors, Carl Albert, Tip O'Neill, and Jim Wright. Every Speaker owes a great deal to those who have been there before. Each of these three Speakers helped me on the path to leadership and educated me at critical steps along the way. In these pages, that education continues. Speaker O'Neill has died since he wrote his chapter, but his wisdom remains a legacy to me and to all who will follow in the speakership.

The Constitution of the United States of America puts the legislative branch of the government in first place. It is the Congress and especially the House of Representatives that must perform the truly representative function under our system of government. It is the Speaker's obligation to make the representative process work, to ensure that the House is a productive place to do the people's business. This book offers valuable lessons for citizens, members, and not least for Speakers about this powerful and challenging office. I hope that it will be read widely.

Thomas S. Foley
The Speaker
United States House of Representatives
December 1994

Contributors

Carl Albert was the 46th Speaker of the U.S. House of Representatives. Born in Bug Tussle, Oklahoma, in 1908, he was educated at the University of Oklahoma and at St. Peters College, Oxford, where he was a Rhodes Scholar. First elected to the House in 1947, he was selected as Democratic whip in 1955 and elected Democratic majority leader in 1962. Elected Speaker in 1971, he presided over the most significant House reforms in the modern era. Speaker Albert retired from the House in 1977 and lives in McAlester, Oklahoma.

Lynne P. Brown is director of government relations and serves on the adjunct faculty at New York University. Before coming to NYU she worked in Washington, D.C., on the leadership staff of Representatives John Brademas (D-Ind.) and Thomas S. Foley (D-Wash.). She has written numerous articles on leadership in Congress and is coauthor of *The Politics of Education: Conflict and Consensus on Capitol Hill* (1987).

William F. Connelly, Jr., is associate professor of politics at Washington and Lee University in Lexington, Virginia. He recently coauthored with John J. Pitney, Jr., *Congress' Permanent Minority? Republicans in the U.S. House* (1994). He was an American Political Science Association congressional fellow in 1985-1986 and a guest scholar at the Brookings Institution during 1991-1992.

Roger H. Davidson is professor of government and politics at the University of Maryland and coeditor of *The Encyclopedia of the United States Congress* (1995). He has served on House and Senate staffs studying committee reorganization and as senior specialist in American national government and public administration at the Congressional Research Service, U.S. Library of Congress. Among his books on Congress and national policy making are *The Postreform Congress* (1992) and (with Walter J. Oleszek) *Congress and Its Mem-*

bers (4th ed., CQ Press, 1994). He specializes in legislative innovation and workload and is a fellow of the National Academy of Public Administration.

Joe S. Foote is dean of the College of Mass Communication and Media Arts at Southern Illinois University at Carbondale. Foote was administrative assistant to Rep. Dave McCurdy (D-Okla.) and press secretary to House Speaker Carl Albert. He is author of *Television Access and Political Power: The Networks, the Presidency, and the "Loyal Opposition"* (1990). He is currently working on a book concerning global news media.

Thomas P. "Tip" O'Neill, Jr., was the 47th Speaker of the U.S. House of Representatives. Born in Cambridge, Massachusetts, in 1912, he was educated at Boston College. In 1936 he was elected to the Massachusetts House and in 1948 became its first Democratic speaker. In 1952 he was elected to the U.S. House seat vacated by John F. Kennedy. Appointed to the Rules Committee by Speaker Sam Rayburn in 1955, he served there until his appointment as Democratic whip in 1971. He was elected majority leader in 1973 and Speaker in 1977. Tip O'Neill served as Speaker for ten years, the longest continuous period of service in the history of the office and second only to Speaker Rayburn in total time of service. Speaker O'Neill retired in 1987 and passed away in 1994 just after completing his chapter for this book.

Daniel J. Palazzolo teaches political science at the University of Richmond. He is author of *The Speaker and the Budget: Leadership in the Post-Reform House of Representatives* and several articles on congressional leadership and budget policy making. He is currently working on a study of budget politics in the states.

Robert L. Peabody is professor of political science at Johns Hopkins University. He has been a student of Congress for several decades. His major book is *Leadership in Congress* (1976).

Ronald M. Peters, Jr., is director and curator of the Carl Albert Congressional Research and Studies Center and chair of the Department of Political Science at the University of Oklahoma. He is author of *The American Speakership: The Office in Historical Perspective* (1990) and *The Massachusetts Constitution of 1780: A Social Compact* (1978). He is editor of *The Next Generation: Dialogue Between Leaders and Students* (1992) and coeditor of *The Atomistic Congress: An Interpretation of Congressional Change* (1992).

John J. Pitney, Jr., is associate professor of government at Claremont Mc-Kenna College. He has held several positions in Washington, including congressional fellow of the American Political Science Association. He has written a number of essays on Congress, campaign strategy, and the Republican Party. He is coauthor of *Congress' Permanent Minority? Republicans in the U.S. House* (1994).

Barbara Sinclair is professor of political science at the University of California, Riverside. Her publications on the U.S. Congress include *Legislators, Leaders and Lawmaking: The U.S. House of Representatives in the Post-Reform Era* (1995), *The Transformation of the U.S. Senate* (1989), *Majority Leadership in the U.S. House* (1983), and *Congressional Realignment* (1982). She served as an APSA congressional fellow in the office of the House majority leader in 1978-1979 and was a participant-observer in the office of the Speaker in 1987-1988.

Steven S. Smith is professor of political science at the University of Minnesota. He is author of *The American Congress* (1995), and coauthor of *Call to Order: Floor Politics in the House and Senate* (1989), *Managing Uncertainty in the House of Representatives* (1988), and *Committees in Congress* (CQ Press, 1984, 1990). He is writing books on the Senate filibuster, Senate party leadership, and Russian parliamentary institutions.

Mark Watts is a Ph.D. candidate at the University of Minnesota. His dissertation concerns media coverage of Congress.

Jim Wright was the 48th Speaker of the U.S. House of Representatives. Born in 1922, he spent much of his childhood in Weatherford, Texas. After serving in World War II, he became mayor of Weatherford. He was elected to the U.S. House in 1954 and served for many years on the House Public Works and Transportation Committee. In 1977, he was elected Democratic majority leader and served in that role during Thomas P. "Tip" O'Neill's tenure as House Speaker. Elected Speaker in 1987, Wright led the House to a remarkably productive legislative record in the 100th Congress. Speaker Wright resigned from Congress in 1989. He resides in Fort Worth, Texas, where he teaches a course in political science at Texas Christian University. He is currently preparing a manuscript that will chronicle his service with eight American presidents—Eisenhower through Bush.

Acknowledgments

This book had its genesis in plans for a symposium on the speakership which was to have been held on the Norman campus of the University of Oklahoma. The sponsors of the symposium are the Carl Albert Center, the College of Continuing Education, and the Political Communication Center of the University of Oklahoma. I am indebted to Mark Ashton, Leroy Bridges, Ken Sue Doerfel, Cindy Eckart, Lynda Kaid, Julian Kanter, Linda Norton, Jim Pappas, and LaDonna Sullivan for their efforts in planning. Thanks also go to Loise Washington of Speaker Albert's office.

The scholars who have contributed to this book are among the most careful students of the speakership. Some are old friends and acquaintances while others are new-found friends and acquaintances. I want to thank all of them for their timely and excellent work in preparing their respective chapters.

I am especially grateful to Speakers Albert, O'Neill, and Wright for their contributions. The inclusion of work by these former Speakers adds a rare dimension to this book. My debts to Speaker Albert are uncountable and they continue to accrue. Speaker Wright took an early and active role in planning the symposium, and without his active participation this book would not have been undertaken. Since completing his chapter, Speaker O'Neill has passed away. He will be missed by all Americans. Speaker Foley took time from the pressures of office to contribute a substantive foreword that places today's speakership in context. I want to thank Danney Goble and Gary Hymel for their assistance to Speakers Albert and O'Neill, respectively.

The photograph of the four Speakers is believed to be the only one to include four Speakers of the House in one photograph. I am indebted to Joel Jankowsky for making it available.

LaDonna Sullivan lent her great skill to the preparation of the final manuscript, making both substantive and stylistic suggestions. If I do anything well at the Carl Albert Center, it is typically as a result of her assistance. I am grateful to my acquisitions editor, Jeanne Ferris, editorial assistant Megan Davis, and copyeditor Debbie Hardin. Thanks also to Alexa Selph for preparing the index.

Finally, thanks to Glenda, and to John and Julie—the speakers of our house.

From left: Carl Albert, Thomas P. "Tip" O'Neill, Jim Wright, and Tom Foley. This photograph was taken at the Democratic National Convention in 1992 through the efforts of Joel Jankowsky, former aide to Speaker Carl Albert, and now a Washington, D.C., attorney.

1 The History and Character of the Speakership

Ronald M. Peters, Jr.

Through its history, two basic outlooks have been expressed on the fundamental character of the U.S. House of Representatives. One is an impression of the House as a collection of individual members loosely aggregated into party collectives. On this view, the main purpose of the House's rules and procedures should be to ensure fairness to these members and the parties with which they are associated. The other impression is of the House divided between majority and minority parties, with the majority party having the responsibility to govern. During most of the history of the House since the inception of the two-party system in 1860, the Republicans have favored the latter or the party view and the Democrats have favored the former or the representative view. However, during the past two decades the parties have switched positions—the Democrats of late have favored the party view and the Republicans have favored the representative view.

This switch indicates that the division in outlook is caused by factors that go beyond party philosophy. It has much to do with the composition of the parties and the relative situation of the majority and minority. The Democrats argued the representative view in part because their party's caucus was deeply divided along geographic and ideological lines. Since they did not have a cohesive majority, they could not stand on the principle of party governance, even when in the majority. This began to change after the civil rights revolution of the 1960s, as more and more white southerners moved to the Republican party. When southern Democratic constituencies began to be more like northern Democratic constituencies, the party began to govern like a party. The Republicans, always more cohesive, have not been in the majority since 1954. They have shifted from the party governance view to the representative view because they have not had the chance to govern for more than forty years.

The speakership of the House is differently conceived on these two outlooks. As the constitutionally defined presiding officer of the House, the Speaker has the obligation to ensure the fairness and efficiency of the House's deliberative process. As the leader of the House's majority party, the Speaker has the obligation to build coalitions capable of enacting party legislation and to protect majority party interests against tactics employed by the minority. In the position of Speaker of the House, the two views of the speakership come together and define a uniquely American political office.

This book provides an analysis and evaluation of several aspects of the speakership as it functions today. Contributors are among the leading scholars of the speakership and the House. Chapters trace the selection of Speakers (by Lynne P. Brown and Robert L. Peabody); the role of the Speaker as the leader of the majority party (by Barbara Sinclair); in relationship to the minority party, (by John J. Pitney, Jr., and William F. Connelly, Jr.); and in the budget process (by Daniel J. Palazzolo); in foreign policy (by Steven S. Smith and Mark Watts); to the media (by Joe S. Foote); and in relationship to institutional change (by Roger H. Davidson). The book is particularly enhanced by chapters written by three former Speakers of the House—Carl Albert, Tip O'Neill, and Jim Wright. Their unique perspectives capture the evolution of the office from the point of view of those who have known it best.

This chapter traces the main patterns in the evolution of the speakership since 1789, provides a generic examination of it, and offers a framework within which to consider the office. In a concluding chapter the office is reconsidered in light of the analysis provided by the other authors.

The Evolution of the Speakership

The American speakership is more complicated than any other. This is true of the state speakerships but it is especially true of the federal speakership. Other speakerships cover the spectrum from the nonpartisan models of Great Britain and Canada to the independent power that sometimes has been exemplified in revolutionary regimes such as that of Iran. Parliamentary regimes incline toward impartial speakerships, while presidential regimes foster more independence. But the form of the regime is not the only or the dispositive variable. In Japan, for example, the Speaker of the Diet served the interests of the Liberal Democratic party during much of the postwar period. Since 1973 the Japanese Speaker has become more of a neutral arbiter as a result of the development of a true multiparty system.[1] Much depends on political and cultural circumstances unique to the country and the period of its history.

The American speakership evolved initially under circumstances that fostered independence. In the seventeenth and eighteenth centuries, the Speakers of the colonial assemblies emerged as leaders of colonial opposition to the policies of royal governors. Some were long serving and wielded great power. In Virginia, for example, Speaker John Robinson served for more than twenty-five years and held a virtual lock on legislation, including control of the governor's salary. For a time he also served as the colony's treasurer. It is no coincidence that the speakership of the British House of Commons was also quite partisan during this period, as the nature of the British regime itself underwent a radical transformation.

By the convening of the Constitutional Convention in 1787, Americans had no experience with a truly impartial speakership. During the interregnum under the Articles of Confederation, the state Speakers typically represented political parties or factions. They were politically ambitious and aimed for other offices at the state or federal levels. They surely did not remove themselves from politics. It may come as a surprise that during the first Congress there was some degree of ambivalence about the role the Speaker should play.

The Constitution mentions four specific offices: president, vice president, Speaker, and chief justice of the United States. There was a great deal of power and prestige to these constitutionally defined offices. It was inevitable that the large states would squabble over the allocation of these constitutional plums. Virginia, with George Washington, won the presidency. Massachusetts garnered the vice presidency. New York landed the chief justiceship. This left Pennsylvania out in the cold, and its representatives caucused to demand the speakership. Frederick A. C. Muhlenberg was their choice and became the first Speaker. In a system without well-defined parties, Muhlenberg had some difficulty figuring out his proper role. The dignity of the office demanded that he stand aloof from the raw partisanship. His duty as presiding officer implied an obligation of fairness to members. Yet as a representative of a district, he obviously had political obligations as well. The challenge was in balancing the various demands that seemed embedded in the very character of the office.

The challenge of obtaining that balance has remained central to the speakership during its entire history. There are four main periods in the evolution of the speakership, which I have defined in other works: the parliamentary era, the partisan era, the feudal era, and the democratic era.[2] The period prior to the Civil War, which I have called the "parliamentary era" was characterized by an infirm constitutional order and an unstable party system. During this era Speakers could not often rely on stable partisan majorities and frequently faced severe challenges to parliamentary order and the orderly processes of representative government. Henry Clay of Kentucky was the only strong

Speaker of the era. Clay established a firm grip on the House, used the office to advance policies and to further his own presidential ambitions, and established the office as a force in the political system. Other Speakers, such as Nathaniel Macon of Virginia during the Jefferson administration and Andrew Stevenson of Tennessee during the Jackson administration, worked effectively on behalf of their party's president. Occasionally a Speaker such as James K. Polk (later elected governor of Tennessee and then president of the United States) seemed to manage the shoals of office better than did others. Yet during the turmoil of the 1840s it was all that Polk could do to maintain a semblance of order in a House that was badly divided by party, faction, and region. Still, no one then or since regards this period as having witnessed the emergence of a strong institutional speakership.

By contrast, the fifty-year period dating from the Civil War, which I have dubbed the "partisan era," witnessed the emergence of a strong two-party system in which the speakership eventually emerged as the strongest of partisan political offices, holding firm institutional control over the House. There can be little doubt that the solidity of the party system itself was the main factor influencing the development of an institutionally powerful speakership, but the relative weakness of the presidency in relation to the Congress, as well as the temperament of some of the Speakers of this period, also had significant effects. Any roster of the most notable Speakers of the House would include several of this period. Republicans James G. Blaine of Maine, Thomas Brackett Reed of Maine, and Joseph G. Cannon of Illinois were giants in the House. Democrats Samuel J. Randall of Pennsylvania, John G. Carlisle of Kentucky, and Charles F. Crisp of Georgia were also strong figures, although presiding over less cohesive partisan majorities. This period in the evolution of the speakership culminated in "Cannonism," the virtual absolute control of the House agenda by Speaker Cannon and his appointed Rules Committee, against which the House eventually revolted in 1910.

The revolt against Cannon precipitated the emergence of the third era in the history of the speakership, which I call the "feudal era." This era took root during the second decade of the twentieth century at a time when senior members were revered and given power to the point that the committee system and the senior members who headed it dominated the House. This tendency toward the dominance of senior members via the committee system was most pronounced in the Democratic party and especially its southern wing. After 1933, when the Democrats became the governing majority in the House (the Republicans elected majorities only twice after 1928), the feudal era was firmly ensconced. This period lasted until the reform movement of the 1960s and 1970s, discussed in detail in Chapter 8. There were two strong Speakers during this period. Nicholas Longworth of Ohio led Republican-controlled Houses in the late 1920s, when party governance was still possible, and provided effective leadership of House Republicans. Sam Rayburn of Texas, the House's longest-serving Speaker, presided over an awkward coalition of southern conservative and northern liberal Democrats for the better part of two decades. Rayburn became an icon by working through the committee system rather than by challenging its power.

It was only on Rayburn's death in 1961 that the most recent epoch in the history of the speakership began, which I have labeled the "democratic era." Liberals in the House Democratic Caucus chafed under the control of southern conservatives, who dominated the committee system and worked with Republicans on the floor in the "conservative coalition" to control legislation. The last political battle of Rayburn's life occurred in 1961 as he led the fight to break the Rules Committee free from conservative coalition control. As more and more liberals were elected through the decade of the 1960s, the balance of power shifted toward them and the institutional reforms they favored. Beginning with the Legislative Reform Act of 1970 and the House Democratic Caucus reforms of the early 1970s, a new system of internal governance emerged that was essentially democratic but unfortunately schizophrenic. On the one hand, power was widely diffused at the committee and subcommittee levels and on the floor where individual members gathered in policy-specific coalitions, but on the other hand, the institutions of central party leadership were strengthened.

During the parliamentary period, there was no one person or one party in charge of the House; during the partisan era, the Speaker was in firm control; during the feudal epoch, the committees and their chairs were dominant; in the new democratic era the decentralized policy-making system has made it necessary for the Speaker to work continually to generate legislative majorities for a variety of policy issues. No single institutional power controls the House and no majority has coalesced to provide stability; instead, issue-specific majorities have to be generated by extensive and complicated leadership management of the House. The task of the Speakers is to translate their partisan majority into legislative majorities. It is this most recent version of the speakership that we will examine in this book.

Throughout its evolution, even as the speakership has undergone these various transformations, its fundamental character has not mutated. Indeed, in some respects it has remained remarkably the same. The demands on the speakership come from our system of governance. The circumstances in which those demands are expressed have changed over time, but their central character has not. The Speaker now, as in the past, is a presiding officer, a party leader, a representative of a constituency, and a constitutional officer obligated to do what can and should be done so that the government functions on behalf of the American people.

The Character of the Speakership

The Constitution does not require that the Speaker be a member of the House, but no nonmember has ever been considered for the post. Should a transformation of American political culture lead to a demand for a nonpartisan Speaker, then perhaps the House would have to look beyond its membership for candidates. As it now stands, however, the Speaker will be a member of the House and therefore will always have a constituency to represent. Should the American political system produce multiple competitive parties, then perhaps the Speaker would emerge as a coalition candidate rather than as the leader of a partisan majority. But until such a change happens, the Speaker will always be a party leader. Should the Constitution be amended to eliminate bicameralism and the separation of powers, thus moving in the direction of parliamentary government, then the speakership might be driven in the direction of nonpartisanship or merge into a new kind of ministerial role. But until that happens, the speakership will remain a leading position in a system of constitutionally separated powers.

It is these features of the system that have shaped the speakership over time. The Speaker is at the same time the presiding officer of the House, the leader of a party, the representative of a district, and an ambitious politician. In recent times, the Speaker has also become the chief administrator of a large and complex organization and a public personality who is often the focus of media attention. How do these various elements of the speakership merge to produce a unique American hybrid? Let us consider this question by tracing the path to the speakership and the circumstances in which speakers must govern today.

Recent Speakers typically have come into office after long service in the House. (In Chapter 2 Lynne P. Brown and Robert L. Peabody trace patterns of leadership succession.) The average prior service of the last four Speakers (Albert, O'Neill, Wright, and Tom Foley) is 25.5 years. This lengthy tenure has several typical effects. First, it has ensured that persons elected to the speakership will have been "men of the House" (to paraphrase the title of Speaker O'Neill's autobiography). This means that they will have been socialized into the norms and folkways of the House and will have established many enduring friendships as well as a few adversarial relationships with other important members. Second, Speakers have typically served in other leadership capacities, such as committee chairs or in other leadership positions. Third, Speakers have very rarely been major legislators during their careers. Instead, they have more commonly tended to serve as apprentice leaders (as task force chair, whip, caucus chair, majority leader, or some combination of these positions). Fourth, most Speakers have, by the time of their elections as Speaker, established safe House seats. Speakers Wright and Foley experienced close elections during the course of their careers, but not during or immediately preceding their services as Speaker. Fifth, recent Speakers have all served as their parties' majority leaders and were chosen in uncontested party elections; therefore, their rises to the speakership were "automatic" and the real battle for the leadership of their parties had taken place some years previously when they won election as majority leaders. The Democrats have preferred stability in leadership succession.

Thus, the Speaker is likely to be a seasoned legislator from a safe district with prior service in party leadership and an established network of political allies. A Speaker is very likely to be a person who is well established in the House and experienced in party leadership. As indicated previously, the leadership ladder is a training ground for Speakers, but no period of apprenticeship suffices. Speakers soon discover that the office is much more complicated than they had anticipated. In Chapter 11, Speaker Wright, who had served as majority leader for ten years before becoming Speaker, notes how much greater are the demands of the speakership.

The Business of the Speakership

The Speaker is the chief parliamentary officer of the House, responsible for the day-to-day management of its business. While the party's majority leader does the daily tasks of scheduling legislation, it is the Speaker who must ensure that the rules and procedures of the House are fully and fairly administered. With the support of the House parliamentarian, the clerk of the House, the sergeant at arms, and the doorkeeper, the Speaker's office must manage a very complicated organizational and legislative process. This means that the Speaker's office is beset on a regular basis by requests, inquiries, demands, and obligations that only it can meet. While a staff and organizational infrastructure facilitates the Speaker's tasks, the speaker alone is responsible for the orderly conduct of business.

Closely associated with the role as chief parliamentary officer is that of chief administrator. Some administrative tasks are the direct product of the Speaker's parliamentary role. These include maintaining the records of the House, working with the Senate and executive branch in processing legislation, and making numerous appointments to boards, commissions, and special committees. Other tasks are purely administrative, a result of the fact that the House is a large and complex organization. The Speaker is responsible for assigning office space and for security on the House side of the Capitol. He authorizes member travel on official business in some instances. Until recently, he was directly accountable for the management of the House post office, House bank, and House restaurant. Because of recent problems in these three areas, the House has created a professional staff position of director of nonlegislative and financial services, who is appointed by the Speaker, the majority leader, and minority leader, but answers to the Speaker alone.

While these administrative tasks may seem mundane, they can occupy a significant amount of time, involve the expenditure of political capital, and bring political trouble for a Speaker who is inattentive. When Carl Albert was Speaker during the early 1970s, requests to his office included one to permit the makers of Mercury automobiles to videotape an advertisement with a live cougar on the steps of the Capitol. He also received a complaint by one member that he was being driven from his House office by an invasion of cockroaches. On one occasion two senior members came to near blows over a prized parking spot. On another, a senior member of the House was accused of using House office space for assignations. The Speaker, then, must be a zoologist, an entomologist, a referee, and a judge. These tasks are onerous and sometimes repugnant to Speakers, even though they are otherwise proud to hold the office. Once in late 1970, Rep. Morris Udall (D-Ariz) wandered into the majority leader's office and found Carl Albert sitting on some boxes as he prepared to move into the Speaker's offices. "Carl," said Udall, "you don't look too happy today." "Space," Albert replied as he gazed around at the boxes. "Now I've got to deal with space!"

Strategies of Leadership

The first formal task Speakers undertake are their inaugural statements. These have ranged from the very terse to the decidedly verbose; they provide an opportunity for the Speaker to state legislative goals and articulate his approach to office. The members will have varying expectations of the Speaker. The members on the minority side want most of all a Speaker who will be fair and impartial in conducting the business of the House. At the beginning of every Congress, leaders on both sides usually pay lip service to comity and bipartisan harmony. The Speaker encounters a different set of expectations from the members of the majority party, however. These members want a leader who will protect their electoral interests and provide leadership for party policy positions. Speakers are expected to strike an appropriate balance between these conflicting demands. How they do so will depend on contextual factors that are unique to each speakership.

Speaker Rayburn, for example, led a Democratic party that was deeply divided between its southern conservative and northern liberal wings. The House at that time was dominated by a strong committee system led largely by southern conservatives. Rayburn supported the national program of the Democratic party, but also had strong southern roots. He needed to straddle the divide between the party's northern and southern factions. In order to do so, he found it necessary to be very selective in defining leadership positions, and to rely occasionally on Republican votes. As a consequence, his good relationship with Republican leader Joseph W. Martin, Jr., of Massachusetts was a product of both temperament and the demands of practical politics. By contrast, Speaker Wright, another Texan, found himself differently situated and of a different temperament. Wright's Democratic party was more cohesive and, on the whole, more liberal than Rayburn's. At the same time, the Republicans were also more cohesive and more ideologically conservative. Rayburn and Senate Majority Leader Lyndon Johnson of Texas had found it possible to work with the relatively pragmatic Dwight Eisenhower, but Wright was not able to work with the more dogmatic Ronald Reagan. As a result, Wright had to use the powers of his office to build winning coalitions within the Democratic party, much to the distress of Republicans, as noted by John J. Pitney, Jr., and William F. Connelly, Jr., in Chapter 4.

The Speaker must make a calculation about the best strategy of leadership available. This will depend on the relation in which he stands to the majority party membership, the attitude of the minority, his relationship with the president, and his personal disposition and goals. The choice of strategic approach comes somewhat naturally from the Speaker's prior experience, commitments, and initial coalition, but the approach must be adapted to the actual circumstances in which he is called to lead. Since all of these things vary from Speaker to Speaker, no Speaker is typical.

Defining the Party Program

While the speakership today is not the bastion of party control it was at the beginning of the twentieth century, it is nonetheless a vital organ of party leadership. It has been common in recent years for Speakers to define the main legislative components of a party program. The specific content of the legislation will depend on several factors. Usually there are several major legislative items pending, carried over from the preceding Congress. These may be ready for early floor consideration. Sometimes the election has defined main issues that the Congress must address. The Speaker may have specific legislative objectives. In the 92nd Congress, Speaker Albert defined legislation on jobs, agriculture, and the environment as components of the party program. In the 95th Congress, Speaker O'Neill moved President Jimmy Carter's energy bill through the House in six months as a party program bill. In the 100th Congress, Speaker Wright moved a raft of legislation that addressed transportation, health, welfare, and drugs to enactment, in some instances despite presidential vetoes. In general, Speakers will accept policy leadership from presidents of their own party. When the presidency is held by the opposition, Speakers assume a special role in defining party issues. In this instance, Speakers will make an early determination about their stands relative to the program of the president and the demands of the legislative party.

In some cases bipartisan cooperation is possible and desirable. Some issues cut across party lines, and some national emergencies transcend partisan politics. Sometimes a majority coalition can only be achieved with bipartisan support. For this reason, as well as because of a general concern for fairness, Speakers maintain lines of communication to the minority leadership. Relationships between Speakers and minority leaders have differed as a result of personality and context. Speakers Rayburn and Martin led their respective parties for almost two decades and had a very close cooperative relationship. Speaker Rayburn packed the Rules Committee in 1961 so that John F. Kennedy's program could reach the House floor. Rayburn's narrow margin of victory was provided by New England Republicans led by his old friend Joe Martin. While subsequent Speaker-minority leader relationships were not as close as that between Rayburn and Martin, most have been cordial. Republican leader Robert Michel of Illinois served longer in the House minority than any other member in its history; yet he used to lead members in singing "Happy Birthday" in his rich baritone voice to Speaker O'Neill. Speakers must, then, define their attitudes toward the minority party and its leadership. In the highly partisan House environment of the 1980s and 1990s, every concession to the Republicans could be questioned by Democrats, and every effort to preserve and protect Democratic seats could be challenged by Republicans. Speakers who insult the minority on one issue may find themselves in need of minority votes on another. Yet Speakers who befriend the minority too often may appear weak and vacillating to members on their side of the aisle. Good personal relations can take the edge off of partisan conflict, but they cannot eliminate it entirely.

The Committee System

The Speaker is in the middle of a very complex legislative organization, the backbone of which is the committee system. Since political scientist Woodrow Wilson first described the Congress in 1885 as a collection of committee baronies, it has been widely accepted that the work of the Congress is done in its committees. At the helms of those separate ships sit committee chairs who have a great deal of independent power in the House. During the House's feudal era, the committee chairs were hegemonic in their domains. In the post-reform House the power of these committee chairs has been constrained, but is still often formidable.

Speakers must reckon their relationships with the committee chairs. In doing so they will discover that their relationships with committee chairs will vary according to the circumstances of the committee and the character of the chair. The Rules and Budget Committees, for example, are now basically arms of the leadership and typically chaired by a member who supports the Speaker. The Energy and Commerce and Ways and Means Committees, by contrast, are large and independent fiefdoms that together control most of the legislative jurisdiction of the House. Their chairs are always power players in the House and sometimes are at odds with the leadership. In the 1980s and 1990s, the Energy and Commerce Committee has been headed by John Dingell (D-Mich.) and the Ways and Means Committee has been led by Dan Rostenkowski (D-Ill.). Both of these members are strong willed and have enjoyed strong constituencies in the House. Their relationship to the speakership has varied by personality and issue, but each has been a force with which to be reckoned. Other committee chairs enjoy varying degrees of power and autonomy. In some instances, the work of a committee may be largely irrelevant to the Speaker's legislative goals. Occasionally, a committee becomes relevant because it has jurisdiction over a bill or issue that becomes important. Speakers must array their relationships to the committee chairs like pins on a map. The big pins might connect the Speaker to the committee chairs, but lying around and below them are the threads that tie the Speaker to the members of the committees. The Speaker's relationship to House committees is complex and overlaps with the Speaker's coalition in the majority party caucus. These relationships are the ties that bind, but they can be broken by the force of political events.

External Forces

Thus far we have viewed the Speaker in relationship to the internal dynamics of the House, but the House is merely a solar system in a larger universe. Today the press of events demands that the Speaker pay close attention to the external environment of the House. The main forces in that external environment are the public at large, the media, the Senate, and the presidency.

Speakers have the best lines of communication to the American public—435 members of the House. The constitutional founders aimed to ensure that the House would hold tight to its constituencies, and they succeeded beyond their most optimistic expectations. Speakers soon learn from members the issues important to the American public. But this representational avenue is supplemented now in two other main ways. The first is through direct campaigning. The obligation of Speakers to canvass on behalf of their party's members extends back well into the 1800s. Today that burden is shared with the party majority leader. Speakers will, by the time they assume office, have traveled to perhaps a majority of the districts in the country on behalf of party incumbents and challengers. Speakers must balance their politicking with other demands on their time, of course, but a sitting Speaker will still travel widely on behalf of members, coming to know their many constituencies in the process.

These representational and electoral links to the public are now supplemented by scientific techniques. Modern presidents typically employ full-time pollsters to track public opinions. The information that the professional opinion trackers provide is used to plan campaign strategies, legislative strategies, and media management. During the Reagan and Bush administrations, Speakers O'Neill, Wright, and Foley found it necessary to develop a parallel capacity. Speakers now commonly draw on the advice of professional pollsters, and will from time to time commission polls of their own to better track public opinion in order to develop more effective legislative and public relations strategies.

The Speaker's access to the public is affected by members and by the media. In following longstanding precedent, the Speaker conducts a fifteen-minute daily press conference when the House is in session, and will hold longer press conferences periodically to announce major legislation, to respond to issues of the day, and to stake out a political or policy position. Since Speaker Albert, all Speakers have employed full-time press secretaries or other staff members operating in that capacity. Speaker Rayburn used to say that a Speaker who could not feel the mood of the House was lost. That remains true today; however, the Speaker will be unlikely to rely too heavily on such feelings. And unlike Rayburn, Speakers today will often face the necessity of managing the news rather than merely reading it in a newspaper.

Unlike the spin-control events at the White House, however, the Speaker will find it very difficult to shape the image of the House and its legislative activities, or the events and issues of the day. Although media interest in the speakership has increased dramatically over the past two decades, it still does not rival that which comes in natural course to the presidency. Speakers have to develop an approach to the media, taking into account their own personalities and styles, the opportunities afforded to them by circumstance, the expectations of their members, and the demands of the moment. Speaker O'Neill, for example, was able to take advantage of the fact that the House alone was controlled by the Democrats in the early 1980s to establish a very high media profile. Speaker Wright reached out to the media but expressed frustration because negative attention seemed to outweigh his best efforts (see Chapter 11).

Except for the members of the House and the Speakers' own constituents at home, the most significant players for Speakers will be the president and the members of the Senate. The president, whether of the same or opposing party, will have much to say about the House agenda. The president will shape considerably the climate of public opinion within which the House must do its work. If the president is of the same party as the Speaker, the president will expect the Speaker to help pass legislation. Speakers have generally acknowledged their obligations to support a president of their own party unless their consciences or district stand in strong opposition. If the president is of the opposing party, the Speaker will inherit an obligation to develop an opposition legislative program while at the same time working with the administration in order to ensure that the orderly processes of government continues. In foreign policy, Speakers have often supported presidents of the opposite party. However, this norm seems to have weakened considerably since the Vietnam War.

The Speaker in all likelihood will view the Senate about the same way that the House in general does—cautiously. In the history of the American republic, no tension has been more consistent than that between the House and the Senate. From the House point of view, senators are often prima donnas; the Senate is an incubator of presidential ambition but not of presidents. After all, how many sitting senators have been elected president? [3] This caricature is something in which some members of the House so deeply believe that they seem to think it their obligation to move over to the Senate in order to clean it up. When they get there, they become strangely corrupted by the place and soon start their own exploratory campaigns for the White House. Speakers have a better balanced view of the Senate than the other members of the House because they bear the constitutional responsibility of conducting the House's relations with the Senate and of standing up for the House's prerogatives as a coequal body. This obligation forces the Speaker to recognize that the Senate is the other coequal body and to respect its prerogatives. The relationship between the Speaker and the Senate and its leadership will, then, be fundamentally defined by the constitutional roles of the two bodies, but also by the Speaker's personal relationships with the Senate leaders. This may or may not follow party lines. Speaker O'Neill, for example, was often said to have a better relationship with Republican leader Howard Baker than with Democratic leader Robert Byrd. There may have been a personal element in this, but as importantly, O'Neill's relationships were with the leader who was responsible for the Senate's work, the Republican majority leader, and not with Senator Byrd, the Democratic minority leader.

A Framework for Understanding the Speakership

This overview of the history and character of the speakership enables us to develop a framework of the office that may help us to consider the evidence presented in this book. The framework is built around four basic questions that probe the core of any speakership.

1. How is the Speaker identified as a product of:
   - character,
   - background and life experience,
   - socialization into the peculiar culture of the House,
   - a political constituency, and
   - a particular legislative coalition?

2. In what situation does the Speaker serve the:
   - historical period,

- character of the political system,
- institutional rules and norms of the House,
- partisan control of the government (united or divided), and
- current political and policy situation?

3. What are the priorities of the speakership:
   - personally,
   - legislatively, and
   - politically?

4. What are the strategies of the Speaker
   - legislatively (coalition building),
   - publicly (enhancing the Speaker's personal image and that of the House), and
   - in dealing with the home constituency?

These questions help define the tasks of any Speaker and hence the nature of the speakership itself.

As our historical overview and analysis of the character of the speakership suggest, the essence of the office involves elements of continuity and change. A Speaker can control some things but not others. Speakers cannot easily change the political system, the norms of the House, nor their own political coalitions. It is probably too much to expect Speakers to change character very much as well. However, Speakers can adapt their goals and strategies to the circumstances in which they find themselves. This is the art of being Speaker.

It is an art by virtue of both method and substance. The techniques of art can be taught, but artistic creativity cannot. Nor can artistic vision be reduced to a formula. As the chapters in this book abundantly demonstrate, the techniques of House leadership have become finely honed in the past two decades. Any Speaker coming to office today will have ready-made machinery of party governance. This is as true of the Republicans as of the Democrats. However, it is one thing to have the car, another to know how to drive it, and still another to know where to go.

A theory of the speakership must address the main question that every Speaker must ask: what should be the goals of the Speaker? Recent Speakers have been described as institutional facilitators (Albert), party voices (O'Neill), policy initiators (Wright), and policy facilitators (Foley). Should a Speaker's main goal be fairness to members, preserving his or her own office and reputation, preserving the reputation of the House, making public policy, or electing the next president? Recent Speakers have had each of these goals in view, but none has been able to attain all of them—they are sometimes irreconcilable. So how should Speakers decide what their goals should be?

Theory fails us, in part because more than one theory applies and in part because it is not we who are asked to make the decisions. Machiavelli once wrote a primer for princes, but he was never a prince. A prince smart enough to take the "cold-faced Florentine's"[4] advice might perhaps have been smart enough to have figured it all out for himself. The essence of leadership lies in the ability to assess the possibilities offered by political office in order to chart a career path as well as a course of action. I have given a good deal of thought to the speakership of the House and to those who have come to fill it. As I consider each case, I am most struck by the thought that must also strike them: they made it to the top. They did so not merely by Fortuna, the advice of others, or the force of arms, as Machiavelli might suggest;[5] they did it by understanding themselves, the House, and the opportunities presented.

So one answer to the question of what goals Speakers should seek is that they must apply the same intelligence that brought them to the speakership to the obligation to fill it. They, not we, must decide what the office and the circumstances demand. We Machiavellis can only offer some things for them to keep in mind. Among those that our theoretical framework suggests, three seem most salient.

First, a Speaker in a legislative body must be a *Speaker*. The Speaker has an obligation to ensure that the conditions of deliberative governance prevail. This normally will entail a balancing of obligations to majority preference and minority rights.

Second, a Speaker today must bear a special responsibility for the institutional health of the House. This will involve considerations of legislative and administrative efficiency, public image, and relationships with external entities. The Speaker must weigh the obligation to organizational leadership.

Third, the Speaker has an obligation to effective governance in the broadest sense. Sometimes circumstances will elevate him to national prominence while at other times he may operate in the shadow of the presidency or of the House itself. But he cannot escape the constitutional obligation to ensure that the needs of the country are met by its political institutions.

Other goals that a Speaker might have—to win elections, to enact favored policies, to shine in the media, to serve constituents, to make friends, to avoid conflict—ought to be subservient to these main obligations. Precisely how a Speaker might accomplish the main obligations of office or any of its lesser aims is, however, something that only the Speaker of the moment can determine. We may point to the nature of the office and the choices that it poses, but we cannot provide the answers to the main questions that Speakers must ask. This they must do themselves, and in doing so, they will confront the challenges of their office and of their time.

Notes

1. Ellis S. Krauss, "Conflict in the Diet: Toward Conflict Management in Parliamentary Politics," in *Conflict in Japan,* ed. Ellis S. Krauss, et al. (Honolulu: University of Hawaii Press, 1984), 243-293 at 266ff.

2. Ronald M. Peters, Jr., *The American Speakership: The Office in Historical Perspective* (Baltimore: Johns Hopkins University Press, 1990).

3. Two. Warren G. Harding and John F. Kennedy were elected president while serving as senator. Two others, Harry S. Truman and Lyndon B. Johnson reached the White House from the Senate via the vice presidency. See Robert C. Byrd, *The Senate: Historical Statistics, 1789-1992* (Washington, D.C.: U.S. Government Printing Office, 1993), 446-447.

4. Robert Penn Warren, *All the King's Men* (New York: Harcourt Brace Jovanovich, 1974), 393. Machiavelli, of course, thought that he knew more than any prince; but it was he, not they, who was put to pasture.

5. Machiavelli, *The Prince* (New York: Norton, 1977), 16-28.

2 Choosing the Speaker

Lynne P. Brown and Robert L. Peabody

This chapter will explore patterns of leadership selection in the U.S. House of Representatives that lead to the choice of its Speakers, focusing especially on the past four Speakers—Carl Albert (1971-1977), Thomas P. "Tip" O'Neill (1977-1987), Jim Wright (1987-1989), and Thomas S. Foley (1989-1995).*

Patterns of Succession in Party Leadership

Party leadership is a central fact of congressional life. Who sits where in the hierarchy of the House—especially who occupies the speakership—affects the political fortunes of other members, how the institution is organized, and what it achieves. If we concede that Speakers make a difference to the organization and outcomes of the legislative branch, then it is worthwhile to ask by what method of selection Speakers are chosen. What are the implications of that selection process for the type of leadership that emerges?

For most, if not all, of the nineteenth and early twentieth centuries, House leadership was relatively fragmented if not unstable. Seldom did a Speaker serve for more than two consecutive Congresses. Even Henry Clay, who served for a total of ten years, had his tenure spread out over five interrupted Congresses.

Late in the twentieth century, along with the development of seniority as a norm and the growth in institutionalization of the House, the trend has been toward continuity rather than change in congressional leadership. This was most starkly revealed by the service of Speaker Sam Rayburn and Majority

---

* While every effort has been made to maintain scholarly objectivity, the authors have benefited from insights gained from partisan observation, including a 1965 internship with Majority Whip Hale Boggs (D-La.), and eighteen months as a staff assistant to Speaker Carl Albert (D-Okla.) (Peabody); and four years on the staff of the majority whip's office, John Brademas (D-Ind.), 1978-1980, and Thomas S. Foley, (D-Wash.), 1981-1982 (Brown).

Leader John McCormack, who served in tandem for twenty-one years, from 1940 to 1961, except for two Republican-controlled Congresses, the 80th (1947-1949) and 83rd (1953-1955).

Since 1940 there has also been a strong proclivity for floor leaders, majority or minority, to advance to the speakership (Table 2-1 provides an overview of leadership selection since 1940.) And beginning in January 1955 with Albert's appointment as majority whip, a ladder of leadership advancement, at least in the Democratic party, began to emerge. Crucial to this emergence was the increasing viability, strength, and organization of the whip system.[1] Advancing from majority whip to majority leader in 1961 and to the speakership in 1971, Albert became the first person to traverse these steps in that order in the history of the House. (McCormack of Massachusetts dropped to minority whip from majority leader for both the 80th and 83rd Congresses, and then reverted back to majority leader in 1949 and 1955.) Following Albert, all consecutive Speakers and prospective Speakers—such as majority leader Hale Boggs of Louisiana (1971-1972)—solidified their party leadership careers by getting on the ladder as whip. Wright is a partial exception, advancing from *deputy* whip to majority leader in 1976. The analysis that follows will concentrate on the beginnings of formal party leadership and how these four Speakers got their leadership careers underway.

The four Speakers were initially *appointed* as whips by the Speaker or the Speaker and majority leader working in consort. It was not until 1986 that the Democrats began to *elect* their whips. No elected majority whip has, as yet, advanced to Speaker.[2]

A relatively ambiguous aspect of the House leadership process involves how aspiring leaders advance from being just one of 435 members to inclusion in a much smaller and select pool of talent. Two quotations from the biographies of Speakers Albert and O'Neill are highly suggestive, however. Albert stressed the importance of devoting a lot of time on the floor:

In my first term [1947-1949], I do not believe I missed a single day of the House's proceedings. I was there when the chaplain opened the day's work with a prayer. I was there when the Speaker's gavel sounded adjournment. In between, I stayed on the floor, because that is where I had wanted to be all my life.[3]

O'Neill took a slightly different tack. He had been advised by John F. Kennedy, his predecessor: "Whatever you do, don't make the mistake I did. Be nice to John McCormack." Dutifully—and probably eagerly—O'Neill took the future president's advice:

Table 2-1 Speakers of the House of Representatives: 1940-1993

Name and state	Dates of service as Speaker	Years of service	Years in House before election as Speaker	Age at election as Speaker[a]	Prior leadership positions	Reasons for vacating office
Sam Rayburn, Texas (D)	1940-1947 1949-1953 1955-1961	17	28	58	Majority Leader, 1937-1940; Chair, Democratic Caucus, 1921-1923	Party became minority 1947, 1953; Death (Nov. 16, 1961)
Joseph W. Martin, Mass. (R)	1947-1949 1953-1955	4	22	62	Minority Leader, 1939-1947	Party became minority
John W. McCormack, Mass. (D)	1962-1971	9	33	70	Majority Leader, 1940-1947, 1949-1953, 1955-1961; Minority Whip, 1947-1949, 1953-1955	Retirement
Carl B. Albert, Okla. (D)	1971-1977	6	24	62	Majority Leader, 1962-1971; Majority Whip, 1955-1961	Retirement

Thomas P. "Tip" O'Neill, Mass. (D)	1977-1987	10	24	65	Majority Leader, 1973-1977; Majority Whip, 1971-1973	Retirement
Jim Wright, Texas (D)	1987-1989	3	32	65	Majority Leader, 1977-1987; Deputy Whip, 1973-1977	Resignation
Thomas S. Foley, Wash. (D)	1989-1995	6	24	60	Majority Leader, 1987-1989; Majority Whip, 1981-1987; Chair, Democratic Caucus, 1977-1981	Defeated in re-election, Party became minority
Average (Mean)		7.8	26.7	63.1	—	—

[a]Except in cases of mid-Congress leadership selection, age is given as of the expiration date of the Congress prior to selection as Speaker.

Source: *Biographical Directory of the United States Congress, 1774-1989* (Washington, D.C.: U.S. Government Printing Office, 1989). Adapted from Randall B. Ripley, *Party Leaders in the House of Representatives* (Washington, D.C.: Brookings Institution, 1967), 14-15; Robert L. Peabody, *Leadership in Congress* (Boston: Little, Brown, 1976), 32-33.

I was a regular at the McCormack breakfast table in the House dining rooms where he would hold forth every morning between 8:30 and 9:55, when it was time for the committee meetings to begin. . . . The talk was mostly business—politics, legislation—and gossip about members of the House.[4]

These two quotations reveal that potential leaders follow a variety of tactics in coming closer to being viewed as prospective leaders, especially: (1) getting to know an increasingly wide range of members, and (2) ingratiating themselves with top leaders, especially the Speaker.

As the selection of the immediate past four Speakers convincingly demonstrates, the House Democratic party, long the ruling party in the House, has developed an almost inviolable pattern of succession to top leadership: (1) appointment (now election) to whip; (2) election to majority leadership, which is sometimes contested; and (3) advancement to Speaker, which is almost never challenged.[5] As already suggested, the practice of advancing from majority whip to majority leader to Speaker is relatively recent. At least from 1955 on, but arguably from 1940 on, House Democrats have institutionalized leadership selection patterns. The means of recruitment and advancement have been highly dependent on personal, geographical, and ideological ties, epitomized in the famed "Boston-Austin" axis. It began when Rayburn (strictly speaking representing Bonham, not Austin, Texas) was elected Speaker in 1940. In the earlier contest for majority leader in 1937, McCormack—who represented the Boston end of the axis—had supported Rayburn in his fight against the chair of the Rules Committee, John J. O'Connor of New York.[6] Three years later, having been elected Speaker, Rayburn would reciprocate by throwing his support for majority leader to McCormack.[7] After Rayburn's death twenty-one years later, McCormack was elevated to the speakership without opposition, despite less than universal support.[8] In 1970, McCormack, approaching 80 years of age, resigned. Albert, from McAlester, Oklahoma, moved up to Speaker, and leadership shifted back along the axis from the northeast to the southwest.

The 1971 election of Boggs of Louisiana as majority leader to serve with Speaker Albert was an exception to this alternating regional pattern of leadership selection. Both Albert and Boggs were from the South, but they chose O'Neill of Massachusetts as their whip. After Boggs's death, the axis would be reestablished from 1973 to 1977 with Albert and O'Neill and from 1977 to 1987 with O'Neill and Wright. But with the election of Foley of Washington as majority leader in 1986, and three years later as Speaker, the Boston-Austin axis became a historical relic. Indeed, after 1989 the South, long represented in House Democratic leadership circles, no longer had *any* member in the top hierarchy.

What accounted for the earlier sustained pattern, a pattern that lasted for nearly fifty years? First, the alignment of New England and the Southwest—especially Texas—combined two large and fairly cohesive House voting blocs. The South, if it remained unified, could deliver ninety or more votes, often as many as one-third of House Democrats. Probably a more basic reason behind the continued success of the Boston-Austin axis was the seniority that flowed from stable, one-party politics in Texas and Massachusetts. Three Texans have served as Speaker since 1930, occupying the office more than one-third of the time. Democratic Speakers from Massachusetts have held the office nearly twenty years. At least one close observer of the House stresses a liberal-urban and conservative-rural connection, including ties to oil and gas money.[9] But such an interpretation fails to account for why Boston, not Chicago or New York, was a part of the axis.

A final and less visible reason for perpetuating the Boston-Austin axis was mentor-protégé relationships, many of which extended back generations. Junior members sought (or, in some cases were prodded into) an ongoing relationship with a senior colleague from the same state or region who was already a part of the leadership hierarchy.

A consistent thread that helps explain the dynamics of leadership selection in the House is the phenomenon of tapping, a process by which established party leaders identify, encourage, and help shape the careers of newer members along lines of leadership service.[10] This pattern of mentor-protégé relationships is a strong one among Democratic House leaders and has had an important bearing on the choice of future Speakers.

The histories of the past four Speakers underline the fact that, in the House, most leaders come to office through a process of appointment and apprenticeship. According to House Democratic party rules and precedents, the Speaker is chosen in party caucus by a majority of his or her colleagues. However, the real process of selection stretches back years in time to a point well before the convening of a given Congress's organizing caucus, as candidates are selected and eliminated in a gradual but continuous narrowing of the field of potential candidates.[11]

A second point to make about tapping is that it is clear that members are both selected *and* self-appointed for leadership careers. The process involves a seeking out by the mentor as well as a willingness to be found by the protégé.

In the case of each of the past Speakers examined here, the future Speaker declared himself available for a lower leadership office early in his career, attempting to win the willing approval of those above him on the leadership ladder. The corollary of the desire by aspirants to be noticed by leaders is the decision by incumbent leaders to sponsor relatively junior members.

The tapping process can vary in intensity depending on the personalities involved and individual calculations of political opportunity. Some leadership aspirants such as Tony Coelho of California and Richard Gephardt of Missouri were more assertive on their own behalfs, although even Gephardt relied on the sponsorship of fellow Missourian Richard Bolling and caucus chair Gillis Long of Louisiana to draw him into higher party councils. And until he became chair of the Democratic Congressional Campaign Committee (DCCC), Coelho worked closely with two other old hands in campaign fund-raising, Tip O'Neill and Dan Rostenkowski (D-Ill.).

The phenomenon of tapping proceeds along a continuum with fluctuations in levels of sponsorship and self-promotion. On one end may be an Albert, patiently waiting to be plucked from the back bench by an impressed senior leader. On the other end may be a Coelho, eager to interject himself into the leadership equation. In between are different variations for individual leadership careers. But the point remains that the road to the speakership over the past half-century has involved mentorship as well as moxie.

In any organization, the promotion of the careers of others can be a double-edged sword: grooming the next generation of leaders versus advancing potential challengers. In the House of Representatives, the sponsorship of ambitious and talented members is perhaps not as threatening a proposition as in other organizations. Challenges to incumbent leaders are rare; successful challenges rarer still. Nevertheless, it would be naive to assume that party leaders, in choosing their protégés, are unaffected by the prospect of being overshadowed or outmaneuvered by them—if not immediately, perhaps at some point in the future. As a result, in the tapping process there is a tendency on the part of leaders to sponsor careers in a selective fashion. The recruit is usually one who combines emerging ability with similar political background, a professed loyalty to the House, and a proper measure of deference. These criteria were strongly operative in the Rayburn-Albert and McCormack-O'Neill connections; they appear in more or less pronounced form in other leadership pairings in the contemporary House. Furthermore, such traits are often absorbed and internalized by the aspiring leader. A lower-ranking leader, once in line, knows the path to promotion lies in working hard, showing initiative, but almost always deferring to the norms of loyalty, tradition, and seniority.

This does not mean that the selection process leading to the speakership yields recruits of mediocre talent or undeveloped ambition. In this regard, House leaders are more in line with a practice observed by Kenneth Prewitt in his study of recruitment of city council members in California: "The potential tension between recruiter and recruited is managed not through selection of low quality but through selection of like-minded individuals." [12]

While being tapped is not sufficient to ensure later leadership advancement,[13] it is clearly an advantage for it brings a member into contact with the movers and shakers of the House and begins a process of institutional mastery. Furthermore, through the process of tapping, a complicated pattern of relationships is formed, woven from numerous personal and professional loyalties (and animosities) that continue to influence leadership selection and operation over decades.

Of all the factors contributing to Democratic stability of leadership and well-developed patterns of succession, perhaps the most important has been the party's near continuous control of the House. Since 1931 only two Congresses, the 80th (1947-1949) and the 83rd (1953-1955), operated under Republican control. Moreover, over the past forty years, Democrats have controlled the House by an average majority of three-to-two.[14]

Majority party leaders work within a climate of expanding resources. They have many ways, large and small, to assist their colleagues in achieving their objectives. There are more committee assignments to be distributed. Majority members chair the committees and subcommittees. With positions come staff, superior access to interest groups and executive officialdom, and greater influence on legislative outcomes. Since there are more benefits to go around, majority members are apt to be more satisfied and less critical of the leadership. Continued majority status promotes searching for compromise and accommodation, and maintaining established patterns of leadership succession.[15]

And what of the minority Republicans? In contrast to the majority, the minority party operates in an environment of continuing frustration and contracting resources. In general, there are fewer choice committee assignments to go around; political patronage and staff assistance are harder to come by. Opportunities for constructive participation in drafting and implementing major legislation are increasingly limited.[16] Fewer numbers, constrained resources, inability to reward adequately the party faithful, prospects for continuing defeat in committee and on the floor—all foster internal dissension and tend to undermine the minority leadership.[17]

Jim Wright: The Partial Exception That Proves the Rule

Much has been made of the dramatic 1976 contest for House majority leader in which moderate Jim Wright of Texas defeated liberal Phil Burton of California by one vote, 148 to 147.[18] Four Democrats sought to succeed the popular O'Neill as majority leader. (O'Neill had advanced to the speakership with no opposition.) In addition to Wright, a deputy whip, and Burton, a former Democratic Caucus chair, the field included senior Rules Committee member Bolling of Missouri and John McFall, the majority whip, also of California. As was often said, "Everybody liked Jack McFall," but could he make the large leap from *appointed* majority whip to *elected* majority leader? One problem was his connections to a South Korean rice agent named Tongsun Park, who later became the subject of investigation for throwing lavish parties and making substantial campaign contributions to members of Congress. Even with broad-scale support from the large California delegation and fellow Appropriations Committee members, there was little consensus that he could make the shift from a relatively passive, service-oriented whip to an aggressive, outgoing, policy-oriented majority leader. His thirty-one votes on the first caucus ballot only served to confirm this interpretation.

It is intriguing that in the second ballot Burton failed to advance by more than one vote even though fellow Californian McFall dropped out. Some believed that Burton threw votes to Wright in order to ensure Bolling's defeat on the second ballot. Burton would emphatically deny this.[19] On the third and final ballot, Bolling was urging his supporters to back Wright. Personality, ideology, and regional balance all figured in the outcome, but the one-vote victory was a result, above all, of Wright's active campaigning for votes from first-term members and to his Public Works Committee record of assistance to other members over the years.

In the 95th Congress (1977-1979), John Brademas of Indiana, the chief deputy whip under McFall, would be appointed majority whip by newly elected Speaker O'Neill. Brademas's party leadership career, cut short by an electoral defeat in 1980, provides another example, one of four, in which a majority whip would fail to advance to the majority leadership.[20]

The 1976 contest shows that the succession from whip to majority leader was far from automatic. Holding the appointive whip slot was an advantage *if* its occupant used this leadership status to build support and to engender admiration among party colleagues. Albert, O'Neill, and, to a lesser extent, Boggs had done this.[21] McFall had not. The "Koreagate" scandal was a final (and probably fatal) blow to an already ailing candidacy. McFall's weakness, in turn, drew into the race three of the most ambitious and assertive members of the House. Once McFall was out, *any* of these three, once elected, would be an exception to the pattern that had been building since Albert, Boggs, and O'Neill.

Opening Up the System: Making the Whip Elective

The position of whip is third in the House Democratic majority party hierarchy, a nominal second in the minority Republican party. For the nearly eighty years of the position's existence, up until 1986, the whip was appointed by Democratic Speakers in consultation with their majority leaders. The recruitment process for party leaders favored a balancing act between assertiveness and deference. A potential whip had to demonstrate leadership capabilities, preferably through floor activity. As junior members, Albert, Wright, and Foley all made a mark for themselves managing legislation; this was true for O'Neill also, but to a lesser degree.

As already suggested, future House leaders also have strong bonds with those on the party hierarchy above them. Aspiring whip candidates can best be seen as cautious aggrandizers of influence. Their roles were not subservient, but neither could they afford to be revolutionaries. Again, a relationship of mentor-protégé was the standard practice.

This is not to say that potential whip candidates could not express ambition. When O'Neill became majority leader in 1973, more than two dozen members approached him and indicated their interest in serving as majority whip. But O'Neill honored ambition within the constraints of traditional hierarchy. At the January 2, 1973, Democratic Caucus he spoke against a resolution sponsored by Burton of California to create an elective whip. Largely because of O'Neill's opposition, the resolution failed 123 to 114. Albert and O'Neill then elevated the two floor whips from the previous Congress, McFall to be whip and Brademas to be chief deputy whip. As long as the level of entry remained appointive, leadership styles would remain mainly conciliatory and conforming.

But junior members, increasingly unhappy with the process of selection, continued to urge that the position be made elective. Finally, on January 29, 1985, the Democratic rank-and-file earned a greater voice in shaping the entry level of its party's hierarchy. The vote in favor of making the whip an elective position was a lopsided 133 to 36. The plan was not to take effect until the position was vacant, after Foley had relinquished the post (presumably to seek the majority leadership). Neither O'Neill nor Wright, the likely next Speaker, opposed the change. Capitalizing on a strong, take-charge personality and the favors he had acquired through chairing the DCCC since 1981, Coelho of California won a six-way contest in December 1986 and became the first elective whip.[22]

New Competitive Forces in Congress

A whole genre of literature has dealt with the major congressional reforms of the 1970s, encompassing the Democratic Study Group, the Bolling and Hansen Committee reforms in the House, and the Stevenson Committee modifications in the Senate. An even more discernible trend has been to incorporate the post-reform House as the baseline of developments since the 1970s.[23] Discussion of the differences between the pre- and post-reform House is beyond our mandate. For our purposes, the most critical observations are threefold: (1) the House has become more open, decentralized, democratic, and truly representative; (2) at the same time, the party leadership has made modest gains in strengthening its powers; and (3) methods of selecting top party leadership remain markedly incremental in nature.

Both causing and accompanying these major reforms of the 1970s has been the arrival of a new breed of politician, so-called careerists in action. The new breed of politician was well represented in the Democratic Class of 1974, the "Watergate class." House Majority Leader Gephardt, first elected in 1976, has often been cited as the "archetypical new-style politician." [24] As Alan Ehrenhalt suggests:

The professional talent that has built a Democratic majority in Congress . . . has transformed Congress into a place whose members arrive young and independent, make it the consuming passion of their lives in their most productive working years, and leave only when they reach retirement age or feel the temptation to seek some higher office.[25]

What does this new breed of activists want from their leadership? According to Barbara Sinclair, the building of successful legislative coalitions and party maintenance or "keeping peace in the family" are uppermost.[26] For many of the newer members, keeping peace within their families also meant more consistent scheduling of legislation.

As Rohde, Sinclair, and others have noted, the late 1970s, 1980s, and early 1990s also have witnessed a dramatic increase in the resurgence of partisanship.[27] Increased Democratic voting cohesion, use of closed rules to benefit consideration of legislation, and Speaker Wright's willingness in the 100th Congress (1987-1989) to wield new institutional powers generated one of the most successful legislative records in a decade—at a cost of House Republican participation.

The Loosening Grip of Geography

Regional considerations continue to affect Democratic leadership contests but are significantly less decisive than in prior decades. All things being equal, members would prefer to vote for someone from his or her own region, someone with whom they would have access, someone who approaches issues in a similar manner. But over the years regional demarcation has broken down. Even the "solid South" is no longer solid. In 1986 when Coelho ran successfully for the elective whip, he argued that his prior duties as chair of the DCCC and his appearance in the districts of almost all of his colleagues had given him a national perspective.[28] In this he was joined by many junior Democrats who felt that if they were ever to forge unified and comprehensive policy positions they needed to look beyond mere state or regional agendas.

In the House Democratic leadership elections of 1986, geographical factors received strong rhetorical play. But the end result—Speaker Wright of Texas, Majority Leader Foley of Washington, and Majority Whip Coelho of California—gave the House three leaders from districts west of the Mississippi for the first time in history.

In 1989, following Wright's forced resignation, regional considerations continued to play a role, if a diminished one. Two southerners, Ed Jenkins of Georgia, a candidate for majority leader, and Beryl Anthony of Arkansas, a candidate for majority whip, both made relatively poor showings. The new set of leaders—Speaker Foley of Washington, Majority Leader Gephardt of Missouri, and Majority Whip William Gray, III, of Pennsylvania—was balanced geographically, but this was more an artifact of the strong personal appeal of the winners. It is significant to note that no one from the traditional Boston-Austin axis was represented. Except for the chair of the DCCC and chief deputy whips, no Sunbelt states were represented in the hierarchy.

When it seemed that once more the House had stabilized its leadership, perhaps for another decade, reshuffling took place again. On June 20, 1991, Majority Whip Gray surprised his colleagues by announcing he would resign from the House to accept the presidency of the United Negro College Fund. In the contested whip race that followed, two members of the existing party leadership sought the position. On July 11, 1991, Chief Deputy Whip David E. Bonior of Michigan, an earlier opponent to Gray, defeated the chair of the caucus, Steny Hoyer of Maryland, 160 to 109. For the first time in many decades, two of the top three Democratic leaders were midwesterners. Given the waning nature of regional impact, geographic roots are likely to play less of a role in deciding who occupies future top leadership in the House.

The Influence of Money

A study of recent House Democratic leadership contests leads to the conclusion that the establishment of political action committees (PACs) by House leaders or leadership aspirants plays a significant but not determinate role in the selection of party leaders.[29] Prior to the 1970s and the passage of the Federal Election Campaign Act, House party leaders working through interest groups sometimes helped to raise funds for members, but the process was often informal and haphazard.

In the contest for majority leader in 1976, both Burton and Wright raised substantial amounts of money to distribute to their colleagues in the hopes it would gain their gratitude—and votes. Bolling, who was edged out by Wright 95 to 93 on the second ballot, purposely eschewed fund-raising and redistribution.[30]

With greater frequency, members within the formal party hierarchy and without have formed PACs, which may contribute as much as $10,000 per election cycle per candidate.[31] While members are quick to discount the impact of such an amount on elections that cost $400,000 to $600,000 or more, a simple fact of the House is that members are running full-time for office, and campaign contributions from whatever source are desirable. Within the context of House leadership races, money is another means by which aspiring leaders endeavor to show their colleagues that they care about them and their electoral fates. Increasingly, such contributions have become like the ante in a poker game, a minimum stake put up before the deal to show one's seriousness.

Implications for the Speakership: Personality, Stability, and Leadership

Paths to the speakership, though different in detail for each individual, pass by remarkably similar milestones. Successful candidates also display similar traits: running from generally safe seats; a patient waiting-for-one's-turn; loyalty to the institution of Congress and to those members who are higher in the hierarchy; ambition for advancement played out within the context of deference to one's mentors and sponsors; an interpersonal style with colleagues that is persuasive but nonthreatening; and skillful balancing of district, party, and national interests.

These are attitudes and skills important for the man (and perhaps someday, woman) who would be Speaker in the contemporary House. But are they the attitudes and skills needed to be successful once elected to office? What *are* the implications of the process of selecting Speakers for the leadership styles they adopt?

The question of the link between the skills needed to get elected and the skills needed to exercise effective leadership in the House is a variant of the campaigning versus governing debate on the senatorial and presidential levels. From the vantage point of the speakership, the occupant must fulfill two somewhat conflicting roles simultaneously: presiding officer of the House and leader of the party. The first role, rooted in tradition, calls for conducting the business of the chamber in a fair and impartial manner. As was discussed in Chapter 1, this canon of fairness and evenhandedness is sometimes at odds with the expectations surrounding the Speaker's role as party leader. But Speakers violate the norms of presiding officer at their peril.[32]

As partisan standard bearer and strategist, the Speaker performs along these dimensions of leadership: affecting policy outcomes, projecting the party's message and image, anticipating new or emerging demands or opportunities, looking after one's colleagues, reforming or readapting the institution or larger political system. The careers of the four most recent Speakers reveal that the selection process by which they rose to prominence, while providing an important training ground for the development of leadership abilities, is certainly not a guarantee that the members who prevail will possess high-order skills as legislative craftsmen, media stars, or even adept administrators.

The route to the speakership often dictates that policy interests take a back seat to matters of procedure and personality. Albert, O'Neill, Wright, and Foley had different formative experiences in the legislative arena. Albert and then Foley served on the Agriculture Committee and both performed ably in managing legislation in the committee and on the floor. But given the narrow issues involved, the stage was a small one. O'Neill was not very engaged in the work of crafting legislation; he left matters of substance to others. But his perch on the Rules Committee allowed him to help direct the flow of traffic to the floor and, in that way, affect policy outcomes. Wright had a somewhat broader legislative scope from the base of the Public Works and Transportation Committee, but the focus was often parochial and centered on channeling federal projects to particular districts (and keeping track of the horse trading). Representing Texas also involved him in gas, oil, and energy legislation.

For all four it was their tenure as floor leaders that helped temper and hone their skills as legislative strategists. Having relinquished their original committee assignments by that point, their role as majority leader was to assist the Speaker in setting the agenda and achieving victories on the floor. Moreover, Speakers often cede to their floor leaders responsibility for important legislative packages such as the budget. With its substantial and visible floor responsibilities, the majority leadership is both a proving ground and showcase for its occupant. Majority leaders often take to the hustings to help members raise campaign war chests. Members, in turn, become comfortable with their leaders. The longer they have been in office, the less the probability that majority leaders will be challenged for the speakership. And, indeed, all four Speakers we are studying advanced to the top rung of the ladder without serious opposition.

Once reaching the speakership, these people displayed a broad range of styles as leaders of the House. Albert assumed a relatively low profile on the legislative front, largely ceding control of the policy agenda to the committee chairs, as had McCormack and Rayburn before him. O'Neill, whose first four years as Speaker coincided with a Democrat in the White House, followed President Jimmy Carter's legislative lead. With the election of Ronald Reagan as president in 1980 and the switch to Republican control in the Senate, House Democrats assumed a more assertive stance on legislation. O'Neill went along with Reagan when the president seemed unbeatable, but O'Neill was prepared to exert influence when the House voting margins were narrower, especially after 1982.

Wright was the most aggressive of the four and was initially successful in shaping and pushing through the House a legislative program that was comprehensive, coherent, and strongly reflective of his own views on where the Democratic party should position itself. He also assumed an active involvement in Central American foreign policy. As Speaker, he performed as a legislator, which was probably presaged by his activist stance as majority leader, particularly on energy and conservation issues. The record of the 100th Congress included the overriding of four Reagan vetoes—an accomplishment of which later Congresses, faced with multiple Bush vetoes, fell far short. Foley

has not carried forward with Wright's high-profile, high-pressure performance in the legislative arena; a low-key style better suits the sitting Speaker's
personality and might be seen as a strategic response to the partisan excesses of
the 100th Congress.

As spokesperson for the party and institution of the House, the Speaker
occupies a visible position on the national political scene, especially when the
opposite party controls the White House. Such exposure, heightened by television, now comes to the Speaker as a matter of course. O'Neill probably represents the transitional figure in the move toward a job description for Speaker
that includes talent as a media personality. Neither prepared for the role nor
comfortable with it, O'Neill nonetheless felt compelled to present a counterpoint to the daily scripted messages, press conferences, and photo opportunities emanating from the Reagan White House. That O'Neill fell short of the
performance of "The Great Communicator" did not hurt him among his
Democratic colleagues and, in a development that probably surprised the
Speaker more than anyone else, he became a national celebrity.[33]

At the same time, in a not unrelated development, the emergence of media
skills as a criterion for selection of lower ranking leaders can be seen. In Foley's
unopposed ascent to the majority leadership in 1986, Gephardt's rise to that
post two and a half years later, Coelho's victory over a crowded field for whip
in 1986, and Gray's successful whip race in 1989—in all these contests the
winning candidate was helped by the perception that each could perform cred-
ibly on a national stage, including television, and could help craft and deliver
themes with national scope and appeal. In this way are seen the expanding
demands of the job reflected in the changing dynamics of the selection process.

In large measure, the story of House majority leadership has been one of
stability and succession. Competition has not characterized the races for the
top leadership posts, including the Speaker. Will this trend continue? Under
what circumstances might leadership races grow more competitive?

Upheaval in patterns of succession might accompany a serious political or
electoral setback that is seen to result from a collective failure of congressional
party leadership. A series of scandals, especially those that threaten sitting
members in their districts (such as the House bank scandal, for example),
could fall into this category. Strategic political missteps that cause the Democrats to lose or drastically narrow their majority in the House might be another
example. In the wake of a public relations disaster or defeat at the polls, the
rank and file might be led to widen its search for leaders beyond those already
poised on the ladder.

Times of crises may have the opposite effect, however, and lead to a desire for stability and trust in known quantities. This was the sentiment widely expressed at the time of the forced resignation of Wright, leading to the selection of Majority Leader Foley to assume the speakership. Moreover, heavy party losses at the polls might come at the expense of more liberal, more change-oriented members. Those returning to Congress may reinforce, not overturn, the status quo.

On a less apocalyptic scale, the history of leadership races shows competition increasing when the incumbent or heir-apparent has no singular or compelling claim on the position. In the majority leadership race of 1976, sensing Majority Whip McFall's weaknesses, Bolling and Burton decided to throw their hats in the ring. Once they entered the race, Jim Wright, the eventual winner, saw no reason not to lay equal claim to the position.

This aspect of competition is related, in the case of the Democrats, to limited turnover in leadership positions. The longer the tenure of a member in a leadership post, the better the chance of proving one's value and service to colleagues. If turnover increases in Democratic leadership circles, either through electoral defeats or resignations, the competition for positions could heighten.

Finally, competitive leadership races hinge on the structure of opportunities within the House and whether that structure is sufficiently broad to accommodate the ambition of its members. Most members of Congress do *not* choose a career in leadership; most seem content, as Peabody has observed, to cultivate their own constituencies and pursue legislative interests through committee work or floor activity.[34] But in the face of an expanding cohort of members ambitious for leadership, incumbents may justifiably begin to worry about the security of their places in the hierarchy. The growth of the whip system throughout the late 1970s and 1980s and the increasing use of extra-leadership entities such as task forces can be seen as leadership's response, not only to a fractious family, but to one composed of ambitious members. Broadening the leadership circle serves to give more members a stake in the party and the institution;[35] it also serves to expand career possibilities.

When the range of possibilities fail to keep pace with individual demands for advancement, however, House leadership positions can become more hotly contested. In recent times, such competition, when it has come, has occurred at the lower levels of the party hierarchy. For example, the contest for majority whip in 1986 (the first time that post was open to election) was a hard-fought battle among six members. The 1989 whip race saw a four-candidate field reduce itself to a tough two-way race. The caucus chair that year attracted three contestants and no fewer than four candidates actively campaigned for vice chair. Competitive leadership elections seldom destabilize the party or lead to rival factions. Instead, in almost all instances, members revert to their legislative tasks and the winner settles quickly and easily into a new equilibrium.

A final line of inquiry concerns the *type* and *quality* of leadership a selection system produces. The process described herein mainly produces Speakers who are middle-of-the-road, nonideological, consensus-seeking bridge-builders attuned to the needs of the members. This prototype was epitomized by O'Neill; Foley is another example.

The process—the patient waiting-in-line, the need to curry favor across a range of political camps, the balancing act between staying in the shadows of those higher on the ladder and making a name for oneself—seldom tends to promote policy innovators or self-styled intellectuals or charismatic figures. In a legislative body such as the U.S. Congress, the limits of power are more obvious than the opportunities for power. Holding a leadership position in such an environment conditions the occupant to approach problems cautiously, to build a base of support before taking action, and to risk the minimum necessary to achieve the ends. The resulting leadership style is mainly reactive, not anticipatory; prosaic, not visionary; transactional, not transformative.[36] Contemporary Speakers have seldom been "strong" leaders in the way that term would be used in other realms, such as business, athletics, or the military.

Those members who successfully advance within the ranks of majority party leadership also feel strong bonds to the institution of the House, which sometimes limit their abilities to see beyond the needs of the institution or to reach out to wider audiences. For session after session, this may lead to few or no problems. The House and its members are forgiving—up to a point. But when members feel that their own reelection prospects are threatened—in the face of scandal or public disapproval or unpopular votes—they put more pressure on their leaders "to do something." When confronted with extraordinary challenges, party leaders unfortunately may not always be up to the task.

If House majority leadership elections were more competitive, what would be the result? Certainly, there is a good chance that more impressive candidates, as judged by intellect or personality or drive, would prevail. Stellar Speakers might be the norm. But could they, in turn, prevail over their colleagues? To ask the latter question is to go to the heart of the dilemma of leadership in Congress: strong leaders come at a price that rank-and-file members are rarely willing to pay—that is, the constraint of their own freedom of action.

The Speakers in the Twenty-First Century

Following Wright's controversial tenure (1987-1989), the speakership moved into a consolidating phase marked by a solidification, not expansion, of power.

The election of a Republican majority in 1994 abruptly and dramatically shifted the mantle of leadership to the GOP. The first Republican Speaker in forty years, Newt Gingrich of Georgia, stepped up the leadership ladder on that side of the aisle. He was elected his party's whip, the number two spot, in 1989 by a close 87-85 margin and was in line to rise to the top party post to replace the resigning Bob Michel of Illinois. On the Democratic side, with Foley defeated for re-election, Gephardt and Bonior are likely to become minority leader and whip, respectively. The pattern of succession among House Democrats will probably continue, at least for the short term.

Of course, predictions are hazardous when dealing, on the one hand, with the careers of individual politicians (each with his or her own agenda, assets, and limitations) and, on the other, with national trends that may lead to inter-party turnover. The House Democratic party leadership, as this research confirms, has demonstrated a remarkable stability over the last half of the twentieth century. The question now is whether the Republicans will evidence a similar stability—both in their electoral victories and in the selection of their leaders.

Notes

1. Randall B. Ripley, "The Party Whip Organizations"; Lawrence C. Dodd, "The Expanded Roles of the House Democratic Whip System: The 93rd and 94th Congresses," *Congressional Studies 7* (Spring 1979): 17-56; "The History and Operation of the House Majority Whip," H.R. Doc. 93-126, 1973); Lynne P. Brown, "Dilemmas of Party Leadership: Majority Whips in the U.S. House of Representatives, 1962-1984," (Ph.D. dissertation, Political Science Department, Johns Hopkins Univ., 1985).

2. Tony Coelho (D-Calif.) won that first elective race for whip, but then left Congress in 1989. William H. Gray, III, (D-Pa.), after winning a tough race to take Coelho's place, only served two years before announcing that he, too, was retiring from Congress. The opponent Gray had prevailed over in the 1989 contest, David E. Bonior of Michigan, was next elected whip and is still the incumbent.

3. Carl Albert (with Danney Goble), *Little Giant: The Life and Times of Carl Albert* (Norman, Okla.: Univ. of Oklahoma Press, 1990), 163.

4. Thomas P. O'Neill (with William Novak), *Man of the House* (New York: Random House, 1987), 118-121.

5. Robert L. Peabody, "Party Leadership Changes in the United States House of Representatives," *American Political Science Review* 61 (Sept. 1967): 675-693; Robert L. Peabody, *Leadership in Congress: Stability, Succession and Change* (Boston: Little, Brown, 1976), 475-480; Garrison Nelson, "Partisan Patterns of House Leadership Change, 1789-1977," *American Political Science Review* 71 (Sept. 1977): 918-939; Lynne P. Brown and Robert L. Peabody, "Patterns in House Democratic Leadership: The Choices of Wright, Foley, and Coelho, 1986" (Paper delivered at the annual meeting of the American Political Science Association, Chicago, Sept. 3-6, 1987): 51-53; and Lynne P. Brown and Robert L. Peabody, "Patterns in House Democratic Leadership: Foley, Gephardt, and Gray, 1989" in *New Perspectives on the House of Representatives*, 4th ed., ed. Robert L. Peabody and Nelson W. Polsby (Baltimore: Johns Hopkins Univ. Press, 1992), 356-357.

6. Anthony Champagne, "Sam Rayburn: Achieving Party Leadership," *Southwestern Historical Quarterly* 90 (1987): 373-392.

7. D. B. Hardeman and Donald C. Bacon, *Rayburn: A Biography* (Austin: Texas Monthly Press, 1987), 245-246.

8. Nelson W. Polsby, "Two Strategies of Influence: Choosing a Majority Leader, 1962," in *New Perspectives on the House of Representatives*, 260-290.

9. John Barry, *The Ambition and the Power* (New York: Viking, 1989), 16-17.

10. The discussion of tapping is drawn from Brown, "Dilemmas of Party Leadership," 138-142.

11. The counterpart of "tapping" by leaders is "blocking." The recent past yields several examples of members whose rise to leadership was blocked—either by circumstance or by the intervention of incumbent leaders. One of the more striking examples was Speaker Albert's refusal to allow Hale Boggs to select Dan Rostenkowski as whip in 1971. Another example of an interested and competent member blocked for higher leadership was Morris Udall (D-Ariz.), who conducted a largely symbolic campaign against the incumbent Speaker, McCormack, in 1969; ran and lost for majority leader in 1971; and considered running for whip in 1973 if the post had been made elective. Phillip Burton (D-Calif.) clearly had leadership ambitions as well; he ran for majority leader in 1977 and four years earlier had mounted a serious effort to make the whip elective. There were different reasons for each person's failure to ascend the leadership ladder, but in each case the opposition or, at best, coolness, of incumbent leaders worked against their chances.

12. Kenneth Prewitt, *The Recruitment of Political Leaders: A Study of Citizen-Politicians* (Indianapolis: Bobbs-Merrill, 1970), 120.

13. A good example is Richard Bolling (D-Mo.) a Rayburn protégé and member of the Rules Committee (later its chair: 1977-1983), who failed in bids for majority leader in 1962 and 1976-1977.

14. Post World War II Democratic majorities range from a high of 295 to 140 in the 89th Congress (1965-1967) to a low of 243 to 192 in the 91st (1969-1971) and 93rd (1973-1975) Congresses.

15. Peabody, *Leadership in Congress*, 302.

16. David W. Rohde, *Parties and Leaders in the Postreform House* (Chicago: Univ. of

Chicago Press, 1991), 127-129.

17. Only the House Republicans have undertaken revolts against incumbent floor leaders—Charles Halleck of Indiana versus Joseph W. Martin, Jr. of Massachusetts, 1959; and Gerald Ford of Michigan versus Halleck, 1965. Peabody, *Leadership in Congress*, 100-148.

18. Barry, *The Ambition and the Power*, 11-40. Barry builds on Bruce I. Oppenheimer and Robert L. Peabody, "The House Majority Leadership Contest, 1976" (Paper delivered at the annual meeting of the American Political Science Association, Washington, D.C., Sept 1-4, 1977) For that research all four candidates, their staffs, and more than thirty House members were interviewed.

19. Oppenheimer and Peabody, "The House Majority Leadership Contest, 1976," 70; Richard Bolling, "Learn from My Losses: How Not to Run for Speaker," *Washington Post*, July 27, 1986, D-1.

20. In addition to McFall and Brademas, two other recent whips, Coelho and Gray, resigned from the House and therefore took themselves off the leadership ladder. If the current whip, Bonior, ascends the ladder, he would reestablish the pattern set by Albert, O'Neill, and Foley, but would be the first *elective* whip to follow the path of his predecessors.

21. Boggs's own performance as whip was sometimes considered erratic, and his attempt to ascend to majority leader in 1971 was challenged by four of his colleagues. Unlike McFall, however, Boggs eventually prevailed. Peabody, *Leadership in Congress*, 157-161.

22. Brown and Peabody, "Patterns in House Democratic Leadership," 1986 27-50.

23. See for example, Ronald M. Peters, Jr., *The American Speakership: The Office in Historical Perspective* (Baltimore: Johns Hopkins Univ. Press, 1990), 209-286; Rohde, *Parties and Leaders in the Postreform House*, 1-16.

24. Nelson W. Polsby, "The Institutionalization of the House of Representatives," *American Political Science Review* 62 (1968): 144-168; Charles S. Bullock, III, "House Careerists: Challenging Patterns of Longevity and Attrition," *American Political Science Review* 66 (1972): 1295-1300; Burdett Loomis, *The New American Politician* (New York: Basic Books, 1990), 1-29; John R. Hibbing, *Congressional Careers: Contours of Life in the U.S. House of Representatives* (Chapel Hill: Univ. of North Carolina Press, 1991), 12-20, 176-184; John R. Hibbing, "Careerism in Congress: For Better or for Worse?" in *Congress Reconsidered*, ed. Larry C. Dodd and Bruce I. Oppenheimer (Washington, D.C.: CQ Press, 1993), 67-88.

25. Alan Ehrenhalt, *The United States of Ambition* (New York: Basic Books, 1990), 228.

26. Barbara Sinclair, *Majority Leadership in the U.S. House* (Baltimore: Johns Hopkins Univ. Press, 1983), 22-29.

27. "Party voting peaked at 64 percent of the votes taken in 1987, more than double the 1970/1972 low point. Democratic party unity, which had declined to a range of 70 to 72 percent in the four years of Nixon's first term, climbed sharply to a maximum of 88 percent in 1987 and 1988." Rohde, *Parties and Leaders in the Postreform House*, 14.

28. Brown and Peabody, "Patterns in House Democratic Leadership," 36-38.

29. Ibid., 52-55, 358-360.

30. Oppenheimer and Peabody, "House Majority Leadership Contest, 1976" 26-33.

31. Ross K. Baker, *The New Fat Cats: Members of Congress as Political Benefactors* (New York: Priority Press, 1989).

32. Critics of Wright's speakership felt that it weighed more on the partisan side at the expense of the role of an impartial presiding officer. Barry, *The Ambition and the Power*, 467-474.

33. O'Neill (with Novak), *Man of the House*, 355-356.

34. Peabody, *Leadership in Congress*, 4-7, 50-55.

35. See Sinclair, *Majority Leadership in the U.S. House.*

36. For a discussion of transactional versus transformative leadership, see James MaGregor Burns, *Leadership* (New York: Harper & Row, 1978), 4, 355-363, 425-426.

3 The Speaker as Party Leader

Barbara Sinclair

Although formally elected by the entire House membership, the Speaker actually is selected by the majority party membership and, as a consequence, is its agent. As the presiding officer of the House, the Speaker has an obligation to all members, but it is the expectations of majority party members that shape the job. Since 1955, the Democrats have controlled the House. The study of the Speaker as party leader, then, is to date the story of Democratic party leadership.*

Members of the modern House can advance their goals of reelection, policy, and influence by passing legislation, which requires collective action; they can also do so through activities that they can carry out as individuals tending and voting the district, for example, or engaging in entrepreneurial policy activism. Members expect their leaders to facilitate the collective action necessary to pass legislation that will further the membership's goals, but to do so without imposing unacceptable constraints on members' pursuit of their goals as individuals. How much constraint members consider acceptable varies with the political and institutional context. Depending on the circumstances, members may expect their leaders to use the powers and resources delegated to them aggressively to produce collective goods, especially legislation, or they may expect leaders to use their powers and resources with restraint and avoid limiting members as they pursue their goals through individualistic means.

Changes in the political and institutional context in the 1970s and 1980s altered the expectations Democratic members to have of their party leaders. By the mid-1980s, there emerged a highly active House majority party leadership that is now routinely involved in all stages of the legislative process and much

---

* This chapter is based, in part, on a fifteen-month period of observation in the Speaker's office in 1987-1988. My thanks to Jim Wright and his staff for providing me a unique opportunity for seeing the speakership in action. This chapter is also based on interviews with members of Congress, their staffs, and numerous informed observers—all of whom I owe a debt of gratitude.

more engaged than its predecessors in political discourse on the national stage. The Speaker is the leader of this group.

How the Speaker of the House as chief of the party leadership team goes about attempting to meet the very considerable and often not easily reconciled expectations of his or her members is the subject of this chapter. We begin by examining the tasks of leadership; proceed to examine leadership organization, resources, and strategies; and then discuss leadership involvement in the various stages of the legislative process and the role of the leadership in national political discourse.

Tasks and Expectations: The Job of the Contemporary Speaker

Lawmaking depends for its adequate performance upon a number of tasks being satisfactorily carried out. From the many problems confronting society, a manageable subset must be selected for serious consideration. Policies must be formulated and legislation crafted. A majority of the chamber must be assembled to approve each piece of legislation. Setting the agenda, formulating policy, and mobilizing votes are all prerequisites to lawmaking, and each in turn depends on a variety of subsidiary activities.

To make legislating possible, the House is organized on the duel bases of committee and party. Committees are charged with primary responsibility for policy formulation in their areas of jurisdiction; party leadership, the only central leadership in the chamber, is charged with the assembling of majorities and with coordination. Beyond these very broad outlines, however, the distribution of tasks, powers, and resources has varied over time.

The reforms of the 1970s, as discussed in Chapter 8, weakened committee chairs, instituted the referral of legislation to more than one committee, and increased amending activity on the floor. These changes made committees less capable of formulating legislation that can command a House majority without help from the Speaker; as a consequence, the Speaker is now more often drawn into the pre-floor legislative process. The lesser ability of committees to protect their legislation on the floor and the increasing level of partisanship in the House have made it necessary for the party leadership to mount more frequent and more intensive efforts to mobilize votes. Unlike the Speakers of the past, the contemporary Speaker is also expected to play a prominent role in legislative agenda setting and in national political discourse. During the recent period of divided party control of government, Democrats came to understand that the president's great access to the media gave the executive office an enormous advantage in political and policy struggles; they also realized that they as individuals could never compete with the president in the realm of public opinion. The skill with which Ronald Reagan used the president's media access to further his policy and political agenda and denigrate Democrats made congressional Democrats realize they needed spokespersons to counter the president. Democrats came to expect the Speaker to use the access to the media the position brings to promote the membership's policy agenda and to protect and enhance the party's image.

Organization and Resources

House Democrats now expect their Speaker to play a highly active role in the legislative process in the House and in the national political process more broadly, shaping debate and facilitating the passage of legislation to further their policy and reelection goals. They still, however, expect the Speaker to do so without constraining too much their own opportunities to participate in the legislative process and to pursue their goals as individuals in other ways as well. The strategies post-reform Speakers have developed for meeting these expectations depend heavily on new powers and resources that the Speaker gained during the reform era and on the creation or elaboration of a set of party organizations that provide the Speaker with assistance and information.

To sustain the high level of legislative activity expected by the members, the Speaker needs assistance, which has led to an expansion of the leadership inner circle. In the 1940s and into the 1950s, the inner circle really consisted of just the Speaker and the majority leader; by the early 1970s, it had expanded to include the whip as a full-fledged member. Now, in addition, the chair and vice chair of the Democratic Caucus and the four chief deputy whips are part of the inner circle.

Although the inner circle has grown, the Speaker remains the undisputed leader. To be sure, the majority leader, the whip, and the caucus chair and vice chair are each independently elected and thus have their own constituencies in the House. Strong-minded people tend to win these highly prized positions and some tensions are inevitable. Yet all realize that their members have elected them to a leadership team under the captaincy of the Speaker. To a considerable extent, the Speaker controls the composition of the inner circle, which is not a formally designated grouping. It consists of those members who regularly attend leadership meetings, and the Speaker determines this.

The current core leadership group—Speaker Tom Foley of Washington; Majority Leader Richard Gephardt of Missouri; Majority Whip David Bonior of Michigan; Chief Deputy Whips Butler Derrick of South Carolina, Barbara Kennelly of Connecticut, John Lewis of Georgia, and Bill Richardson of New Mexico; Caucus Chair Steny Hoyer of Maryland; and Caucus Vice Chair Vic Fazio of California—is not only relatively large but also diverse. Diversity sufficient to give the leadership ties to all segments of the membership is important to successful coalition-building.

The division of labor among members of the inner circle is in part institutionalized and in part a function of the interests of a particular leader and the wishes of the Speaker who oversees and is responsible for the entire leadership enterprise.[1] Leaders even more than ordinary members of Congress are generalists. Given the still modest size of even the expanded inner circle, the fluid and ill-defined division of labor among the leaders facilitates handling a legislative workload of considerable size and immense scope. When an intensive effort to mobilize votes on top priority legislation is underway, everyone is expected to pitch in. Leaders also take on various nonroutine leadership tasks as their interests and the Speaker's wishes may dictate.

Even the expanded inner circle is far too small to carry out unaided the frequent efforts to mobilize votes that members now expect. The leadership's need for assistance with gathering information and mobilizing votes led to a massive expansion of the Democratic whip system. Consisting of the majority whip, a deputy whip, and approximately eighteen regionally elected zone whips in the early 1970s, the whip system has grown to about 100 members. As of the 103rd Congress (1993-1994), the whip system consists of the majority whip, four chief deputy whips, fifteen deputy or other special whips, fifty-six at-large whips, and nineteen zone whips; all but the majority whip and the zone whips are leadership appointees.

The whip system is centrally involved in the process of mobilizing the votes needed to pass legislation important to the party. This effort is orchestrated through the whip system. As we will discuss later, a special whip task force that includes a subset of the large whip system membership oversees the effort to pass each major bill.

The whip organization also serves as a central conduit for information between members and leaders. For the exercise of legislative leadership, information about the preferences—and the moods, activities, and plans—of the membership is critical. The whip system provides the leaders with such information in two distinct ways. When the leaders instruct, the whips conduct a formal whip poll of members' voting intentions on upcoming legislation. The results of whip polls are an important guide to legislative strategy. A poll may indicate that a vote had better be postponed until a few more members can be brought around or even that substantive changes must be made in the bill at issue if it is to pass; conversely, it may show a solid majority in favor of the legislation and so indicate that no more resources need go into the effort.

Whip meetings, which take place every Thursday morning when the House is in session, are a key mechanism for the exchange of information between leaders and members. For leaders, the meetings provide information on the wishes and moods of their members and an opportunity to explain their decisions to a cross section of the membership. The whip meetings give members a regular opportunity to convey their concerns to their leaders on the whole spectrum of issues, to question them, to confront them, and to require them to justify their decisions; the meetings give members an opportunity to influence their leaders and shape party strategy.

When an even more inclusive forum is considered necessary, the Democratic Caucus—the organization of all House Democrats—provides it. The caucus meets prior to the beginning of each congress to select the party's candidate for Speaker, elect other party leaders, and to make a variety of other organizational decisions. Party rules specify that thereafter the caucus meets monthly and on petition of fifty members. Meetings vary enormously; some are pro forma with no business whatsoever, while others are gatherings of almost the entire Democratic membership for the exchange of information and for debate on issues of deep concern to all. Caucuses are called sometimes to discuss general party policy and sometimes to discuss specific legislation. Committee and party leaders can use the caucus to explain the politics and the substance of legislation, often in blunter terms than they might use in a public forum, and members can state their positions and ask questions more pointedly as well.

The Steering and Policy Committee, a committee of the Democratic Caucus, provides still another forum for discussion and information exchange; its most important function is, however, making Democratic committee assignments. When, in the mid-1970s, the reformers gave Steering and Policy that function, they greatly enhanced the Speaker's resources. During the 1950s and 1960s, an era of committee government, the Democratic party's top leaders— the Speaker and the majority leader when the party was in the majority—were not formally members of the party committee that assigned Democratic representatives to standing committees. Although they certainly influenced committee assignments, their influence was indirect.[2] The 1970s reforms greatly expanded the leaders' formal powers in the committee assignment process. The Steering and Policy Committee to which that task is now entrusted is chaired by the Speaker; the majority leader, the majority whip, and the four chief deputy whips are members ex officio, as are the chair and vice chair of the Democratic Caucus and the chair of the Democratic Congressional Campaign Committee. The Speaker appoints a number of the remaining members (in the 103rd Congress, nine of twenty-five).

The Speaker can use the clout in the committee assignment process that this heavy leadership presence provides to shape committee memberships or to apportion choice assignments as favors, or both. Because committee seats are so crucial to representatives' careers, the Speaker's increased influence over assignments is important; but, for the same reason, member expectations constrain the Speaker's use of this clout. Because members care so much about these decisions, the Speaker must be particularly sensitive about balancing criteria derived from the dictates of collective action versus those derived from the desire of members to be free to pursue their goals as individuals.

The single most important new power the Speaker was given as a result of the reforms of the 1970s was the right to nominate the Democratic members and the chair of the Rules Committee, subject only to ratification by the Democratic Caucus. Democratic members of the Rules Committee are now dependent on the Speaker for their positions, and the Committee has become an arm of the leadership. Control of the Rules Committee gives the leadership substantial control over floor scheduling, something it lacked when the Rules Committee was independent.[3] In addition, because the rule under which a bill is brought to the floor sets the conditions for floor consideration, control of the Committee can be used to structure the choices members face on the floor, sometimes to the advantage of a particular outcome.

When, in the mid-1970s, the House adopted multiple referral, that is, the requirement that legislation be referred to all committees with jurisdiction, it gave the Speaker the power to set time limits on committees for reporting the bill out. Reporting deadlines force committees to act or lose jurisdiction and, thus, prevent them from using delay to kill legislation or from extracting an exorbitant price for reporting it.[4]

During the 1970s and in the succeeding post-reform years, the leadership gained still other resources that enhanced its capacity to exploit its powers, old and new, to the limit set by member expectations. Because of the labor-intensive character of the legislative enterprise, staff is an important resource, and leadership staffs grew significantly. As with other members, the leaders may hire as many as eighteen full-time and four part-time employees. In addition, in the early 1990s, staff designated specifically for the leadership totaled approximately eighty-nine for House Democrats. The Speaker employed about twenty-four aides in his speakership offices and another twelve at the Steering and Policy Committee; the majority leader had twenty-three employees on his leadership payroll; the majority whip, thirteen; the chief deputy whips, six; and the Democratic Caucus, eleven.

Leadership professional staff perform a variety of functions, one of the most important being information gathering. They serve, as one aide said, "as the eyes and ears" of the leaders. "Our job," said another, is "to make sure the leadership is not surprised." Effectively using the powers the leadership commands to facilitate the passage of legislation the membership wants clearly requires information. Because of broad member participation in the post-reform House, more information is needed to plan strategy, and staff information gathering activities are critical. Beyond that, staffs perform on the leaders' behalf a range of activities extending from seeing that business flows smoothly on the House floor to negotiating on legislation to dealing with the media. Thus, staff greatly extends the range of matters in which the leadership can be involved.

Leadership Strategies

Using these new powers and resources and the restructured and reactivated party organizational entities, post-reform Speakers have developed strategies for meeting their members' expanded expectations. The provision of selective benefits—favors—to members has been a central leadership strategy during most of the history of the House. The Speaker controls "goods" useful to members in the pursuit of their goals. Members' knowledge that leaders can help them obtain a desired committee assignment, raise campaign funds, or get a locally important project included in a bill gives leaders' requests for cooperative behavior added weight. The reforms of the 1970s increased the selective benefits at the Speaker's command. As Speakers became more central to the legislative process, the assistance they could give members as individuals increased further. With the administration now in Democratic hands, the Speaker's access to the White House and the departments further augments the assistance the Speaker can provide individual members.

To be sure, the Speaker's supply of selective benefits is limited, and member expectations further constrain how they may be used. To help one member, the Speaker cannot inconvenience a majority or distort policy outputs to the detriment of the party image. Members' conception of fairness, which dictates that all geographical regions be represented on the major committees, constrains how the Speaker's influence in the committee assignment process can be employed. However, Democrats increasingly believe that party loyalty should be a major criteria for assignment to the most important committees, and this belief aids the Speaker in using assignments to foster cooperative behavior.

In addition to doing favors for individual members, post-reform Speakers emphasize, much more than their predecessors, the provision of services to their members collectively. Legislative scheduling is carried out with much greater attention to members' needs for predictability and time in the district. The whip system distributes a plethora of information, including timely and easily digestible summaries of the legislation up for floor consideration. In providing these services, the leaders respond directly to members' expectations. In addition, by making it possible for members to tend their districts more efficiently, such services may give members greater leeway in their pursuit of goals other than reelection.

Speakers developed a strategy of inclusion in response to the increased participation of members since the reforms of the 1970s. The Speaker tries to draw as many Democrats as possible into the leadership's orbit. As it evolved over time, the strategy reshaped the whip system and the process of mobilizing votes. The strategy of inclusion, especially as it manifested itself in the task force device, made it possible in the late 1970s for the Speaker to satisfy to a reasonable extent his members' potentially conflicting expectations. Task forces gave the core leadership the help it badly needed in the unpredictable environment of the immediate post-reform House. By increasing the number of people working in an organized way to pass the bill at issue, a task force increased the probability of legislative success. Task forces also gave a large number and broad variety of Democrats, and especially junior Democrats, an opportunity to participate meaningfully in the legislative process but in a way that contributed to, rather than detracted from, the leadership's effort to pass legislation.

Facing Republican administrations in the 1980s, Democrats became willing to accept some constraints on their autonomy, particularly limitations on the offering of floor amendments. The price in terms of policy of maintaining the wide-open, participatory process that characterized the period immediately following the reforms of the 1970s had proved to be too high. But with floor participation more restricted, the value to members of task force participation increased. Task forces provide Democrats the opportunity to become significantly involved in legislation they care about, even if they are junior or not on the committee of origin—an opportunity otherwise seldom available on the House floor.[5]

Structuring the choices members face is a quintessential legislative strategy. By making the Rules Committee an arm of the leadership, the reformers gave the Speaker true control of the flow of legislation to the floor and provided the Speaker with a powerful and flexible tool for structuring members' floor choices. In the immediate post-reform period, Democrats were unwilling to allow their Speaker to use these powers aggressively. But by the late 1970s, many Democrats had become concerned about the costs of the wide-open floor amending process that the reforms had established, and a number began urging the leadership to use restrictive special rules to bring some order and predictability to floor consideration.[6] The leadership responded to its members' changing expectations and needs by increasing its use of rules to structure choices. While in the mid-1970s most major legislation was considered under a simple open rule allowing all germane amendments, by the late 1980s most bills were brought to the floor under complex and usually restrictive rules.

On its face, the strategy of structuring choices via restrictive rules seems coercive, but the leadership generally uses it prudently. Since approval of a rule requires a majority of the House membership and thus usually a much larger proportion of Democrats, members must acquiesce in having their choices constrained. They usually do so because the leadership has skillfully crafted the rule so that approval furthers on balance most members' goals. Frequently, the leadership attempts to provide "cover" or protection for Democrats to enable them to vote their policy preferences without paying too big a reelection price. Sometimes the rule makes possible the passage of a bill that all members know must be enacted but that is unpalatable on both policy and reelection grounds. And, if a significant group of Democrats needs a vote on an amendment for constituency reasons, the leadership will provide the opportunity, though it will structure the choice to minimize the policy damage.

The strategy of "going public" was thrust on the Democratic party leadership by changing member expectations during the long period of divided control of government. Unlike rank-and-file House members, the Speaker does have considerable access to the national media. Members have come to expect the Speaker to use it to shape the political agenda and party images to their advantage. Because House party leadership had traditionally been defined as an insider job, the leaders of the 1980s and 1990s have had to invent the means for carrying out their members' mandate. Structures and tactics had to be developed, tried, and refined—a process still underway. With a Democratic president, the Speaker's visibility and role as party spokesperson inevitably declines, yet encouraging House Democrats to "all sing from the same hymn book," one of the aims of the leadership's media strategy, remains important.

Shaping Legislation

To further the Democratic membership's policy and reelection goals, legislation must satisfy the most intensely interested Democrats, it must be acceptable to most members of the party, and it must be at minimum defensible in the public arena and preferably broadly attractive. The complexity of satisfying all these criteria simultaneously varies across legislation. If the visibility of the legislation is low and the group of intensely concerned Democrats relatively small and homogeneous, the committee can usually do the job without help. On high visibility, high stakes legislation, committees now often need leadership assistance. Committees face a more contentious and more partisan climate on the floor. Much legislation is referred to more than one committee, thus requiring cross-committee bargaining and coordination at the pre-floor stage.

For a variety of reasons, a committee may not report in timely fashion a bill that the party membership or even its own party contingent wants. The committee's membership may be unrepresentative of the membership at large; the committee may be beset with internal leadership problems; the various parties to a dispute may all believe strategic advantage is to be gained by waiting out their adversaries. When such a problem arises, members now expect the Speaker to induce the committee to act.

Much of the Speaker's time is devoted to persuading members to compromise and prevailing on committee leaders to be responsive to the needs of significant segments of the Democratic membership or to the sentiments of the party as a whole. Most often, these efforts occur behind the scenes, but sometimes a more public forum is employed. Usually the leaders' approach is direct: they talk to, cajole, and lean on those causing the problems. Sometimes such efforts are supplemented by indirect means: others from inside or outside the chamber are enlisted to aid in the persuasion effort.

In October 1991, going into a presidential election year with criticism of the House at a high, the House Democratic party needed a solid legislative accomplishment before adjourning for the year. The big highway bill that would benefit all parts of the country fit the need nicely. When the chair of the Public Works Committee expressed doubt about reconciling the House and Senate versions by the Thanksgiving adjournment target, the Speaker called him into his office. As Speaker Foley reported at an October 30 news conference, "I had a conversation with Mr. Roe last night, and we agreed the highway bill will be done by Thanksgiving." [7] Earlier in the year, the Speaker had prevailed on a reluctant Ways and Means Committee chair to move legislation extending unemployment benefits. When more than one committee is involved in formulating legislation, committee leaders may not be capable of providing the intercommittee coordination and mediation needed to bring an acceptable bill to the floor. During the 101st Congress, the Ways and Means Committee and the Education and Labor Committee were at loggerheads over child care legislation; each came up with a distinct approach and refused to budge. After exhorting and pressuring the committees to compromise to little avail, the party leadership intervened directly; Speaker Foley "personally brokered the final package," an aide explained. Because many members very much wanted the legislation and the Democratic party needed to show it could produce, the leadership had no choice but to step in. Foley had, in fact, been subjected to considerable criticism from within his party for not doing so earlier.

Omnibus legislation almost always requires leadership brokering and coordination. Budget resolutions, reconciliation bills, continuing resolutions, and bills such as the omnibus trade bill of 1988 and the various omnibus drug bills of the 1980s involve an enormous number of consequential issues, some of which always land in the leadership's lap because other actors cannot resolve them.

Any high stakes legislation is now likely to require leadership involvement at the pre-floor stage. Decisions about the substance of highly salient and controversial legislation can have significant repercussions for the image of the Democratic party and thereby may affect members' electoral fates. Such legislation needs to be readily defensible in the public arena. When committee leaders are not sufficiently sensitive to such concerns or are not capable of doing what is necessary, Democrats expect their party leaders to intervene. Thus, during the Bush administration, the party leadership was deeply involved in drafting minimum wage and civil rights legislation that was acceptable to both the most intensely interested Democrats and the party membership at large and that was defensible in the public arena. In the early months of the Clinton administration, the leadership brokered an agreement with conservative Democrats that made passage of the reconciliation bill possible. Failure of this legislation, which implemented Clinton's economic program, would have delivered a devastating blow to the new administration and to the image of the Democratic party.

As these instances suggest, the Speaker's active role in shaping legislation is more than simply a by-product of behind-the-scenes efforts to mediate conflicts and coordinate action. When the Congress considers bills of great substantive scope and political consequence, it is not simply the party leadership's coordinating capacities that dictate its involvement. Members are often unwilling to rely solely on committee leaders to interpret their will and to protect their political and policy interests. On such legislation, only the party leadership as the elected agent of its members possesses the legitimacy to speak and make decisions for the membership.

When agreement must be reached with political actors outside the House, a similar logic often dictates that the party leaders represent their members. When a bill reaches conference, differences between the chambers and with the administration must sometimes be worked out under great time pressure. "Summit" negotiations between the president and Congress only take place when agreement through normal processes has proven impossible and on policy matters of great consequence.

Relatively formal negotiations between congressional leaders and high ranking administration officials representing the president directly are a recent phenomenon. President and Congress have resorted to summits when normal processes are, for one reason or another, incapable of producing an agreement and the costs of failing to reach an agreement are very high. During the 1980s and early 1990s, the deficit and the budget process often provided the sense of emergency and the statutory deadline that made inaction politically costly. The sharp differences in policy preferences between Republican presidents and congressional Democrats and the tough decisions that had to be made often stalemated normal processes and made summits necessary. Invariably, the party leadership has represented its membership in these negotiations. With a Democrat in the White House, such relatively formal summits are much less likely, but the Speaker does play a central role as go-between, conveying the Democratic members' views and interests to the president and the president's to House Democrats. Inevitably, the Speaker is drawn into questions of policy substance.

Contemporary Speakers are much more deeply and regularly involved in the pre-floor legislative process than were their predecessors. Democratic committee leaders countenance such leadership activity because it is aimed at passing the committee's legislation, because the party leadership in its dealings with the committees represents the sentiments of the Democratic membership, or both. Party leaders almost always work with committee Democrats to shape a legislative vehicle that increases the probability of success. The strategy of inclusion makes the decline in autonomy easier for committee Democrats to accept.

Recent speakers have differed somewhat in how quick they are to intervene in the pre-floor legislative process. Speaker Jim Wright used the leverage his position gave him quite expansively. Foley, as a former committee chair, defers to chairs more and tends to wait longer before he intervenes. These are, however, differences at the margin. House Democrats expect their leaders to produce legislative results; when doing so requires pressuring committees and their chairs, they expect their leaders to do so.

Assembling Floor Majorities

Changes in the House and in the political environment in the past two decades have resulted in much more frequent demands on the leadership to become actively involved in floor-passage efforts. The House floor is the party leadership's traditional province and assembling floor majorities its traditional responsibility. Yet in the pre-reform House, committees could usually pass their bills without much help from the party leadership. Floor passage is now much less certain. Democratic committee contingents and the Democratic membership more often need help from their party's leadership to pass legislation on the floor.

To meet member expectations, the Speaker needs to engineer the passage of legislation but to do so without constraining too much the members' desire to participate in the legislative process. The strategies of structuring choices and of inclusion as currently employed make possible a balance roughly satisfactory to most Democrats.

The floor amending process on a bill is governed by a special order or rule reported by the Rules Committee; a rule may, for example, bar all amendments or make only certain specific amendments in order. In response to the explosion of amending activity on the House floor, the party leadership in the 1980s increased its use of rules that restrict amendments in some way. In the 95th Congress (1977-1978), 12 percent of rules were restrictive; by the 102nd Congress (1991-1992), 66 percent were.[8]

The rule for the reconciliation bill implementing Clinton's economic program in 1993, for example, allowed only a vote on a comprehensive Republican substitute; amendments to delete various unpopular elements of the package—the Btu tax and the tax on social security payments to high income recipients—were not made in order. Many Democrats would have found it very difficult to explain votes against such amendments back home, especially in response to thirty-second attack advertisements, so allowing such amendments would have confronted Democrats with the unpalatable choice between casting a series of politically dangerous votes or contributing to the picking apart of the package on the floor.

The leadership frequently employs carefully crafted and often restrictive rules to enable their members to vote their policy preferences without paying too big a reelection price. Closed rules, for example, may provide cover for members by making the crucial vote a procedural one. Unpopular but necessary measures may be bundled with more popular provisions and voted on as a package under a restrictive rule. Thus members could justify a vote for a congressional pay raise by including in the package a stringent ethics code. When Democrats really need to offer an amendment for policy or reelection reasons, they are given the opportunity to do so. On the 1991 civil rights bill, for example, the Black Caucus and a group of women members were given the chance to offer a liberal substitute to a more moderate version drafted to have broad appeal.

Republicans complain bitterly that restrictive rules unfairly curtail their opportunities to participate meaningfully in the legislative process, that the rules are means for preventing the House from working its will. (For the Republican perspective, see Chapter 4.) During the debate on the 1993 reconciliation bill, for example, Republicans argued that any rule that did not allow them to offer a series of amendments, including ones knocking out the Btu tax and the tax on social security benefits, was undemocratic. Democrats believed that such a rule would simply allow Republicans to play irresponsible political games; they could put Democrats on the spot by forcing them to vote on the least popular components of the deficit reduction plan and possibly manage to unravel the carefully constructed compromise. Reminding their opponents that in 1981 Republicans had insisted on considering Reagan's economic program under a highly restrictive rule, Democrats passed a rule that allowed Republicans to offer only a comprehensive substitute.

The frequent partisan floor battles over rules indicate how important the decision on the character of the rule is. Rules are never neutral in their effects; any rule—whether open or closed or somewhere in between—provides an advantage to some outcome over others. Of course, the majority party leadership will structure rules to provide advantages to its party members rather than to the opposition party. Republican frustrations are understandable. Major legislation increasingly splits the membership along partisan lines, and meaningful participation in shaping the legislation and amassing support takes place within the majority party. So long as Democrats remain reasonably unified and willing to allow their leadership to use its tools aggressively, the minority party is irrelevant. A commentator has called Republicans' complaints the "shrieks of the eunuchs."

Any Democrat, no matter how junior, can take part in the leadership's efforts to mobilize votes as long as he or she supports the legislation at issue and is willing to work. The regionally elected zone whips carry out the initial count of Democrats' voting intentions. The bulk of the work of mobilizing votes is performed by a whip's task force constituted by sending out a broad-based invitation to all whips and to other potentially interested Democrats. The members of the task force refine the count by checking personally on the voting intentions of members not contacted or undecided on the initial count; by one-on-one contacts, they attempt to persuade members not committed to the party position to support it; they "work the doors"—standing at the chamber doors to ensure that members know what the party position is on the vote and to answer questions if necessary; they "work the floor"—attempting some last-minute persuasion if necessary.

Task forces provide leaders with badly needed assistance, and they provide members, especially more junior ones and those not on the committee of origin, with an opportunity to participate meaningfully in the legislative process on issues of special interest. Of course, party and committee leaders are very much involved in planning strategy and, when necessary, in last minute persuasion. The more consequential the legislation and the more uncertain its passage, the more likely the top party leadership and the Speaker personally are to get directly and centrally involved.

The battle to pass the reconciliation bill in May 1993 is a case in point. Success was critical for the Clinton administration in its early days and for the Democratic party, and yet, because the package contained some unpalatable provisions, passage was difficult. Whip Bonior himself headed up the task force, which started work several weeks before the bill got to the floor. Members of the task force and then the top leaders themselves unrelentingly pursued every House Democrat; anyone who might have influence with an undecided or recalcitrant member—state party chairs, governors, union officials, personal friends—were enlisted whenever possible to help in the persuasion effort. The administration was, of course, very much engaged. Cabinet secretaries called and visited Democrats; Secretary of the Treasury Lloyd Bentsen, for example, came to the Texas delegation's lunch meeting. The president personally called close to sixty members—some of them repeatedly. The Speaker himself closed floor debate for his party, telling members that "this is a time to stand and deliver; this is a time to justify your election." [9]

Given the level of effort, Democrats could hardly fail to understand that how they voted on the bill would affect their futures in the House. This vote would count heavily, everyone knew, in the leadership's consideration of committee assignments. As Rep. Barney Frank (D-Mass.) said, "Nobody got a pass on this." [10] The pressure was unusually overt in this instance: first-term members circulated a petition demanding that any committee or subcommittee chair who voted against the party position be stripped of his or her position by the caucus. Within hours, more than eighty Democrats, including several influential committee chairs, had signed.[11] Committee leaders were thus sharply reminded that they are agents of the Democratic membership and that, in their importunings, the party leadership was reflecting the wishes of the majority of Democrats.

Through its command over special rules and over the whip system, the Democratic party leadership can increase very significantly the likelihood of legislation passing intact on the House floor. The leadership's use of these tools depends on its members' acquiescence and is most effective when, as in this case, it is clear that the leadership is acting as the agent of its membership.

Setting the Agenda and Shaping Debate

In December 1986, immediately after being chosen the Democrats' nominee for Speaker, Wright outlined a policy agenda for the majority party and the House: deficit reduction achieved in part through a tax increase, clean water legislation, a highway bill, trade legislation, welfare reform, and a farm bill were included. In his acceptance speech after being elected Speaker on

January 6, 1987, and in his televised reply to the president's state of the union address on January 31, Wright further specified and publicized the agenda, adding aid to education, aid to the homeless, and insurance against catastrophic illness.

Over the course of the 100th Congress, Wright continued to call attention to and raise expectations of action on these items in a variety of public and House forums. He used his powers as Speaker to assure that these bills were given preferential consideration in the chamber. As items were enacted, they were cited repeatedly as accomplishments, and some new issues were added to the agenda. By and large, though, the Speaker kept the focus on the original agenda, and by the end of the 100th Congress every item on that agenda had become law.

Although special political conditions facilitated Speaker Wright's aggressive agenda setting, Democrats have come to expect their Speaker to play an active agenda-setting role when control is divided. When the opposition party controls the White House, congressional Democrats will usually be dissatisfied with the president's agenda. Yet even when the president's party is a minority in Congress, the president has great advantages in the struggle to define the national and the congressional agenda. To get their issues on the agenda, House Democrats need their leadership's aid. Furthermore, during the 1980s most Democrats became convinced that, under conditions of divided control, the congressional majority party receives little credit for the legislation it does produce unless it has a clear, publicly enunciated agenda. Of course, Wright's agenda-setting function was shared in part with Senate Majority Leader Robert Byrd of West Virginia, but because of the more decentralized character of the Senate, the House Speaker typically is able to have a greater impact on agenda setting.

It became increasingly clear during the 1980s that the party leadership could not rely solely on insider strategies to pass legislation. How the issue in question is defined often determines the electoral risk inherent in a particular vote and, as a consequence, the opposing sides' probability of legislative success. Moreover, specific legislative battles and broader controversies may leave residues on party images. Which party ultimately benefits and which loses in the court of public opinion, which gets the credit or which bears the blame, is largely determined by how the issue has been defined. House Democrats expect their Speaker to participate effectively in national political discourse, influencing the terms of the debate to further the immediate legislative goals of the Democrats and to protect and enhance the party's image.

The Speaker has available numerous forums for enunciating the party's message; however, because the press do not consider the Speaker as intrinsically newsworthy as the president, coverage is seldom guaranteed. When the Speaker delivers the party's reply to an opposition president's state of the union address, the Speaker has the rare opportunity to speak directly and at some length to a large national audience. The Speaker's address at the beginning of a Congress will also receive considerable press coverage. The Speaker and other members of the leadership team are invited to appear on the morning news shows occasionally and on the *MacNeil/Lehrer NewsHour* and the weekend interview shows more frequently, but in these cases the press determines the topics of discussion. Every day that the House is in session, the Speaker holds a short news conference a few minutes before the chamber convenes. The Speaker can command a reasonable press turnout, though not necessarily extensive coverage, for a special news conference. As has been discussed in an earlier chapter, each of the top leaders employs at least one press aide who is in constant touch with the Capitol Hill press corps. Because the halls of the Capitol are open to the press, impromptu, informal contact between reporters and leaders is frequent.

Although the Speaker has a great deal of contact with the press and a certain amount of access to media forums for putting forth the party's message, the Speaker is at a severe disadvantage compared to an opposition party president with whom the Speaker must compete for press attention. The Speaker's own members' tendency to blur the clear message the Speaker would like to convey further hinders the leadership in its attempt to shape debate. Although members want their Speaker to take a lead role as their agent in national political discourse, they are not willing to abstain themselves. The result can be a cacophony of disparate voices that not only garbles the message but also prompts "Democrats in disarray" stories. Getting everyone "to sing from the same hymn book" is a perpetual problem.

Employing the strategy of inclusion, the leadership has attempted to alleviate the problem by involving a large number of the members in an organized message effort. The "message group," consisting of a score or so of Democrats—most of the core leadership and a number of media-savvy, mid-seniority activists—meets each morning that the House is in session to develop a message for the day and plan its dissemination. To actually get the message out, especially via the one-minute speeches any member may deliver at the beginning of a House session, the smaller strategy group relies on a pool of 90 to 100 members known as the "message board." A badly split party cannot be unified or made to appear united by such efforts but, when the party is reasonably united, such coordination assures that Democrats get the maximum public benefit and may even amplify the members' unity.

The president, as leader of the party, is its preeminent agenda setter and spokesperson. Thus, with a Democratic president, the Speaker's public position changes, but media strategies do not become less important. The leadership must now coordinate the message it attempts to communicate with that of the White House. In private the Speaker conveys the party members' views and interests to the president, but publicly any seeming or actual difference of opinion between the Speaker and the president almost certainly becomes a media disaster. By reiterating and reinforcing the president's message, the Speaker can contribute directly, if modestly, to shaping national political discourse to the advantage of the party. In addition, for a president attempting to bring about major policy change, having House Democrats unified in support of the president's message is crucially important, and in this endeavor the House Democratic leadership can help.

The Challenge of Party Leadership in the 1990s

House Democrats expect their party leadership to advance their policy and reelection goals by aggressively promoting the collective action necessary to pass legislation. They also expect to be free to advance their goals as individuals and expect their leadership to refrain from hindering them unduly in that endeavor. The challenge the Speaker as party leader faces is reconciling these two potentially conflicting expectations.

The two most recent Speakers answered this challenge in somewhat different ways. Wright made highly aggressive use of leadership tools to promote his membership's collective interests by setting the agenda and passing legislation; Foley has been somewhat less aggressive and more attentive to members' desires for autonomy to promote their goals as individuals. House Democrats lauded Wright for a phenomenally successful legislative record and criticized him for sometimes being heavy-handed. Foley has been praised for his willingness to listen, his conciliatory approach, and his sensitivity to the individual member's needs; he also has been criticized for not being assertive enough in setting forth an agenda and pushing committees to deliver. Certainly these two very different personalities affected their leadership styles but so, too, did the political context. The special circumstances of the 100th Congress—President Reagan weakened by his lame-duck status, the IranContra scandal, the loss of

Republican control of the Senate, and an accumulation of legislative proposals on which Democrats agreed—made Wright's highly aggressive leadership possible; had he not been forced to resign, his leadership style would have been somewhat lower keyed during newly elected President Bush's first two years. Political circumstances—a new president with limited but nevertheless greater resources than the one he replaced and the passage in the previous Congress of much of the accumulated consensus agenda—would have dictated the change—not member discontent, which was never very severe. Becoming Speaker under these political circumstances, Foley was less aggressive than Wright had been in the previous Congress. Over time, as political circumstances changed, Foley became more assertive in taking on the president and promoting the party and its agenda.

Although there are stylistic differences between the two Speakers, what they have in common is more important for understanding the character of party leadership in the House of the 1990s. To satisfy the members' expectations, the contemporary Speaker must be highly active, routinely involved in all stages of the legislative process, and much more engaged than previous Speakers have been in political discourse on the national stage. Because members' expectations of policy results and of autonomy are potentially conflicting, no Speaker will escape criticism.

The election of a Republican House majority after many years of Democratic control opens a new chapter in majority leadership. Although he leads a different party, Speaker Gingrich faces the same problem of striking an acceptable balance between the two imperatives. After forty years out of power, Republican House members have high expectations of participating fully in the legislative process and of quickly producing major policy results. Reelection concerns loom large for the enormous number of junior House Republicans. And the party must show it can act as a responsible majority. Even though the members the new speaker leads are ideologically quite homogeneous and believe themselves to be mandated to bring about policy change, meeting their expectations over the course of the 104th Congress will be no easy task.

Notes

1. Barbara Sinclair, *Majority Leadership in the U.S. House* (Baltimore: Johns Hopkins University Press, 1983), chap. 3 and 6. See also Barbara Sinclair, "The Emergence of Strong Leadership in the 1980s House of Representatives," *Journal of Politics* 54 (Aug. 1992): 658-684; David W. Rohde, *Parties and Leaders in the Postreform House* (Chicago: University of Chicago Press, 1991), 58-60.

2. Nicholas Masters, "Committee Assignments," *American Political Science Review* 55 (June 1961): 345-357.

3. For a more complete discussion of rules, see Stanley Bach and Steven Smith, *Managing Uncertainty in the House of Representatives* (Washington, D.C.: Brookings Institution, 1988). For more on the changing relationship between the Speaker and the Rules Committee, see Bruce I. Oppenheimer, "The Changing Relationship between House Leadership and the Committee on Rules" in *Understanding Congressional Leadership*, ed. Frank Mackaman (Washington, D.C.: CQ Press, 1981); Sinclair, *Majority Leadership in the U.S. House*; Barbara Sinclair, "Strong Party Leadership in a Weak Party Era—The Evolution of Party Leadership in the Modern House" in *The Atomistic Congress*, ed. Allen D. Herzke and Ronald M. Peters, Jr. (Armonk, N.Y.: M.E. Sharpe, 1992).

4. Gary Young and Joseph Cooper, "Multiple Referral and the Transformation of House Decision Making" in *Congress Reconsidered*, 5th ed., ed. Lawrence C. Dodd and Bruce I. Oppenheimer (Washington, D.C.: CQ Press, 1993).

5. David Price, *The Congressional Experience* (Boulder, Colo.: Westview Press, 1992).

6. Bach and Smith, *Managing Uncertainty in the House of Representatives*, 41.

7. Quoted in Chuck Alston, "The Speaker and the Chairmen: A Taoist Approach to Power," *Congressional Quarterly Weekly Report*, Nov. 2, 1991, 3178.

8. Don Wolfensberger, "Comparative Data on the U.S. House of Representatives," compiled by the Republican staff of the House Rules Committee, Nov. 10, 1992.

9. George Hager and David S. Cloud, "Democrats Pull off Squeaker in Approving Clinton Plan," *Congressional Quarterly Weekly Report*, May 29, 1993, 1341.

10. Ibid.

11. Ibid., 1345.

4 The Speaker: A Republican Perspective

John J. Pitney, Jr., and William F. Connelly, Jr.

On January 5, 1993, the House elected Democrat Tom Foley to another term as Speaker. House Republicans saw this day as a bitter landmark, for no one in their party had won such an election in forty years. None of the 176 Republicans in residence at the time had ever served with a GOP Speaker, and eleven of them had not even been *born* when their party yielded control in 1955. Of the Democrats, all but four—Jamie Whitten (Miss.), Jack Brooks (Texas), William Natcher (Ky.), and Sidney Yates (Ill.)—had spent their entire House careers in the majority.

The four-decade stretch of minority status for the House GOP has no precedent: before 1955, neither party had ever dwelled in the minority for more than sixteen years at a time. In 1989, Republican leader Robert Michel noted that each day, "I am setting a new record for having served longer in consecutive years, as a member of the minority party, than any other man or woman in our history." [1]

House Republicans think that one-party dominance has bred arrogance on the majority side. In 1985, moderate Republican Tom Tauke of Iowa said that Democrats "have no fear of being in the minority—and therefore of limitations being put on their power. The Democrats don't say, 'We'd better not do this to the Republicans because they could retaliate and do the same thing to us when they win the majority.' " [2]

Because of such arrogance, goes the GOP argument, House Democrats have come to regard the speakership merely as a partisan tool. Instead of serving the entire House, recent Speakers have served the Democratic party and especially its dominant liberal faction. Republicans generally acknowledge that the American speakership cannot be as detached from party as its British and Canadian counterparts. In 1983, Richard Cheney of Wyoming, then a member of the House GOP leadership, co-authored a book titled *Kings of the Hill,* which applauded the political strength of several Speakers. [3] Republicans nevertheless contend that the speakership—a constitutional office—carries responsibilities that should restrain partisan interests. Ever since Tip O'Neill, say the Republicans, Speakers have gone too far in favoring their partisan role over their institutional one. In 1984, Cheney said that O'Neill often had demeaned his office with personal insults and procedural tricks:

As institutional leader, the Speaker must preserve the House as a democratic body, which means providing a calm forum where both sides can discuss all the major issues of the day. The Speaker's party names someone else—the majority leader—to be its point man. . . . Just as important, the Speaker symbolizes the House both within the framework of government and in the public mind. By word and deed, he can raise the level of political rhetoric, or drag the House into pettiness. [4]

O'Neill dismissed Cheney's comments as "completely at odds with his recent book," [5] and other House Democrats saw them as the sour grapes of a permanent minority. Republicans could respond by quoting Speaker O'Neill's own statement on his selection as Speaker:

I pledge to be prompt and impartial in deciding parliamentary questions. I pledge to be patient, good-tempered, and courteous toward the individual members. I pledge best to employ the talent of the House for full and fair consideration of issues that come before us. In those "moments of agitation from which no deliberative assembly is always entirely exempt," I pledge to "remain cool and unshaken, guarding the permanent laws and rules of the House from being sacrificed to temporary passions, prejudices, or interests." [6]

In 1978, Speaker O'Neill voiced similar thoughts when apologizing for an attack against a Republican who had questioned his honesty: "When I am interviewed as Speaker, I have an official responsibility to be above the battle. . . . [A]s Speaker, a constitutional officer of this House, I must be more charitable and responsible toward my colleagues than they sometimes are toward me." [7]

These observations by Cheney and O'Neill pose the question of whether a Speaker can exercise strong leadership without excessive partisanship. Cheney praised "kings of the Hill" who "impose order on an institution so large its natural tendency is towards chaos." [8] So who contradicted himself: Cheney or O'Neill? Although it may be hard to tell strong leadership from excessive partisanship, lawmakers believe that such a distinction exists. Democrats and Republicans regularly accuse each other of going out of bounds and hurting the institution. One may be tempted to ignore these charges as partisan claptrap, but House members take them seriously.

To note the thinness of the foul line is not to deny its existence. The principled distinction is rooted in the Speaker's constitutional role, as O'Neill suggested. The House, wrote James Madison, is supposed to "support in the members an habitual recollection of their dependence on the people." [9] Partisan differences, said Alexander Hamilton, "may sometimes obstruct salutary plans, yet often promote deliberation and circumspection; and serve to check excesses in the majority." [10] The Speaker should thus ensure that members can be held accountable for their actions, and that the parties can engage in civilized deliberation.

To a member, House Republicans think that recent Democratic Speakers have neglected these duties. While united in their frustrations with the majority party, they are divided by conflicting approaches to their plights. Some prefer the strategy of accommodation: working within the system to achieve incremental progress and persuade the majority to loosen its grip. Others stress confrontation: sharpening partisan differences to win more seats. House Republicans take positions all across this spectrum, and few believe purely in either approach. Over time, however, House Republicans increasingly have tended toward confrontation.

Democrats scorn the GOP's confrontational wing. During the 1990 budget debate, Steny Hoyer of Maryland said: "The Gingrich wing of the Republican party doesn't want to have an agreement. He wants to destroy the process and the institution." [11] And amid the House Bank controversy a year later, New York's Matthew McHugh said: "People like Newt Gingrich see it in their partisan interest to tear down the institution because they hope from the ashes to rebuild it in their own image." [12] House Republicans note that these complaints echo Richard Nixon, who accused *his* critics of seeking to undermine the presidency. They make a strong distinction between assailing the institution and faulting its current management. It is the Democrats, they say, who have hurt the House by abusing their power; and it is the GOP that wants to put the House back in order.[13]

Before examining the House Republicans' views of the recent speakership and House GOP proposals for reform, we should sketch the relationship between the parties in the decades before O'Neill. We shall see that the House has not always been filled with rancor.

Before O'Neill

During the era of strong Speakers (1890-1910), Speakers such as Joseph

Cannon appointed the committees and enjoyed other powers that let them control legislative outcomes. In 1987, Vin Weber (R-Minn.), wrote that the House was reverting to Cannonism "and its propensity to both ignore the national interests and abuse the rights of the minority party." [14] He exaggerated: in comparison with the days of Reed and Cannon, today's House stands as a model of participatory democracy. A less sweeping statement would have come nearer the truth; namely, that in the years between Cannon and O'Neill, the House was less centralized and less partisan.

One prominent Speaker of this period was Republican Nicholas Longworth (R-Ohio), the whose chapter in the Cheney book is titled "Slick Nick Longworth's Fist of Iron." [15] Despite his political toughness, Speaker Longworth preferred persuasion to coercion. Every morning, he rode to work with Democratic Leader John Nance Garner (Texas), and they used their daily commutes to negotiate partisan differences. "He has been so fair to the Democrats," said one observer, "that many good Republicans have protested." [16]

For much of the 1930s, House Republicans worried less about influence than survival: in the 75th Congress (1937-1939), the Democrats outnumbered them 333 to 89. Then the Republicans made a comeback and by the early 1940s stood within grasp of a majority. Their lot in the House also benefited from the selection of Sam Rayburn as Speaker in 1941. Rayburn both reflected and sustained the norms that ruled the institution in the mid-twentieth century: comity, fairness, honesty, diligence, and devotion to the House.[17]

Rayburn built close ties with Republican Leader Joseph Martin of Massachusetts, who went on to hold the speakership in the 80th and 83rd Congresses. Their partnership stemmed both from their personal characteristics and their knowledge that each might stand in the other's place after the next election. When Martin handed the gavel to Rayburn in 1955, Rayburn suggested that they not trade offices because they could soon just have to switch again. Martin sometimes persuaded Republicans on the Rules Committee to help Rayburn get around the implacable chair, Howard W. Smith. At the end of the 1958 session, Martin offered a resolution praising Rayburn for his "able, impartial, and dignified manner." Rayburn replied: "I want to say there has never been an unpleasant moment between us." [18]

Martin *did* have unpleasant moments with the White House. The 80th Congress marked the first (and thus far, only) time since Woodrow Wilson that a Republican Speaker served under a Democratic president. Martin inaugurated his speakership with words that would later sound odd to Republican members accustomed to GOP presidents and a Democratic Congress: "Our

American concept of government rests upon the idea of a dominant Congress ... a Congress which will protect the liberties of the people and not delegate its fundamental powers either to the Executive or to arrogant bureaucrats." [19] He fought the domestic policies of President Harry S. Truman, who responded by damning the "do-nothing Eightieth Congress." Martin backed a bipartisan foreign policy—up to a point. In 1951, back in the role of minority leader, he persuaded General Douglas MacArthur to write a letter criticizing Truman's conduct of the Korean War, an incident that ended with MacArthur's firing.

Under Dwight Eisenhower, Martin generally supported administration policies, yet clung to his belief in congressional independence: "I was not disposed to change my colors and ask Republicans who had served under my leadership to leap blindly behind every suggestion trotted down from the White House. This attitude did not endear me to the President's staff." [20] After the GOP's 1958 losses, Eisenhower aides lent quiet support to an anti-Martin movement within GOP ranks, which arose because some Republicans thought that Martin had grown too friendly with Rayburn. The movement succeeded in replacing him with Charles Halleck of Indiana.

Though less cordial with the Speaker, Halleck generally did not criticize Rayburn's leadership. At the end of the 1960 session, Halleck said about Rayburn: "Never have I found him unfair. Never have I found him arbitrary." [21] Soon after, Rayburn died and was succeeded by Majority Leader John McCormack of Massachusetts. Years later, a promising House Democrat named Jim Wright thought back to McCormack's rise:

[S]ome members at first felt that McCormack might be more partisan than Rayburn, more eager to pick a fight and less inclined to conciliation. What they overlooked was that the nature of his job [as majority leader] had required him to be. While the Speaker must be a fair and impartial judge, the majority leader must be an advocate. The Speaker's office itself can profoundly mellow and alter the outlook of the strongest-willed men. [22]

Halleck had only tribute for McCormack, both as majority leader and Speaker: "John McCormack always was a worthy and formidable antagonist who fought hard—but always fair. . . . We can fight without malice or rancor." [23] Gerald Ford, who defeated Halleck for the GOP leadership after the 1964 election, also revered McCormack. [24]

The next Speaker, Carl Albert of Oklahoma, had a similar style. Before he was a partisan leader, he was first of all "spokesman for the entire House of Representatives, including the Republicans and Democrats, the conservatives and the liberals, the young and the old, the ambitious and satisfied." [25] John Rhodes of Arizona, who became Republican leader when Ford became vice president, lauded Albert's "fair-minded approach towards all members regardless of party," [26] and aimed his criticism instead toward committee chairs and other Democratic party leaders.

As the Republican leaders' comments suggest, Rayburn, McCormack, and Albert all inspired GOP respect because of their willingness to work with the minority. Several other conditions encouraged relative peace between the parties; and by the 1970s, all of these conditions were changing.

First, the stunning loss of forty-eight Republican seats in the 1958 midterm election initially seemed an aberration. Politicians assumed that the GOP would recoup its losses and regain a fighting chance to win a majority. This assumption appeared plausible for a decade or so, as Republicans scored impressive victories in 1966 and 1968. In 1972, demographic shifts and a weak Democratic presidential ticket portended further significant gains. Hopes then fizzled. The GOP picked up only thirteen seats; Republican Leader Ford later recalled, "I had to conclude that I would never become Speaker of the House." [27] As the prospect of a GOP majority dwindled to the level of fantasy (except for a moment after the Reagan victory of 1980), both parties started to see the House GOP as a permanent minority—and they acted accordingly.

Second, Republicans did not regard the House as hostile territory in the 1950s and 1960s because of the composition of the Democratic party. Conservative southerners, who made up a large fraction of the House Democratic Caucus, pulled the Democratic leadership toward the center and sometimes enabled Republicans to build winning legislative coalitions. After 1958, northern liberals started to gain numerical strength and seniority within the Democratic Caucus, a trend that accelerated with the class of 1974. Meanwhile, the enfranchisement of black voters helped bring white southern Democrats into the party's ideological mainstream. As Republicans looked to the other side of the aisle, they saw fewer and fewer friendly faces.[28]

Third, change in the House climate involved the structure of power on the majority side. Even if McCormack and Albert had been more partisan, they lacked the ability to do the GOP much harm. Power was dispersed among the committee chairs, many of whom were conservative southerners. The rising liberal wing of the Democratic party saw the committee chairs as an obstacle and sought reforms to diminish their authority. One such reform consisted of open meetings. "In closed meetings, Republican members used to be able to cut a deal and drive the chairman," a veteran GOP staff member said. "With daylight, the only place power is swapped is in the Speaker's chambers." The reformers also strengthened the party leadership, including the Speaker. Among other things, the Democrats empowered the Speaker to nominate the chair and majority members of the Rules Committee; shifted other committee assignments to the Steering and Policy Committee, chaired and partly selected by the Speaker; and gave the Speaker more latitude over bill referrals.[29] From the viewpoint of the Democratic reformers, these changes restored unity and order to their party. From the viewpoint of Republicans, they enabled the majority to trample the minority. In this way, the reforms would make the speakership a symbol and target for GOP frustrations.

Fourth, the changing identity of the Democratic leadership encouraged partisanship in the House. Just as the Democratic liberals were strengthening the speakership, they wanted to fill the post with a vibrant champion of their cause. In 1976, they found such a person in Majority Leader O'Neill. GOP Leader Rhodes called O'Neill "the most partisan man I have ever known," and remembered O'Neill's blunt warning: "Republicans are just going to have to get it through their heads that they are not going to write legislation!"[30]

Whatever their personal inclinations, future Speakers would now have to consider the O'Neill model and heed members who saw the speakership as their shield and hammer. Speaker O'Neill had few reservations about partisan combat.

O'Neill and the Dogs of War

During the early years of O'Neill's tenure, Republicans still could wield some influence on the House floor. In the early 1970s, the House had started recording votes on amendments in the Committee of the Whole. Up to then, the *Congressional Record* had not published individual members' votes on amendments. The push for recorded votes had come from liberal Democrats who thought that their side would win in the sunshine. But Republicans used recorded votes to bog down Democratic bills and force the majority to take public stands on touchy issues.[31]

The House Republicans thought their activities were fostering deliberation and accountability. Robert Bauman of Maryland said that GOP victories on amendments revealed "the ability of Republicans to develop responsible and meritorious legislative alternatives that transcend mere partisan considerations."[32] The Democrats thought the Republicans were hindering the chamber's work. John LaFalce of New York wrote the Speaker and the Rules chair that "without relief of some kind, we won't be able to do the jobs for which we were elected and the ultimate result will be inefficient Members in an inefficient institution." [33] With O'Neill's encouragement, the Rules Committee began to make greater use of rules that limited the number and type of floor amendments. Bauman called this practice "the most serious and scandalous blow struck against democratic procedures in the House to date." [34] From now on, restrictive rules would be a major point of contention between Democratic Speakers and the GOP.

The stakes got higher with the GOP victories of 1980, for now each side saw itself as a minority. As Foley put it: "There are two minorities in the House of Representatives—the Democratic minority vis-à-vis the administration, and a Republican minority vis-à-vis the House." [35] To fight Reagan's policies, the House Democrats first had to use procedure against the House Republicans. What the majority saw as a fair fight with a mighty president, the minority saw as a theft of what little influence they had.

Democrats said that Republicans had no right to complain. O'Neill recalled that "I could have refused to play ball with the Reagan administration by holding up the president's legislation in the Rules Committee," as many Democrats had urged; instead, he "decided to give it a chance to be voted on by the nation's elected representatives." [36] The GOP, by contrast, saw a Speaker trying to scuttle Reaganomics. When the House took up the legislation to specify budget reductions, the Rules Committee sought to force separate votes on individual cuts, which the Democrats had altered to make as unappealing as possible. Minority Leader Michel said: "These are no longer our amendments that are made in order. They are bastards of the worst order for which we disclaim parental responsibility. . . . It is a rotten rule. It is what you would expect to cram down the throats of a party of nincompoops." [37] With some conservative Democrats, Republicans won enough votes to defeat the rule and pass Reagan's version of the cuts. In this case, the Democrats argued in subsequent sessions, the Republicans had used a tactic that they later deplored: forcing a single vote on a huge package of economic legislation.

Republican legislative victories grew scarcer after the 1982 midterm elections restored the Democrats' working majority. They reinforced their strength through procedural innovations, including curbs on the ability of members to offer limitation amendments to appropriations bills. (These amendments, forbidding the use of funds for specified purposes, had sometimes enabled Republicans to make political points on the floor.)

The following year, Speaker O'Neill tried to secure repassage of the Equal Rights Amendment (ERA) by bringing it to the floor under suspension of the rules, a procedure usually reserved for noncontroversial bills. Under suspension of the rules, debate is limited to forty minutes and no amendments are allowed. Even pro-ERA Republicans resented the tactic. Hamilton Fish of New York voiced "a mixture of genuine sorrow and outright anger." Considering a constitutional amendment under such a procedure "is an affront to the deliberative consideration which should be accorded the constitutional amendment process." [38] The ERA fell short of the required two-thirds majority. Republicans had a rare victory—and another grievance against the Speaker.

Just as procedural warfare was intensifying, so was personal invective. Republicans thought of O'Neill as a potent symbol of Democratic party ills, and in 1980 the GOP apparatus ran television advertisements that parodied O'Neill with a lookalike actor. David Stockman, a House member who went on to head Reagan's budget office, described the Speaker as "a Hogarthian embodiment of the superstate he had labored for so long to maintain." [39] And New York's John LeBoutillier, a GOP member of the class of 1980, said that O'Neill was "big, fat and out of control just like the federal government" and that he "personifies everything about politics that the public hates today." [40]

Speaker O'Neill took offense at LeBoutillier's comments.[41] Nevertheless, he too had an acid tongue, and during the 1980s he appeared to slip the constraints that he had so eloquently described before. At various times he referred to Newt Gingrich (R-Ga.), Vin Weber (R-Minn.), and Robert Walker (R-Pa.) as "real weirdos," "John Bircher types," and "the Three Stooges." [42] He also needled them by mispronouncing their names: Weber and Gingrich became "Wee-ber and Jin-rich." He saved his most acerbic comments for President Reagan: "It's sinful that this man is President of the United States." [43]

"There's a man that doesn't go to church and he talks about prayer. They ought to put a chapel up at Camp David so he can go." [44]

"The evil is in the White House at the present time. And that evil is a man who has no care and no concern for the working class of America and the future generations of America, and who likes to ride a horse. He's cold. He's mean. He's got ice water for blood." [45]

These statements angered House Republicans. After O'Neill called Reagan "evil," Michel said on the floor:

In almost thirty years in the House, I have never heard such abusive language used by a Speaker of the House about the President of the United States. . . . There are precedents in our House rules forbidding personal abuse of a President on the floor of the House. Surely the spirit of these rules ought to be adhered to by the Speaker off the floor as well as on the floor.[46]

The two fronts in the battle between O'Neill and the GOP—procedural maneuver and personal attack—merged in an incident known as "Camscam." Since 1979, the House had permitted live television broadcasts, which gave a national forum to House Republicans who saw themselves trapped by Democratic rules. Gingrich and his fellow confrontationists frequently used one-minute addresses (with which the House usually starts the day) and one-hour "special orders" (speeches that come at the end of the day, when the chamber has finished its legislative business) to explain their philosophy and flay the Democrats.

In the spring of 1984, Republican aide Frank Gregorsky wrote a report criticizing the Democratic record on communism and national security.[47] On May 8, Republicans Gingrich and Walker read the report during special orders. One subject of the report was O'Neill's friend, Rep. Edward Boland (D-Mass.); the Speaker wanted retribution. On May 10, while making another special order, Walker learned how the Speaker had taken revenge. Walker said: "[T]he cameras are panning this Chamber, demonstrating that there is no one here in this Chamber to listen to these remarks."[48] Until that moment, cameras had only shown the member speaking, not the entire chamber. Without telling anyone, O'Neill abruptly changed the policy in a deliberate effort to make Walker look like a fool.[49]

Republicans said the Speaker had pulled a cheap trick, while Democrats charged Gingrich and Walker with a sneak attack that did not allow the criticized members a chance to respond. When Gingrich took to the floor to answer the latter charge, O'Neill stepped down from the rostrum to rebut him: "You deliberately stood in that well before an empty House and challenged these people, and you challenged their Americanism, and it is the lowest thing that I have ever seen in my thirty-two years in Congress."[50] Republican Whip Trent Lott then demanded that the Speaker's words be "taken down." The parliamentarian ruled O'Neill out of order—the first such rebuke for a Speaker in nearly two centuries.

Republicans resented both O'Neill's camera maneuver and his assault on Gingrich. At a GOP conference, Weber reportedly called O'Neill "one of the cheapest, meanest politicians to occupy that office in this century." [51] In an op-ed published a few days later, Republican Leader Michel called for moderation on both sides, and added:

It cannot be left unsaid that the heaviest burden of leadership in the conduct of the House falls upon the Speaker. He is by history, tradition and rule the leader of the whole House, not the majority, not the minority, but the whole. The Speaker must drop the mantle of partisanship the day he assumes office. . . . I know the pressures to do otherwise are immense, but if we are to contribute something worthwhile to the legislative process and to the American people, it must begin with the Speaker, be sustained by the Speaker, and end with the Speaker." [52]

O'Neill did not back down at the time. Eight years later, he expressed regret for the camera maneuver: "I didn't give them notification and I was wrong on that." [53]

The partisan tension from Camscam worsened during the next session of Congress when a disputed Indiana congressional race roiled the House for months. House Republicans accused Democrats of stealing Indiana's eighth congressional district seat away from GOP challenger Rick McIntyre, whose very narrow defeat of incumbent Democrat Frank McCloskey had been certified by Indiana's Republican Secretary of State. (Republicans blamed the controversy less on O'Neill than on Tony Coelho of California, chair of the Democratic Congressional Campaign Committee.) This rancor, however, still did not pervade every corner of the House. A good deal of work on the floor and in committee proceeded amid bipartisanship, or at least civility. And O'Neill himself could rise above partisanship: he initially supported Reagan on Grenada, though he later criticized the invasion.

From the Republican viewpoint, the bad outweighed the good. By the time O'Neill stepped down in 1986, the House side of Capitol Hill had become a tougher neighborhood.

Wright's Rise and Fall

When O'Neill announced his retirement, Republicans looked with mixed feelings toward his likely successor, Majority Leader Wright. "You watch him and you know when he's going to get partisan," said Michel. "The eyebrows start to rise. The voice begins to stretch out. And the Republicans say, 'Snake Oil is at it again.' " [54] Nevertheless, Republicans also noted Wright's cooperation on issues such as narcotics control. The 1986 drug bill "was a positive sign," said Dan Lungren of California. ". . . Republicans stand a better chance of getting a better hearing of their side." [55] (Lungren's praise had special significance because he and Wright once nearly had a fistfight on the floor.) Republican Whip Lott commented, "I personally think that Jim will be better than Tip was. He's not quite as partisan." He appended a note of caution: "But it won't take much to get the war on." [56]

And the war got on. Some Republicans thought that the majority's liberal faction would draw Wright from his previous centrism toward a hard-line stance. As they saw it, events in 1987 confirmed their misgivings. O'Neill had fought Reagan over Central America and nuclear arms, becoming the first Speaker in the twentieth century who regularly opposed the incumbent administration's foreign policy.[57] Wright went a step further and held his own talks with the Ortega regime in Nicaragua. Michel commented, "For us, as legislators, to get directly involved in what is the prerogative of the president and the secretary of state is just absolutely counter to anything I've perceived during my thirty years around here." [58]

Foreign policy gave Wright occasion to express his opinion of President Reagan. Not quite as hostile as O'Neill, he still looked down on the president: "I've found him good company, but bless his heart, he doesn't have any knowledge." [59] In private, he spoke more harshly. In June 1987, when President Reagan called on the Soviets to tear down the Berlin Wall, Wright told reporter John Barry: "It just makes me have utter contempt for Reagan. He spoiled the chance for a dramatic breakthrough in relations between our two countries." [60]

Wright also took liberal positions on economics and social policy; and to enforce his preferences, he used restrictive rules even more often than O'Neill. At first, Republicans were divided over the proper approach to the new Speaker, with the confrontationists seeking to take him on and the accommodationists willing to give him more time. Wright united them on October 29, 1987, a day Republicans dubbed "Black Thursday." In the consideration of the budget reconciliation bill, Wright had the Rules Committee write a "self-executing" rule attaching ten Democratic amendments to the bill without separate votes. These amendments included a $6 billion welfare-reform package. Republicans, as well as some Democrats, argued that such an important measure should require a separate vote. (Some Democrats recalled that Republicans had objected to separate votes on Reagan's first reconciliation bill in 1981.) Enough opposition surfaced to defeat the rule. Michel then asked the Speaker to set the bill aside pending negotiations with the President and Senate. Cheney, who was then chair of the House Republican Conference, described subsequent events in a 1989 article:

Speaker Wright, in essence, told the minority leader where to get off. He announced that the Rules Committee would meet in a special session immediately to report a new rule for the same reconciliation bill, without welfare reform attached. Under the standing rules, the House is not supposed to bring up a Rules Committee report on the same day it is issued unless two-thirds of the members agree to do so. But the Speaker decided to treat the standing rules as if they were made to be broken.[61]

To bypass the two-thirds requirement, Wright had the House adjourn and immediately declare a new "legislative day"—a maneuver that required a mere majority and on which Democrats felt bound to follow the Speaker. The gape-jawed Republicans said that the Speaker was trying to amend the Book of Genesis by adding a new day to the Lord's seven. (Some Republicans labeled the double day "Black Thursday Thursday.") Astonishment turned to fury after the final roll call. When the Speaker announced that all voting time had expired, the bill stood one vote short, and Republicans thought they had won. Then—even though the clock had run out—Wright had his aide John Mack bring Jim Chapman (Texas) to the floor to switch his vote from nay to aye.

Cheney said: "[H]e's a heavy-handed son of a bitch and he doesn't know any other way to operate, and he will do anything he can to win at any price. . . . It brings disrespect on the House itself."[62] Michel resorted to the rare use of an expletive: "You're getting right on the rim where the Speaker himself is getting mighty damned autocratic."[63] Even Willis Gradison of Ohio, the archetype of bipartisanship, reacted strongly: "It takes a lot to politicize me. Wright's done it. I'm partisan as hell now."[64]

As for holding the clock at the end of the vote, a top House Republican said: "What the heck, they do that all the time, but the notion of John Mack dragging a member down into the well to change his vote, going through that whole exercise to get it passed, struck me as a bad piece of business." Democrats replied that the Speaker had kept to the letter of the rules; as one leadership aide put it, "What went on may have been different, but not unusual."[65]

Unusual events did occur in March 1988, when the House faced a vote on aid to the Nicaraguan Contras. Although the House recently had defeated a military aid plan, Republicans sought again to bring such a proposal to the floor. The *Washington Post* reported: "Several times in the past week Wright has said that the House minority would have an opportunity to have its Contra-aid plan voted on."[66] But the Rules Committee placed a Democratic plan for non-military aid as an amendment to the Republican plan for military aid. Under this restrictive rule, members would vote on the Democratic plan first; if it passed, they would have no chance to vote on the Republican plan.

Republicans believed that, under liberal pressure, Wright had broken a promise. Michel said: "In over thirty years as a member of this institution, I have kept my word. I expect others to do the same." [67]

Democrats said that Republicans had already had their chance on military aid. And Wright denied Michel's charge, saying that he had merely promised an alternative under the rule, not a separate vote. Wright said: "I know that in his heart of hearts, Bob feels I have been fair." [68]

The Democratic amendment passed, but the bill was defeated on final passage by Democrats who opposed all aid and by Republicans who spurned what they saw as a "fig leaf." For the House, that outcome was less important than the Republican belief that Wright had breached a promise. As the Speaker himself had written in *Reflections of a Public Man*: "This assumption of mutual honor . . . is part of the very oxygen which fuels the bloodstream of the Congress. Without it, our national task of legislating would be a vastly different and more difficult thing." [69]

While Wright was fueling Republican rancor, press reports were raising questions about his ethics. During the summer of 1987, Gingrich had begun using these reports to attack the Speaker. At first, Gingrich gained little support for his efforts, outside the ranks of the hard-line confrontationists; then, the evidence and the animosity both mounted. Two months after the 1988 Contra vote, seventy-two House Republicans—including several members of the party leadership—signed a letter asking for a formal investigation of Wright by the Committee on Standards of Official Conduct. In September, Michel and Cheney filed a separate complaint against Wright, charging that he had publicly disclosed classified information about Nicaragua.

In deciding who shall lead them and how much power those leaders will have, members of a legislative party carefully weigh political costs and benefits.[70] If leaders run into the red, they may lose their jobs. Through a variety of missteps, Wright had put his internal Democratic support at risk. Perhaps his most costly error came early in 1989, when his handling of the issue of congressional salaries had resulted in both increased public resentment of Congress and a rejection of a much-desired pay raise. And as the year wore on, the ethics issue was making him a liability to the entire party. With strong opposition from the Republicans and faint support from the Democrats, his fortunes crashed during the spring of 1989. When the ethics committee unanimously approved a statement alleging ethics violations, he tried and failed to rally his partisans. With his political base evaporating, he resigned. In his final House address, he said: "All of us in both political parties must resolve to bring this period of mindless cannibalism to an end." [71]

Wright's speech played poorly with Republicans. "What it sounded like was Richard Nixon," said Lynn Martin of Illinois, accusing Wright of seeking to "blame the ethics committee and the House. But it wasn't the ethics committee or the House that did it. It was the Speaker." [72] On the election of Speaker Foley a few days later, Michel struck discordant notes. He rebutted Wright's description of his fall: "Now, it is a catchy phrase, but the distinguished members of the committee on ethics, equally divided from both parties, are neither mindless nor cannibals." He also gave the GOP diagnosis of the House's problem: "Thirty-five years of uninterrupted power can act like a corrosive acid upon the restraints of civility and comity. Those who have been kings of the Hill for so long may forget that majority status is not a divine right—and minority status is not a permanent condition." [73]

Foley and the GOP: No End to the Conflict

Republicans welcomed Foley's rise to the speakership, and the early months of his tenure saw less partisan conflict than in the preceding years. Mickey Edwards of Oklahoma described one scene:

There is a tradition in the House that when you have a voice vote, no matter how many people shouted "yes" or how many people shouted "no," the Democrats always win. And on this day right after Foley became Speaker, there was a voice vote and the few Democrats on the floor at the time shouted "yes" and the Republicans, in much greater number, shouted "no," and we were all poised to demand a [recorded] vote. And the Speaker—it was Tom Foley in the chair at the time—and Tom ruled that the no's had won. . . . [E]very Republican on the floor rose spontaneously and gave Tom Foley a standing ovation.[74]

Yet in spite of Foley's personal decency, the roots of rancor remained alive. The GOP still appeared to be a permanent minority in the House and, until 1993, House Democrats still regarded themselves as a minority against a Republican president. "Foley will learn," said Dan Glickman (D-Kan.), "there's a limit to fairness when the White House is controlled by the other party." [75]

Hints of conflict emerged as early as August 1989, when a Republican offered a motion to recommit a bill to the Appropriations Committee with instructions to amend it. Based on the 1983 rule curbing limitation amendments, the Speaker ruled the motion out of order. Arguing that the rule did not apply to motions to recommit, Michel challenged the ruling—his first such step in his congressional career. On a party-line vote, the challenge failed. Robert Walker of Pennsylvania later said the ruling "belies all that we have heard about there's going to be [fairness] to the minority. There was no fairness to the minority in that vote." [76]

Republicans gradually concluded that Foley was tightening the procedural screws. In his first Congress as Speaker, open rules (those without special restrictions on amendments) accounted for less than half of all the rules for floor action on legislation. (Even under Wright, open rules still had been the norm, if just barely.) And in his second Congress, the proportion of open rules dropped to one-third. [77] Thanks in large measure to the Democrats' firm procedural control, President George Bush lost most of the House votes on which he took a stand.

Foley's gentlemanly demeanor did not prevent bickering over nonlegislative issues. In 1991, newspapers reported that the House Bank had long given members free overdraft privileges on their checking accounts, or in effect, zero-interest loans. Some of the newer, confrontational Republicans urged disclosure of the overdrafters' names, hoping that the case would convince voters that the House Democrats had grown slovenly during their overly long reign. Debate over the House Bank turned up partisan heat with little partisan gain. Many Republicans had made overdrafts, and a number of them—including three members of the minority leadership—either stepped down or lost reelection bids.

Several other administrative scandals broke open at the same time, and one of them confirmed Republican suspicions about Democratic management of House business. A formal investigation of the House Post Office revealed that House Postmaster Robert Rota had helped House Democrats keep tabs on their opposition. Whenever GOP members circulated a "Dear Republican Colleague" letter, Rota made sure that key Democratic aides and members got a copy—but not vice versa. [78]

Such disclosures prompted reforms of House administration. Republicans argued that the administrative overhaul was merely superficial and that the institution's basic problem remained unsolved: two generations of Democratic control of the House.

The 1992 elections brought conflicting signals about partisan relations in the House. On the one hand, the election of President Bill Clinton meant that

House Democrats could no longer see themselves as a beleaguered minority. Now that the federal government was unified under Democratic control, they perhaps could afford to be magnanimous toward the minority Republicans. On the other hand, the 1992 results caused them to worry about their own electoral safety. Republicans had made modest gains in 1992 and were likely to pick up more seats in 1994. An unusually high number of incumbents had either lost or slipped through with diminished margins. Remembering that GOP floor maneuvers in the late 1970s may have contributed to the Republican electoral triumph of 1980, House Democrats hesitated to loosen the reins on the minority. "If I thought that all Republicans were reasonable and responsible," said a Democratic leadership aide, "I would say that we could allow more amendments. But I am doubtful." [79]

House Democrats launched the new session with proposed rules changes that irked the GOP. At first, Democrats planned to limit televised special orders, but the prospect of disruptive Republican protests led them to defer the idea. They also sought to grant five nonvoting delegates—all Democrats—a vote in the Committee of the Whole. In Republican eyes, the Democrats were trying to negate half of the GOP's ten-seat gain; and some remembered that the last election that produced a Republican gain (1984) had also been followed by an alleged Democratic "theft," namely the Indiana dispute. When the Republican critique won support from such sources as the *New York Times* and *Roll Call*, Foley and the Democrats offered a compromise procedure that effectively nullified the delegates' votes whenever they would change the outcome.

Republicans still criticized floor procedure: during the first session of the 103rd Congress, no open rule reached the House until May 5. They took particular exception to the restrictive rule for the legislative branch appropriations bill, because the House had previously dealt with such legislation under open rules. And in June 1993, they enlisted a potentially important ally who could help publicize the fight against restrictive rules: one-time presidential candidate H. Ross Perot. The war continued.

A Republican Speakership

What will House Republicans do now that they have won the speakership? Over the years, they repeatedly have stressed that they would make procedural reform their first priority. Gerald Solomon of New York, ranking Republican on the Rules Committee, has proposed a number of innovations: elimination of the joint referral of bills to two or more committees; abolition of proxy voting and one-third quorums; and a guarantee that party ratios on committees accurately reflect the party ratios in the House.[80] More important, the Republicans have stressed that they would open up floor procedure to improve deliberation and ensure accountability. In describing what he would do as Speaker, Michel has said:

> I would like to guarantee that all controversial bills come to the floor with rules guaranteeing free and open debate. . . . There may be, just may be, some very isolated cases when we would want in the interest of efficiency, or whatever, a closed rule. But by and large, particularly anything of a controversial nature, ought to have a free, open, and unfettered debate by both sides of the aisle before finally coming to a resolution on a controversial piece of legislation.[81]

According to this view, a legislative majority should have to make a public defense of its actions against alternatives raised by the opposition. If the opposition can thereby score political points, so be it: there *ought* to be a connection between what happens on the House floor and what happens in the voting booth. Defenders of the current system might counter that other national legislatures give their majority parties more control over agendas than does the House. But in other countries party-based electoral systems hold their legislative majorities accountable to the voters; in the U.S. House, the rules diminish accountability instead of enhancing it.[82] Even some Democrats have come to agree with this position. In the 1993 debate over the rule on legislative appropriations, Tim Penny of Minnesota said:

> Mr. Speaker, I do not know why in this Congress we are afraid of more open rules. I do not say they all have to be open, but they do not have to be as limited as this. We seem to be determined to manipulate the outcome by limiting the options. This is not democratic. This is not consistent with the principles of the Democratic Party to which I belong.[83]

In alluding to the principles, including accountability, undergirding the Constitution and the Democratic party, Penny acknowledged a principled distinction between strong party leadership and excessive partisanship.

As a majority, House Republicans may find it quite a challenge to keep up their enthusiasm for reform. After decades of frustrations and slights, many will want to get even. When we asked Republican members what they have learned from the Democrats, one answered: "Don't play fair—When we take control, we should stack Ways and Means, Appropriations and Rules just as the Democrats have done." Such behavior would utterly contradict the Republicans' long-standing arguments for reform, and so the desire to avoid the charge of hypocrisy may temper the thirst for vengeance. Another corrective would be the prospect that the Democrats could regain control and strike back: recall that such an expectation helped keep interparty peace during the 1940s and 1950s.

What if Republicans hold the speakership for twenty or thirty years at a stretch? It would become clear, especially to Democrats, that Republicans also can fall prey to the temptations of power. At first, the Republicans might recognize the challenge of institutional responsibility: balancing the need for action with the need for deliberation and accountability. Over time, however, the balance would shift, and a sense of institutional *responsibility* could easily degenerate into a sense of institutional *ownership*. Consider the New York State Senate, where Republicans have ruled for decades, with only a brief pause in the 1960s. As with the Democrats in the U.S. House, the New York Senate Republicans have used their procedural control to sidestep difficult issues. In 1993, the *New York Times* editorial page observed that a homosexual rights bill might have passed if it had reached the Senate floor for a full debate and recorded vote. "But it never got there. Ralph Marino, the Senate majority leader, let his 35 Republican members decide whether to allow a floor vote—in a closed conference. That's not the way democracy is supposed to work." [84]

Conversely, a long spell in the minority would leave the House Democrats angry and frustrated. They would see the majority dismiss their policy initiatives as irresponsible attempts at partisan politicking. They would complain about their inability to influence policy, and the majority would tell them: "If you want to change the place, go out and win 218 seats." This taunt would infuriate them, because they would learn that winning elections requires the ability to frame issues—which is hard to do when the other side controls the agenda, the amendment process, the cameras, and the clock.

So far this chapter has discussed relations *between* the parties. The Democrats have also given the Speaker enormous power *within* party ranks, through increased control over committee assignments, among other things. In the minority, Republicans have gone only partway in granting parallel authority to their leader, and as of the early 1990s, they could not agree whether to consolidate the diffuse structure of their party conference. Because the prospect of majority status seemed so remote, they had not yet given serious thought to the division of labor between a Republican Speaker and the rest of the party leadership. Factionalism may still make it difficult for them to reach a decision.

Accommodationists and confrontationists have battled over the proper response to the party's minority status; if this problem disappears, they will find new things to fight about. Their differences go beyond style and tactics to deeper issues of governing philosophy. Accommodationists tend to see themselves as part of the government (even when they serve in the minority and under a Democratic president) while confrontationists see themselves as perennial "outsiders" (even when they have held office for many years). This distinction roughly corresponds to the "court" and "country" parties of Georgian England.[85] Some House Republicans see a division within their ranks between "traditional conservatives" and "movement conservatives," between "establishment politicians" and "populists" or "revolutionaries." Both sides agree on the need for internal reforms in the House, but the latter would go much further. During the same special order in which Michel discussed restrictive rules, Gingrich discussed revolution:

> Within this current climate, I believe we need to create a new system and new approach to government. We need to transform the current system through a necessary revolution. This revolution is one of replacing the current welfare state and its side effects of destruction of family values, work ethic, and individual ability and responsibility. This revolution is truly necessary and not merely desirable. It must happen. Our Founding Fathers created a powerful system for each generation to have: to paraphrase Thomas Jefferson, its own necessary revolution. Our civil wars should be fought culturally and politically, not militarily.[86]

Other fault lines divide House Republicans. Some concentrate on party business, while others tend mainly to their committees or their constituencies. Regional and generational divisions persist. Conservatism, which predominates among Republicans, is a source of discord as well as unity. The ideology embraces many schools of thought that look alike to outsiders but seem radically different from within. During elections, commentators make much of the fights between libertarians and social conservatives, yet overlook such distinctions when discussing the dynamics of House Republicans.

A Republican majority will be more than a mere enlargement of the current minority. To grow, the party will have to reach beyond its traditional base of affluent business people and lawyers. Whatever form the new pluralism takes, it will bring new strains, as Gingrich has noted:

> [We] have to recognize that we have to get used to fighting ourselves at times and we

have to recognize that we are in the business of conflict management. We are not in the business of conflict resolution. You only resolve conflicts by kicking people out and that means you become a minority. So, if you intend to be a majority, you have to be willing to live with a lot of conflict because that is the nature of a majority.[87]

This new, diverse majority might be riven by internal animosities. In that case, no faction would trust the others with control of the party, and power would remain dispersed. However, House Republicans might decide that they would all be better off with strong, central leadership. As the Democrats learned under Nixon and Reagan, it is easier to reach such a conclusion under an assertive president of the opposite party.

A GOP House under a Democratic president? During the 1980s, such a combination seemed as fantastic as the idea that New York, Jersey City, and Los Angeles would elect Republican mayors in the same year. Yet the 1993 off-year elections produced such outcomes, and 1994 brought a GOP House. Democrats in both political branches should hope that the majority regards its power as temporary and that the Speaker maintains a sense of limits.

Notes

1. U.S. Congress, House, *Congressional Record*, daily ed., 101st Cong., 1st sess., Sept. 12, 1989, E3000.

2. Norman J. Ornstein, "Minority Report," *Atlantic Monthly*, Dec. 1985, 35.

3. Richard B. Cheney and Lynne V. Cheney, *Kings of the Hill: Power and Personality in the House of Representatives* (New York: Continuum, 1983).

4. Richard Cheney, "Tip's Unseemly Role As Speaker," *Washington Times*, July 31, 1984, C1.

5. UPI wire story, July 30, 1984.

6. U.S. Congress, House, *Congressional Record*, daily ed., 95th Cong., 1st sess., Jan. 4, 1977, 51.

7. U.S. Congress, House, *Congressional Record*, daily ed., 95th Cong., 2d sess., Feb. 21, 1978, 3854.

8. Cheney and Cheney, *Kings of the Hill*, 195.

9. Jacob E. Cooke, ed., *The Federalist* 57 (Middletown, Conn.: Wesleyan University Press, 1961), 385.

10. Jacob E. Cooke, ed., *The Federalist* 70 (Middletown, Conn.: Wesleyan University Press, 1961), 475.

11. Richard Wolf, "Dems Getting 'Act Together,' " *USA Today*, Oct. 8, 1990, 4A.

12. John Machacek, "Lawmaker with Few Enemies Checks Colleagues' Bank Books," Gannett wire story, Oct. 25, 1991.

13. Joseph J. DioGuardi, "Introduction," in *A House of Ill Repute*, ed. Dan Renberg (Princeton, N.J.: Princeton University Press, 1987), 1-3.

14. Vin Weber, "Tyranny of the Majority," in *A House of Ill Repute*, 61.

15. Cheney and Cheney, *Kings of the Hill*, 138.

16. Ronald M. Peters, Jr., *The American Speakership: The Office in Historical Perspective* (Baltimore: Johns Hopkins University Press, 1990), 104.

17. Ibid., 122.

18. Regarding office switch, see Joseph W. Martin, Jr., with Robert J. Donovan, *My First Fifty Years in Politics* (New York: McGraw-Hill, 1960), 228. Regarding Rules Committee, see Alfred Steinberg, *Sam Rayburn: A Biography* (New York: Hawthorn, 1975), 313. Regarding mutual praise, see U.S. Congress, House, *Congressional Record*, daily ed., 85th Cong., 2d sess., Aug. 23, 1958, 19,711.

19. U.S. Congress, House, *Congressional Record*, daily ed., 80th Cong., 1st sess., Jan. 3, 1947, 36.

20. Martin with Donovan, *My First Fifty Years in Politics*, 6.

21. U.S. Congress, House, *Congressional Record*, daily ed., 86th Cong., 2d sess., Sept. 1, 1960, 19,162.

22. Jim Wright, *You and Your Congressman* (New York: Capricorn, 1976), 168.

23. Neil MacNeil, *Forge of Democracy: The House of Representatives* (New York: David McKay, 1963), 328.

24. Gerald R. Ford, *A Time to Heal: The Autobiography of Gerald R. Ford* (New York: Harper & Row, 1979), 81-82.

25. Carl Albert, with Danney Goble, *Little Giant: The Life and Times of Speaker Carl Albert* (Norman, Okla.: University of Oklahoma Press, 1990), 319.

26. John J. Rhodes, *The Futile System: How to Unchain Congress and Make the System Work Again* (McLean, Va.: EPM, 1976), 33.

27. Ford, *A Time to Heal*, 99.

28. Barbara Sinclair, *Majority Leadership in the U.S. House* (Baltimore: Johns Hopkins University Press, 1983), 5; and David W. Rohde, *Parties and Leaders in the Postreform House* (Chicago: University of Chicago Press, 1991), 14.

29. For a thorough study of Democratic centralization, see Roger H. Davidson, "The New Centralization on Capitol Hill," *Review of Politics*, 50 (Summer 1988): 345-364; and Daniel J. Palazzolo, "From Decentralization to Centralization: Members' Changing Expectations for House Leaders," in *The Postreform Congress*, ed. Roger H. Davidson (New York: St. Martin's, 1992), 112-126.

30. Rhodes, *The Futile System*, 32-33.

31. Stanley Bach and Steven S. Smith, *Managing Uncertainty in the House of Representatives: Adaptation and Innovation in Special Rules* (Washington, D.C.: Brookings Institution, 1988), 30-31; Steven S. Smith, *Call to Order: Floor Politics in the House and Senate* (Washington. D.C.: Brookings Institution, 1989), 33-34.

32. Robert Bauman, "Majority Tyranny in the House," in *View from the Capitol Dome (Looking Right)*, ed. Richard T. Schulze and John H. Rousselot (Ottawa, Ill.: Caroline House, 1980), 11.

33. Bach and Smith, *Managing Uncertainty in the House of Representatives*, 31.

34. Bauman, "Majority Tyranny in the House," 12.

35. Kelly Marcavage and Doc Syers, eds., *Congress: Past, Present and Future* (Washington, D.C.: House Republican Research Committee, 1987), 17.

36. Tip O'Neill, with William Novak, *Man of the House: The Life and Political Memoirs of Speaker Tip O'Neill* (New York: Random House, 1987), 344.

37. U.S. Congress, House, *Congressional Record*, daily ed., 97th Cong., 1st sess., June 25, 1981, 14,077.

38. U.S. Congress, House, *Congressional Record*, daily ed., 98th Cong., 1st sess., Nov. 15, 1983, H9856.

39. David A. Stockman, *The Triumph of Politics: Why the Reagan Revolution Failed* (New York: Harper & Row, 1986), 121.

40. Richard L. Lyons, "On Capitol Hill," *Washington Post*, July 14, 1981, A4.

41. In 1982, Democrat Robert Mrazek was recruited to run against LeBoutillier with Speaker O'Neill's support. He won, and O'Neill rewarded him with a seat on the Appropriations Committee, nearly unheard of for a first-term member. See Michael Barone and Grant Ujifusa, *Almanac of American Politics, 1986* (Washington, D.C.: National Journal, 1986), 906-907.

42. O'Neill, with Novak, *Man of the House*, 352; Don Phillips, "Democrats Agree to Debate House Republicans," UPI wire story, June 1, 1984; Elaine Povich, untitled UPI wire story, May 21, 1984.

43. James Reston, "The President Is Going Down the Wrong Road,' " *New York Times*, Nov. 1, 1983, A24.

44. T. R. Reid, "Senate Debate Continues; Prayer Bill Foes Attack 'Election-Year Religiosity,' " *Washington Post*, March 7, 1984, A7.

45. Don Phillips, "O'Neill: Mondale Must Attack 'Cold, Mean' Reagan," UPI wire story, July 19, 1984.

46. U.S. Congress, House, *Congressional Record*, daily ed., 98th Cong., 2d sess., July 25, 1984, H7722. The chamber's procedural manual quotes a 1909 report saying that the House must operate "without unnecessarily and unduly exciting animosity among its Members or antagonism from those other branches of the Government with which the House is correlated." See U.S. House, *Constitution—Jefferson's Manual and Rules of the House of Representatives* (Washington, D.C.: Government Printing Office, 1985), 166.

47. "In the Radical worldview, there is no crime by a Communist army or government that can't either be trivialized or blamed on America." U.S. Congress, House, *Congressional Record*, daily ed., 98th Cong., 2d Sess., May 8, 1984, H3545.

48. U.S. Congress, House, *Congressional Record*, daily ed., 98th Cong., 2d Sess., May 10, 1984, H3762.

49. O'Neill, with Novak, *Man of the House*, 354.

50. U.S. Congress, House, *Congressional Record*, daily ed., 98th Cong., 2d Sess., May 15, 1984, H3843.

51. "Republicans Assail O'Neill; Loss of Comity Is Feared," *New York Times*, May 18, 1984, A15.

52. Bob Michel, "Politics in the Age of Television," *Washington Post*, May 20, 1984, B7.

53. Craig Winneker, "Heard on the Hill," *Roll Call*, Nov. 12, 1992, 1.

54. Craig C. Carter, "Hustling for the House Speaker's Job," *Fortune*, Feb. 17, 1986, 93.

55. Karen Tumulty, "Wright As Speaker: Tough Tactician, Center Course," *Los Angeles Times*, Dec. 8, 1986, I1.

56. Edward Walsh, "The New Speaker: Assertive Style, 'Achievable' Agenda,"*New York Times*, Dec. 15, 1986, A1.

57. Peters, *The American Speakership*, 248.

58. Donna Cassata, "Wright Attacked Anew for Part in Peace Process; He Defends Role," Associated Press wire story, Nov. 16, 1987.

59. Ibid.

60. John M. Barry, *The Ambition and the Power: The Fall of Jim Wright—A True Story of Washington* (New York: Viking, 1989), 486.

61. Richard B. Cheney, "What's Wrong about Wright: When the House Speaker Manipulates the Rules, Democracy Suffers," *Washington Post*, April 9, 1989, B2.

62. James A. Barnes, "Partisanship," *National Journal*, Nov. 7, 1987, 2825.

63. Eric Pianin, "House Republicans Pursue Protest Tactics: Still Angry about Tax Vote, GOP Members Delay Adjournment," *Washington Post*, Nov. 3, 1987, A21.

64. Barry, *The Ambition and the Power*, 482.

65. Barnes, "Partisanship," 2825.

66. Tom Kenworthy, "GOP Opposes Contra Aid Voting Plan; House to Consider Democrats' Bill First," *Washington Post*, March 2, 1988, A4.

67. U.S. Congress, House, *Congressional Record*, daily ed., 100th Cong., 2d Sess., March 3, 1988, H644.

68. Jonathan Fuerbringer, "A House Divided by Political Rancor," *New York Times*, March 16, 1988, A22.

69. Jim Wright, *Reflections of a Public Man* (Fort Worth, Texas: Madison, 1984), 72.

70. Barbara Sinclair, "The Evolution of Party Leadership in the Modern House," in *The Atomistic Congress*, ed. Allen D. Hertzke and Ronald M. Peters, Jr. (Armonk, N.Y.: M.E. Sharpe, 1992), 259-292.

71. U.S. Congress, House, *Congressional Record*, daily ed., 101st Cong., 1 Sess., May 31, 1989, H2247.

72. Don Phillips, "Republicans Bridle at Wright Speech; GOP Urges Clearer Rules, Not Retribution over Speaker's Demise," *Washington Post*, June 2, 1989, A6.

73. U.S. Congress, House, *Congressional Record*, daily ed., 101st Cong., 1st Sess., June 6, 1989, H2283.

74. Mickey Edwards, "Congress in the '90s: Can It Lead or be Led?" Remarks delivered at the American Enterprise Institute conference, Dec. 6, 1989 (Washington, D.C.: Federal Information Service).

75. John M. Barry, "Games Congressmen Play," *New York Times Magazine*, May 13, 1990, 85.

76. U.S. Congress, House, *Congressional Record*, daily ed., 101st Cong., 1st Sess., Aug. 1, 1989, H4676; Kim Mattingly, "Is the New Comity Dead?" *Roll Call*, Aug. 3, 1989, 1, 5.

77. U.S. Congress, House, *Congressional Record*, daily ed., 103d Cong., 1st Sess., Jan. 5, 1993, H24.

78. Glenn R. Simpson, "Rota Mailed 'Dear Colleagues' to Scores of Favored Lobbyists," *Roll Call*, July 27, 1992, 1, 18.

79. Richard E. Cohen, "Challenging the House's Traffic Cop," *National Journal*, April 24, 1993, 1002.

80. U.S. Congress, House, *Congressional Record*, daily ed., 97th Cong., 2d Sess., Jan. 30, 1982, H148.

81. U.S. Congress, House, *Congressional Record*, daily ed., 102d Cong., 2d Sess., January 30, 1992, H147.

82. Michael J. Malbin, "Political Parties across the Separation of Powers," in *American Political Parties and Constitutional Politics*, ed. Peter W. Schramm and Bradford P. Wilson (Lanham, Md.: Rowman & Littlefield, 1993), 75-90; Richard B. Cheney, "An UnRuly House: A Republican View," *Public Opinion*, Jan./Feb. 1989, 41-44.

83. U.S. Congress, House, *Congressional Record*, daily ed., 103d Cong., 1st Sess., June 10, 1993, H3389.

84. "The Gay Rights Debate That Wasn't," *New York Times*, July 9, 1993, A14.

85. James W. Ceaser, "The City and the Country in the American Political Tradition," *Journal of Political Science* 15 (Spring 1987): 21-35; James W. Ceaser and Andrew Busch, *Upside Down and Inside Out: The 1992 Elections and American Politics* (Lanham, Md.: Rowman & Littlefield, 1993), 1-28.

86. U.S. Congress, House, *Congressional Record*, daily ed., 102d Cong., 2d Sess., Jan. 30, 1992, H149.

87. Newt Gingrich, address to Southern Republican Leadership Conference, Raleigh, N.C., March 30, 1990.

5 The Speaker and the Budget

Daniel J. Palazzolo

The Speakers of the House, from Carl Albert to Tom Foley, have faced various challenges in the budgetary process since the passage of the Budget Act in 1974. That act required the Congress to fix budget targets in authorizations and outlays in each of thirteen functional categories for each fiscal year and to reconcile annual authorizations and appropriations to those targets. It created separate budget committees in each chamber and altered the legislative process in an attempt to enforce budget discipline. Some challenges have been defined by the individual Speakers themselves; others have emerged from institutional changes in the budget process, large deficits, and the political context within which budget decisions have been made. Speaker Albert's primary challenge was to meet the formal guidelines of the new budget process. Under Speaker Tip O'Neill, the task of facilitating the formal procedures of the Budget Act gave way to managing various forms of conflict over budget priorities, representing the House majority party in negotiations with Senate leaders and the president, and acting as a spokesperson for the Democratic party. Speaker Jim Wright used the budget resolution to define the priorities of the Democratic party. Speaker Foley's major challenge has been to facilitate passage of two major deficit reduction bills, first under a divided government in which opposing parties controlled the Congress and the White House and then under the leadership of President Bill Clinton.

As we have seen in previous chapters, the Speaker of the House is a leader who represents three different interests—institutional, party, and personal. As an institutional leader the Speaker is expected to carry out the duties of presiding officer and facilitate the legislative process in a fair, efficient, and impartial fashion. As the party's primary leader, the Speaker tries to mediate intra-party conflict over policy preferences, build coalitions in support of the majority party's position, and assist the president in passing legislation if the president is of the same party as the Speaker. If the president is of the opposite party, the Speaker acts as a national spokesperson and representative of the House majority party's interests. Finally, all Speakers have personal interests in representing their electoral constituencies and their own policy preferences. This chapter evaluates the strategies Speakers have adopted to deal with the major challenges in the budget process and discusses how those challenges have affected the Speaker's three major interests.

Looking to the Past:
The Budget Process under Four Speakers

The challenges to leadership in the budget process have made it difficult for each Speaker to balance institutional, partisan, and personal interests. When the interests are incompatible, a Speaker's strategies for dealing with the challenges reveals which of the three interests the Speaker considers most important. The Speaker's strategies, in turn, affect how the budget process operates. Each Speaker's capacity to deal with a challenge depends on how compatible the Speaker's interests are with the challenges. Speaker Albert was ideally suited for facilitating the budget process in its early years, but he was not inclined to use the budget resolution to formulate the majority party's priorities. After 1981, Speaker O'Neill succeeded in blocking attempts by President Ronald Reagan and congressional Republicans to cut domestic spending—but at a cost to the formal procedures of the budget process. Speaker Wright was very effective in using the budget resolution to advance his priorities, but he was accused of acting unfairly to the minority party. Speaker Foley's attempt to reach a bipartisan solution to the deficit problem in 1990 reflected his belief that it was the only way to pass a deficit reduction bill with a Republican in the White House, yet some House Democrats thought he had abandoned the party's principles in the process.

Carl Albert: The Budget Act and the Institutional Speaker

Speaker Albert presided over the first two years of the new budget process, 1975-1976.[1] Albert's central challenge was to help guide the budget process through its formative stages, and his strategies reflected his institutional interest in making the budget process work according to the formal guidelines of the Budget Act. The strategy involved explaining the complex procedures of the Budget Act to participants in the new budget process, organizing the committees for action, and moderating fears about the uncertain potential of the Budget Act. Although his successors would take on more political challenges, Albert played a key role in implementing formal budget procedures at a time when the success of the new process was by no means certain.

Albert's final two years in office followed a period of major institutional reform that simultaneously attempted to broaden the participation of the members and integrate the decentralized and fragmented committee system in the House. One objective of the Budget Act was to coordinate the various authorization, appropriations, and revenue decisions made by the Congress. Yet participatory reforms complicated efforts to coordinate legislative activity by opening up the legislative process and allowing more members to participate in key decisions at the subcommittee level and on the floor.[2] The House needed a patient and skillful Speaker to move the House from a long period of committee government to a wide open, but—it was hoped—a more efficient, legislative body.

In transition periods, leaders often struggle to accommodate conflicting expectations about the course and relative speed of change.[3] As Speaker Albert entered his final two years in office, newer members wanted the reforms implemented quickly, while senior members preferred gradual change.[4] Even though Albert tried to accommodate both views, he was not supported wholly by all factions of the Democratic party. Seventy-five first-term Democrats elected in 1974 created most of the Speaker's problems. These members were intensely independent and eager to participate in the legislative process. The first-term members did not hesitate to complain to Speaker Albert about his failure to initiate creative policy proposals and control committee chairs.[5]

In the context of these major political and institutional changes, Speaker Albert took on the challenge of executing the Budget Act when Congress put the process through its first trial run in 1975. Albert's action reflected both his personal commitment to the new budget process and his institutional responsibility to assist the House with the formal procedures established by the Budget Act. Fortunately for the new budget process, Albert identified his role and ably performed the functions associated with guiding the process through its formative stages.

One of Albert's most important tasks was explaining to House members the new budget procedures and purpose of the Budget Act. In early March, after the House was organized to begin the 94th Congress, Albert and Brock Adams (D-Wash.), Chair of the House Budget Committee, met with all the standing committee chairs and Appropriations subcommittee chairs. Richard Bolling (D-Mo.), former representative and a major player in the enactment of budget reform, described the meeting:

. . . Albert did an incredible job of organizing the leadership of the committees for the transition into the new budget process. In 1975, after we organized the committees, he had a meeting of all the committee chairmen with regard to the Budget Act and it was a phenomenal experience. These guys had all voted for it, it had been going on for about six months, and they didn't know the first thing about the Budget Act. One of them knew a little. So, quite obviously, if it wasn't for the Speaker there wasn't going to be any Budget Act. It wasn't going to last.[6]

Adams credited Speaker Albert for expanding the purpose and limitations of the new process:

The Speaker was incredibly important in communicating the idea that the [Budget] Committee was not designed to compete with the other committees in the House. He wanted to make clear and carry out the view that the first resolution was a planning tool, a response, an alternative to the president's budget.[7]

Albert did not intend to use the budget resolution to challenge the Republican president's budget or to initiate particular budget priorities. The Speaker's primary concern was to pass a budget resolution on schedule, an objective he emphasized on the House floor during the first debate on a budget resolution:

Mr. Chairman, I do not take this time to comment on the amendments either pending or prospective. . . . I am not attempting to make a brief for any particular provision or position. Nevertheless, I must assert, as the elected leader of the House, on behalf of this House and the future of the Nation, that it is essential that we pass a budget resolution, and that we finish our procedures within the time contemplated in the act itself. For only by supporting a budget resolution can we continue the development of the vitally important overall budgetary process in this Congress.[8]

The House passed the budget resolution by a vote of 200 to 196.

Thus, Albert rose to the first major challenge of the Speaker in the budget process: making a credible effort to pass a budget. In Albert's view, "If we didn't make it [the budget process] work we were going to be the laughing stock." [9] As the House accepted the responsibility of enacting its own budget, Albert was committed to getting the process started. Albert preferred Sam Rayburn's style of meeting in small groups or individually with committee chairs. His extensive and cordial relationships with most members enabled him to implement that style effectively.[10] Adams credited Albert for guiding the process in its earliest stages: "The Speaker, at that time, was a primary moving force in the budget process, a great factor in making the budget process successful." [11]

Tip O'Neill: The Emergence of Partisan
and Personal Interests

Speaker O'Neill witnessed more changes and encountered more challenges in the budget process than any of the Speakers since the passage of the Budget Act. During the Carter years, House Democrats were intensely divided over budget priorities, and Speaker O'Neill worked to build support for the Budget Committee's resolutions. In 1981, the problem of unifying House Democrats peaked as President Reagan skillfully built a coalition of Republicans and conservative Democrats and wrested control of the budget process from the majority party in the House. After 1982, party unity on roll call votes increased substantially, making it easier for the Speaker to solidify coalitions in support of the Budget Committee's resolution. Yet large deficits, divided government, and intense partisanship created havoc in the budget process. The formal procedures of the Budget Act were substituted regularly by informal, ad hoc arrangements for addressing the deficit. Ultimately, Congress passed a wholesale revision of the Budget Act with the Balanced Budget and Deficit Control Act of 1985 (Gramm-Rudman-Hollings). That law sought to put teeth into the budget process by requiring that if the budget outlay levels were exceeded in broad functional categories of national defense and discretionary domestic spending, the spending spigot would be closed by automatically sequestering funds across the board. This led to intense conflicts over budget priorities. Speaker O'Neill's challenges shifted from facilitating an orderly process to representing and protecting Democratic budget priorities. As the period progressed, the Speaker's partisan and personal policy preferences superseded his institutional interests.

In the late 1970s, O'Neill's institutional and partisan interests were generally compatible. The Speaker continued to stress the importance of passing resolutions on schedule, and since the Democrats had a majority in both chambers and control of the presidency, it was in the party's interests for the institution to perform as expected. But the party was divided along ideological lines. Speaker O'Neill was often quoted as saying that the Democratic party was really "five parties in one. . . . We've got about 25 really strong liberals, 110 progressive liberals, maybe 60 moderates, about 45 people just to the right of the moderates, and about 35 conservatives." [12]

O'Neill used two mechanisms for dealing with weak party cohesion—the

Speaker's task forces and an expanded whip system.[13] Both devices involved more members in the legislative process, improved communication between the members and the leadership, and facilitated coalition building. And both techniques corresponded with O'Neill's conception of leadership: to provide avenues for broad participation and to recognize the diverse ideological perspectives in the Democratic party. O'Neill used a classic "middleman" leadership strategy to build coalitions among the members of the party. He listened to members and mediated differences between the factions of the party. At the same time, O'Neill maintained an intense commitment to traditional New Deal and Great Society programs. Thus, his two major challenges during the Carter years were to reconcile ideological differences between House Democrats and to balance his personal commitment to preserve traditional Democratic programs with his responsibility to build winning coalitions for the Budget Committee's resolutions.

O'Neill struggled to keep the party together on numerous occasions. In 1977, the first year of O'Neill's speakership, the House initially failed to pass the fiscal 1978 first budget resolution. The biggest problem was a mismatch between the priorities of the liberal Democrats on the House Budget Committee and the House Democratic party as a whole. Conservative Democrats disagreed with the Budget Committee's decision to cut President Jimmy Carter's defense budget by $4.1 billion. The Budget Committee's resolution failed, and the House passed an amendment by Omar Burleson (D-Texas) to restore Carter's original defense estimate. A second attempt at passing the budget resolution succeeded after the Budget Committee redrafted the original budget resolution to include a larger defense budget.

In 1980, congressional leaders worked with President Carter to develop a deficit reduction plan and use reconciliation procedures to enforce spending cuts and tax increases. The budget resolution based on those meetings included $6.4 billion in spending cuts. O'Neill reluctantly accepted the budget resolution, though he did not actively lobby for it, and the House passed the budget resolution with bipartisan support. But after a conference with the Senate produced an increase in defense spending in exchange for more domestic spending cuts, O'Neill publicly denounced the plan, stating, "The budget goes against my philosophy." [14] The House rejected the conference budget by a vote of 141 to 245.

After Budget Committee Chair Robert Giaimo (D-Conn.), Senate Budget Committee Chair Ernest Hollings (D-S.C.), and President Carter worked out a compromise that reduced defense spending by $800 million and added

$1.3 billion for domestic programs, O'Neill became involved fully in the process. He instructed the Steering and Policy Committee to emphasize that the vote on the compromise was a party issue; he met with deputy and at-large whips to develop a strategy for building support for the budget resolution; he sent a letter to all House Democrats stating that failure to vote for the resolution would discredit the party; and he set up a task force to mobilize support on the floor.[15] The House approved the conference report by a vote of 237 to 161.

One year later, the political climate changed dramatically and so did the Speaker's ability to build a winning coalition in support of the Budget Committee's first budget resolution. In 1981, President Reagan rode the wave of a convincing electoral victory that gave the Republicans control over the Senate and a gain of thirty-four House seats. The president exploited the divisions within the House Democratic party, and recruited southern Democrats to join with House Republicans to pass four major budget bills: the fiscal 1982 first budget resolution; an omnibus reconciliation bill including major cuts in domestic programs; a three-year tax plan providing tax breaks for individuals and depreciation allowances for businesses; and additional spending reductions in an omnibus appropriations bill.[16] We will focus on the passage of the first budget resolution, which illustrates the Speaker's strategy for dealing with a fractionalized party and allows evaluation of his performance as a party leader in a divided government.

In the early stages of the budget process in 1981, O'Neill's strategy reflected his middleman style of leadership and his institutional responsibility as Speaker. The strategy was to accommodate as many members of the party as possible so that the House Budget Committee could pass a Democratic budget that offered a reasonable alternative to the president's budget. O'Neill placated conservative Democrats who sought more representation on the Budget Committee and significant increases in defense spending. Meanwhile, O'Neill operated under the assumption that while the president was popular, his election was based more on the public's dissatisfaction with Carter than on a mandate for Reagan's conservative economic philosophy. O'Neill thought that the president deserved a fair opportunity to make a case for his program, but the Speaker assumed that the public would reject Reagan's proposals to cut government programs. O'Neill took a low profile in the early stages of the budget process. Rather than publicly attack the president, he contacted interest groups, requested committees to study Reagan's budget proposals, encouraged the media to expose the specific programs Reagan planned to cut, and promoted a floor amendment by Bill Hefner (D-N.C.) that would add $6.6 billion to the Budget Committee's estimate for defense spending.[17]

Yet when the House voted for the first time ever to reject the House Budget Committee's resolution and proceeded to approve the president's plan, House Democrats criticized the Speaker's strategy.[18] Liberal Democrats complained that Phil Gramm (D-Texas) should never have been appointed to the Budget Committee. Gramm had deserted the party and worked with David Stockman, director of the Office of Management and Budget, and Delbert Latta (Ohio), ranking Republican on the Budget Committee, to develop an alternative to the Budget Committee's resolution. Other Democrats criticized O'Neill for taking a trip to Australia for two weeks while Reagan was developing public support for his budget. Budget Committee Chair Jim Jones (D-Okla.) was startled when on his return O'Neill announced that public opinion in favor of the president was so strong that it was not worth fighting against the president's plan. Finally, many Democrats wondered why the Speaker did not appoint a task force to build support for the Budget Committee's resolution.

In retrospect, most of the charges were hurled in frustration and were exaggerated. Gramm was appointed to the Budget Committee on the promise that ultimately he would support the party leadership. When Gramm broke his promise and began working with Stockman he was barred from attending the Democratic Budget Committee caucus meetings. O'Neill's trip to Australia was planned two years before the budget was taken up by the House. Finally, a task force seemed unnecessary in this case, because members had already made up their minds prior to the vote.[19]

It was probably a valid criticism of O'Neill to complain that he conceded victory to Reagan before the budget even reached the floor. Part of the Speaker's role as the opposition party leader is to defend his or her party's position. Even in the face of defeat, the Speaker would have better served the party by publicly supporting the Budget Committee's plan. O'Neill himself later admitted that he had underestimated the president's popularity and ability to generate support for his program. He said he "wasn't prepared for what happened in 1981." [20] Still, one could argue reasonably that O'Neill's apparent blunders only became significant within the broader context of Reagan's impressive electoral victory, popular economic plan, and effective White House operation. Reagan's grassroots lobbying campaign was particularly successful in recruiting the votes of southern Democrats from districts in which Reagan ran ahead of Carter in the 1980 election.[21]

For Speaker O'Neill, 1981 was a defining moment in terms of how he would approach budget politics. He would no longer trust the president, and he perceived budget politics as a battle over fundamental principles. As Democratic party unity improved in the 1980s, the challenge of passing budget resolutions on the floor was replaced by efforts to define the party's priorities and protect traditional Democratic programs from being cut in the midst of large deficits. O'Neill continued to play the middleman role, but his main personal objective was to block further domestic spending cuts, even if it meant stalling the process altogether. A top staff member of O'Neill's reflected on the Speaker's commitment to maintain and, when possible, to restore the programs Reagan sought to cut:

It is a tribute to O'Neill's management of the process, that under extraordinarily adverse circumstances, when all the pressures were to cut and to get people to vote for programs to help poor people was impossible, he managed to build them back up. . . . He would literally hold up final agreement on a reconciliation bill over one AFDC provision or one Medicaid provision.[22]

Several examples illustrate the point. In 1982, O'Neill used his scheduling powers to oppose an omnibus reconciliation bill similar to the one passed by the House in 1981. When House Republicans sought a rule to block floor amendments to the reconciliation bill, O'Neill said, "We're not going to allow ourselves to be put in that position again."[23] O'Neill announced, for example, that the Post Office and Civil Service Committee was not bound to follow instructions in the first budget resolution to make a 4 percent cap on cost-of-living adjustments (COLA) to civil service pensions. When the committee ignored the instructions, O'Neill said the spending cut could be achieved if the House voted for a separate amendment on the floor. The House approved a rule that would allow the Republicans to restore the cut, but the Republicans decided against the amendment, fearing the adverse political consequences of proposing a reduction in a popular entitlement.

In 1983, as the government was on the verge of shutting down for lack of appropriations by Congress, O'Neill held hostage a continuing resolution in order to pass a $98.7 million package of social welfare benefits. O'Neill exalted: "We showed them that we had a definite means of being able to stop the further cutting of the safety net."[24]

In 1984, O'Neill blocked a Senate Republican plan to impose caps on both domestic and defense spending. O'Neill described the purpose of the Democratic strategy in reference to attempts to cut Democratic programs: "We want to stop the course of the [Reagan] administration. We're trying to stop them from turning back the clock." [25] The conference deliberations remained deadlocked until the Congress was forced to pass an extension of the ceiling on total federal debt. As part of the compromise to pass the debt ceiling, the conferees agreed to drop the caps in the reconciliation bill.

In 1985, the House and Senate were deadlocked for two months over the Senate's provision to freeze COLAs for social security at the prevailing rate of inflation. O'Neill publicly announced, "I am bitterly opposed [to the cap on the COLA for social security] and I will so notify and instruct my conferees." [26] Later, President Reagan asked if O'Neill would accept a cap on the COLAs in exchange for a reduction in the defense budget; O'Neill recalls responding, "I can't go along with this reduction on the COLAs. You can be assured that it's never going to go through the House." [27] Ultimately, the president agreed with O'Neill that the COLA should be retained, and the Speaker won another victory in blocking Republican efforts to cut social security benefits.

By placing partisan policy objectives over formal procedures, O'Neill helped to perpetuate the delays and breakdowns that had become a standard feature of budget process during the 1980s.

Jim Wright: Policy Commitments and Partisanship

If O'Neill's major challenge was to protect and defend traditional Democratic programs, his successor, Wright, sought to propose and advance budget priorities.[28] As one Budget Committee staff person remarked, Wright was an "unrelenting activist" in the budget process.[29] Wright's aggressive leadership style served him well in formulating the fiscal 1988 first budget resolution. At the beginning of his first year as Speaker (1987), Wright defined the challenge—to reduce the deficit and shift priorities from defense to domestic social programs. Yet before the year ended, Speaker Wright experienced the limitations to activist, policy-oriented leadership in the House. And, while Wright was very effective when the conditions called for decisive action, he was criticized for acting too hastily in situations that required patience.[30]

Wright ascended to the speakership in 1986 under conditions that appeared to be favorable to "strong, policy-oriented leadership." [31] The Democrats had just recaptured the Senate in the 1986 elections, House Democrats were demonstrating unprecedented levels of party cohesion on roll call votes, and President Reagan was damaged publicly by the Iran-Contra scandal and the lame-duck status typically associated with a president's final two years in office. The new Speaker took advantage of those conditions by leading the House Budget

Committee to formulate a budget resolution that attempted to reduce the deficit and shift spending priorities from defense to domestic programs. Wright's package included an $18 billion increase in tax revenues, an $18 billion cut in defense spending, and $1.45 billion in new spending for domestic social programs.

Never before had a Speaker used the budget process as an instrument for defining his own agenda, let alone a budget that included tax increases. Many House Democrats were skeptical about proposing a tax increase while President Reagan promised to veto any bills that increased taxes. But Wright believed that revenue increases were necessary in order to meet the deficit ceiling of $108 billion for fiscal year 1988 under the Gramm-Rudman-Hollings law. At the same time, he wanted the party to endorse new spending for welfare reform, health care for the elderly, homeless assistance, AIDS research, drug prevention, and job training. Wright personally lobbied Budget Committee Democrats and the Democratic Caucus to support his budget priorities.[32] The budget passed with a straight party-line vote in the Budget Committee and was approved by the House by a vote of 230 to 192, with all the Republicans and only nineteen Democrats voting against the resolution.

As the budget resolution moved on to further stages of the budget process, Wright's objectives were to preserve the major provisions of the House-passed budget resolution and to keep intact the coalition of Democrats who passed the resolution. The Speaker was only partially successful. Wright's budget was modified in conference deliberations with the Senate and was altered significantly by the reconciliation process and in negotiations with the president.

The first crack in Wright's coalition came during conference deliberations with the Senate, though his priorities generally survived. The main controversy was over defense spending. The Senate's budget resolution included about $13 billion more for defense spending than the House, and liberal Democrats in the House were decidedly against the Senate's defense figure. After several weeks of negotiations, Speaker Wright and Senate leaders agreed to a budget resolution that contained a contingency clause for the defense budget. The budget would include the Senate's defense recommendation under the assumption that the president would sign a bill containing $19.3 billion in new tax revenues. The House approved the conference plan, but by a much narrower margin than the original budget resolution. The vote was 215 to 201, as thirty-four Democrats voted against the conference version of the resolution.

Wright's budget package began to unravel when the House took up the reconciliation bill that would attempt to translate the recommendations of the budget resolution into law. The reconciliation bill consisted of $23 billion in deficit reduction, with roughly half coming from spending cuts and half from new taxes. The bill also contained a package of welfare benefits, the so-called Downey package, that embodied Wright's priorities in the original budget resolution. The package, including a measure that would require states to extend eligibility for the Aid to Families with Dependent Children (AFDC) program to two-parent families in which the primary wage earner was unemployed, would cost the federal government $148 million in fiscal year 1988 and $1.7 billion over three years. Southern Democrats objected to the mix of taxes and spending cuts in the reconciliation bill plus the AFDC mandate on the states. Buddy MacKay (D-Fla.), described the problem for southern Democrats: "It's [the reconciliation bill] got two lightning rod issues [taxes and welfare]; both of which are career threatening in the South. . . ." [33] Wright suffered his first major defeat when the House defeated the rule on the reconciliation bill by a vote of 203 to 217; forty-eight Democrats (thirty-two from the South) voted against the bill.

The aftermath of this vote is described in Chapters 4 and 11. By forceful action Speaker Wright was able to reverse his defeat and pass the budget. However, the original package was compromised even further by a budget summit agreement between the president and Congress. The summit produced a two-year budget plan, including a total of $76 billion in deficit reduction, that set the guidelines for the final reconciliation bill and the omnibus appropriation bill for fiscal year 1988. As the curtain closed on Speaker Wright's first year, he found himself relying on Republican votes to pass both of those bills.[34] And, though he succeeded in getting President Reagan to sign a bill that raised $9 billion in taxes, it was half of what the Speaker originally wanted.

Speaker Wright deserves credit for taking on the challenge of trying to raise taxes to reduce the deficit and defining a Democratic agenda during the final two years of the Reagan administration. Yet his aggressive style was not always consistent with the expectations of House members. The results of Wright's activist leadership reflect both the impressive potential of the Speaker's office and the limitations to strong, policy-oriented leadership in the House.

Tom Foley: Balancing Institutional and Partisan Interests

Compared with Wright and O'Neill, Foley has been a much less partisan Speaker. He has not yet attempted to push his own policy agenda, and he has not engaged in the sort of partisan combat waged by his predecessors. Foley expressed reservations about the partisan element of the opposition party leader role that he assumed during the Bush administration: "I was not elected primarily to be the campaign manager of the next Democratic President. I don't see my job that way." [35] House Democrats have occasionally criticized Foley's nonpartisan style, which seems out of context in the highly partisan, contentious atmosphere that has pervaded budget politics. Foley acknowledges and ignores his critics: "There are people who think I should be more partisan, should be more aggressive, should be more combative. More hard-edged. . . . I don't tend to agree with them." [36] Thus, Foley's speakership has restored an interest in institutional leadership combined with a weaker commitment to partisan interests, and what appears to be almost no interest in pursuing personal policy preferences.

Speaker Foley's major challenges in the budget process have been to help pass the two largest deficit reduction plans in history. In both cases he has acted as a consensus builder rather than an advocate for a particular set of priorities. After Foley suffered an embarrassing defeat on the 1990 bipartisan budget summit agreement, he helped to pass a Democratic-sponsored budget and reconciliation bill later that year. In 1993, he served as an able lieutenant of President Clinton's budget plan and reconciliation bill in the House. He also played an instrumental role in lobbying House Democrats to support the conference version of the reconciliation bill.

In January 1990, President George Bush submitted a budget that recommended $36 billion in deficit reduction to meet the Gramm-Rudman-Hollings deficit ceiling of $64 billion for fiscal year 1991. By April, however, as the House Budget Committee deliberated over the first budget resolution, OMB Director Richard Darman announced that the administration had underestimated the size of the deficit, and at least $50 billion more in spending cuts or revenue increases would be needed to avoid sequestration. Despite Darman's warning, Budget Committee Democrats decided to stick with Bush's original budget assumptions and wait for the president to recommend a way to achieve the additional $50 billion in deficit reduction. Speaker Foley expressed the position of House Democrats, who were unwilling to let the administration off the hook: "The first action has to be taken by the president. First, with the president, then with us." [37]

Recognizing that a sequestration order of at least $50 billion would force deep cuts in defense spending, President Bush called a meeting with congressional leaders on May 6 to talk about a process for negotiating a deficit reduction deal with "no preconditions." Just three days later, however, Bush's Chief of Staff John Sununu stated that "no preconditions" meant the Democrats could propose new taxes if they wanted. Sununu's statement confirmed the suspicions of House Democrats who believed Bush's invitation to negotiate with House leaders was a political ploy to get the Democrats to initiate a tax increase as part of a deficit reduction package. While Foley was open to negotiations with the White House, many House Democrats distrusted Bush and Darman and were opposed to bipartisan talks. The leadership decided to adopt a "go slow" strategy in which Foley insisted that the president must publicly acknowledge the need to increase taxes before the Democrats would go along.[38] This strategy gave Bush an opening to accept a tax increase without alienating House Democrats.

On June 26, after weeks of ambiguity about the president's intentions to revoke his campaign pledge of no new taxes and propose a tax increase, Speaker Foley told Bush: "If you issue this statement [on the need for taxes] we'll agree with it." [39] Following the meeting, Bush made a televised address stating the need to increase revenues as part of a deficit reduction plan, and Foley backed the president at a press conference following the speech. The Speaker said the Democrats were not interested in scoring political points for persuading the president to abandon his "read my lips, no new taxes" campaign pledge. Foley stated, "I think it's important that neither political party attempt to make political capital out of serious bipartisan efforts to reach a budget agreement." [40]

From that point, the budget moved sluggishly through a series of summit meetings involving congressional leaders and White House officials. After failing to reach agreement in August, a group of twenty-three lawmakers took refuge for ten days of private talks at Andrews Air Force base in early September. But a dispute over the president's proposal for a capital gains tax cut undermined chances for a final agreement. As the beginning of the fiscal year approached (October 1), and the threat of an $85 billion sequester became more likely, bipartisan talks continued in Speaker Foley's office, this time with a much smaller group of eight people. On September 30, the group reached a budget agreement that would be debated and voted on by the House. It was a five-year, $500 billion deficit reduction package that reduced discretionary spending by $182.4 billion, cut Medicare by $60 billion, and raised $163 billion from a host of excise taxes, including gasoline, tobacco, alcohol, and luxury items.

But the leaders of the summit recognized that the compromise agreement faced an uphill battle from the day it was announced. President Bush admitted,

"Sometimes you don't get it the way you want, and this is such a time for me."
Speaker Foley noted, "This isn't the kind of thing the political system wants to go racing out in the streets [about] and saying, 'Joy! Joy!' " [41] It did not take long for members to attack the budget and the process used to formulate it. Members of both parties condemned the closed, secretive talks of the summit that prohibited them from having any input. Conservative House Republicans, led by Minority Whip Newt Gingrich (R-Ga.) argued that the plan included too many taxes and would stifle economic growth. Liberal Democrats complained that the excise taxes were regressive and that reductions in the earned income tax credit, delays in unemployment benefits, and increases in Medicare deductibles and premiums were unfair.

Nevertheless, the leaders of both parties attempted to garner a majority of members from their respective caucuses. On the Democratic side, early whip counts showed very little enthusiasm for the budget. Speaker Foley tried to persuade committee chairs to vote in favor of the budget resolution on the premise that they could change specific aspects of the plan in the reconciliation process. He made the same appeal to the Democratic Caucus on the morning of the vote. Finally, in a dramatic end to a long day of debate on the floor, Foley spoke to the House. He described the problem of large deficits; he urged members to look beyond partisan politics; and he reminded them again that passing the budget resolution was only the beginning of the process. Foley stated: "The president said today to me, and I repeated to the press, that it was our conviction . . . that many of the policies established in the budget agreement were for illustrative purposes only, and that the legislative committees had the right as well as the obligation to consider alternative policies to achieve similar savings." [42]

Despite the Speaker's efforts, the House rejected the budget resolution by a vote of 179 to 254. Foley's strategy of trying to mobilize the committee chairs was unsuccessful. Only fourteen of the twenty-seven Democratic committee chairs and only seven of the thirteen subcommittee chairs of the Appropriations Committee voted for the budget. His plea to pass the budget resolution so that the House committees could work out the details of the deficit reduction plan alarmed House Republicans, who believed the reconciliation bill would be even less appealing to them than the budget resolution. Once it was clear that a majority of Republicans would vote against the plan, previously undecided Democrats also had reason to vote against it.

Some Democrats saw the vote on the budget resolution as a referendum on Foley's leadership. Foley's critics charged that he was too willing to compromise the party's principles in order to close a deal with the president. Liberal Democrats, in particular, were surprised that the Speaker expected them to vote for a bill that contained severe cuts in social programs and regressive taxes. The fact that they were not consulted in the process added insult to injury.

Yet Foley believed the vote was as much a failure of bipartisan cooperation in an era of intense partisan politics as a failure of his leadership strategy. The Speaker knew it would be difficult to sell the package to House Democrats and he personally did not like all aspects of the summit package. But he also knew that a strictly Democratic alternative would not have passed in the Senate. The Speaker thought if the Republicans could produce a majority on their side, then a majority of House Democrats would also go along, if only because they feared that voters would be even more angry if they had done nothing.[43]

In the last analysis, although Foley lost the battle over the summit budget, he helped to win the war for the Democrats. House Democrats were able to regroup and pass their own budget resolution just three days after the summit agreement failed. The new plan stripped many of the controversial provisions in the summit bill and turned over the legislative details to the committees. Throughout the next month, as Democrats from both chambers worked through conference negotiations, Foley played an essentially mediating role between House and Senate Democrats. Eventually the Congress and the president agreed to a budget that included a 3 percent increase in the highest marginal rate of taxation; excise taxes on alcohol, fuel, and tobacco; caps on discretionary spending; and much less severe cuts in Medicare than the summit budget had called for. During the process, Democrats painted Republicans as the party of the rich, unwilling to raise the top rate for individual income earners, a theme that Clinton would repeat in the 1992 presidential campaign. Meanwhile, Bush was unable to rebound from his decision to violate his promise not to raise taxes. Ironically, Speaker Foley, who said the Democrats would not turn the president's decision to raise taxes into a political game, played an important role in persuading the president to revoke his promise, and once Bush endorsed a tax increase, the game was on.

When Clinton was elected president, Speaker Foley's role changed from representing Democrats in negotiations with the administration to delivering votes for the president. In 1993, the Speaker participated in a coordinated lobbying effort with the White House to attract wary Democrats to vote for a $496 billion reconciliation package of taxes and spending cuts. Up until the day before the vote, the leadership appeared to be short of the necessary majority to pass the bill. Conservative Democrats wanted more spending cuts and fewer tax increases, and they sought a cap on entitlement spending. House Democrats were also worried that the proposed energy tax would be changed in the Senate, which was scheduled to meet after the floor vote in the House. After House leaders agreed to a provision to control entitlements and a promise by the president to reduce the energy tax and cut more entitlement spending, the House passed the bill by a vote of 219 to 213. As part of an intense lobbying effort by the White House, the Speaker helped to cool tensions within the party and persuaded members to support the bill, but the key decisions regarding the content of the final package ultimately were made by the president.

The Speaker performed a similar role when the House considered the conference version of the reconciliation bill. Securing approval of the conference bill was difficult because of the slim margin of victory on final passage of the House bill, the unanimous opposition of Republicans, and differences between the House and Senate bills. The conference provided recalcitrant members with an opportunity to shape the final details of the budget package before it was sent to the president, and they made the most of this opportunity.[44]

For members who disagreed with the conference bill, the Speaker explained that there was no viable alternative and that the consequences of defeat—a failed Democratic presidency and a shock to financial markets—were too onerous to bear. Yet neither the conference bill nor the arguments made by party leaders were enough to ensure victory. As the floor votes on the conference bill neared, passage of the bill remained in doubt. In an effort to persuade wary Democrats to vote for the bill, President Clinton signed two executive orders that ostensibly made a firmer commitment to deficit reduction (a deficit reduction trust fund and an entitlement review in the event that spending exceeded the targets in the plan) and engaged in a final round of last minute deal-making that included a promise to send Congress more spending cuts in a few months. Meanwhile, party leaders engaged in extensive lobbying efforts to pass the bill and promised members the opportunity to amend the president's next budget package, including amendments that would cut entitlements and discretionary spending and call for a constitutional amendment to balance the budget.[45] The bill ultimately passed by a slim two-vote margin, 218 to 216.

Looking to the Future:
The Speaker and the Budget Process

The Speaker's strategies for dealing with future challenges will depend on prevailing conditions and the individual Speaker. The 1994 midterm elections produced the first Republican majority in forty years, a new Speaker of the House, Newt Gingrich (R-Ga.), and a return to divided party government. The Republicans are expected to be unified and eager to govern. In the near term, if previous patterns of divided government hold, we can expect Speaker Gingrich to play a leading role as the spokesperson of the House majority party. At the very least, the Republicans will propose a constitutional amendment to balance the budget, a key ingredient of the party's "Contract with America." Gingrich and the Republicans should also challenge the basic priorities of Clinton's budgets: the Republicans are especially likely to clash with Clinton over tax policy and the level of defense spending. Gingrich and the supply side wing of the House Republican Party will also need to deal with fiscal conservatives on the Senate side. Majority Leader Bob Dole and Senate Budget Committee Chair Pete Domenici appear to be more concerned with the budget deficit then offering a tax break.

As a party leader, one of Gingrich's primary challenges will be to handle criticism from Democrats about how Republican spending and tax priorities square with a promise to balance the budget. Gingrich will also need to determine how actively to engage in the budget committee's deliberations over the budget resolution. And he will need to decide if and when to engage in budget negotiations with the White House, and how to represent Republicans in those negotiations. Yet his biggest challenge might be adapting to the role of institutional leader. Gingrich has displayed a tendency to be abrasive and confrontational, a style more conductive to a minority party leader than a Speaker. As the Speaker, Gingrich has a responsibility to the House, as well as to the Republican party. Like all speakers, Gingrich will struggle to balance party goals with procedural fairness. The manner in which Gingrich attempts to balance these competing interests will define his role in the budget process. The challenge for Gingrich might be particularly important as a restive public judges the performance of the new House majority party.

Notes

1. For this passage on Speaker Albert's role in the budget process, the author consulted Daniel J. Palazzolo, *The Speaker and the Budget: Leadership in the Post-Reform*

House of Representatives (Pittsburgh: University of Pittsburgh Press, 1992), 54-57.

2. An increase in floor amendments illustrated how eager members were to participate in the process. Steven S. Smith, *Call to Order* (Washington, D.C.: Brookings Institution, 1989), chap. 3.

3. For a discussion of how leaders attempt to manage change, see Roger H. Davidson, "Congressional Leaders As Agents of Change," in *Understanding Congressional Leadership*, ed. Frank Mackaman, (Washington, D.C.: CQ Press, 1981). See also chap. 8.

4. For more on the tension between junior and senior members, see Ronald M. Peters Jr., *The American Speakership* (Baltimore: Johns Hopkins University Press, 1990), 156-157. See also Matt Pinkus, "Albert: From a Cabin in the Cotton Patch to Congress," *Congressional Quarterly Weekly Report*, June 12, 1976, 1492.

5. Elder Witt and Tom Arrandale, "Overestimating the Capability of Congress," *Congressional Quarterly Weekly Report*, June 28, 1975, 1343-1346.

6. Richard Bolling, interview by author.

7. Brock Adams, interview by author.

8. U.S. Congress, House, *Congressional Record*, daily ed., 94th Cong., 1st sess., May 1, 1975, 12,767.

9. Carl Albert, interview by author.

10. See Nelson W. Polsby, "Two Strategies of Influence: Choosing a Majority Leader, 1962," in *New Perspectives on the House of Representatives*, ed. Nelson W. Polsby and Robert L. Peabody (Chicago: Rand McNally, 1969), 334-337. See also Peters, *The American Speakership*, 155-158.

11. Brock Adams, interview by author.

12. Irwin B. Arieff, "House, Senate Chiefs Attempt to Lead a Changed Congress," *Congressional Quarterly Weekly Report*, Sept. 13, 1980, 2696.

13. See Barbara Sinclair, "The Speaker's Task Forces in the Post-Reform House of Representatives," *American Political Science Review* 75 (1981): 391-410; Steven S. Smith, "O'Neill's Legacy for the House," *The Brookings Review* 5 (1987): 28-36; and chap. 3.

14. Gail Gregg, "House Sends Budget Back to Conference," *Congressional Quarterly Weekly Report*, May 31, 1980, 1460.

15. See Barbara Sinclair, *Majority Leadership in the U.S. House* (Baltimore: Johns Hopkins University Press, 1983), 186-187.

16. For more on budget politics in 1981, see Sinclair, *Majority Leadership in the U.S. House*, 190-213; Lance T. LeLoup, "After the Blitz: Reagan and the U.S. Congressional Budget Process," *Legislative Studies Quarterly* 7 (1982): 321-339; Allen Schick, "How the Budget Was Won and Lost," in *President and Congress: Assessing Reagan's First Year*, ed. Norman J. Ornstein (Washington, D.C.: American Enterprise Institute, 1982); and Palazzolo, *The Speaker and the Budget*, chap. 4.

17. Steven S. Smith, "Budget Battles of 1981: The Role of the Majority Party Leadership," in *American Politics and Public Policy*, ed. Allan P. Sindler (Washington, D.C.: CQ Press, 1982).

18. For the following account of O'Neill's problems in 1981, the author consulted Palazzolo, *The Speaker and the Budget*, 100-103.

19. See Sinclair, *Majority Leadership in the U.S. House*, 193-194.

20. Thomas P. "Tip" O'Neill, *Man of the House* (New York: Random House, 1987), 345.

21. See Steven J. Wayne, "Congressional Liaison in the Reagan White House: A Preliminary Assessment of the First Year," in *President and Congress: Assessing Reagan's First Year*, ed. Norman J. Ornstein (Washington, D.C.: American Enterprise Institute, 1982), 49-65.

22. Interview by author.

23. Dale Tate, "Congress Faces Uphill Battle to Achieve Budgeted Savings," *Congressional Quarterly Weekly Report*, June 26, 1982, 1507.

24. Diane Granat, "Congress Clears 1984 Continuing Resolution," *Congressional Quarterly Weekly Report*, Nov. 19, 1983, 2431-2432.

25. Diane Granat, "Legislative Business Proceeds Amidst Hill's Political Battles," *Congressional Quarterly Weekly Report*, July 7, 1984, 1608.

26. Jacqueline Calmes, "House, with Little Difficulty, Passes '86 Budget Resolution," *Congressional Quarterly Weekly Report*, May 25, 1985, 971.

27. Tip O'Neill, interview by author.

28. For a comparison between O'Neill and Wright, see Daniel J. Palazzolo, "Majority Party Leadership and Budget Policy Making in the Post-Reform House of Representatives," *Congress and the Presidency* 19 (1992): 157-174.

29. Interview by author.

30. For a full description of Wright's leadership role in the budget process, see Palazzolo, *The Speaker and the Budget*, chap. 6.

31. Barbara Sinclair, "House Majority Party Leadership in the Late-1980s," in *Congress Reconsidered*, 4th ed., ed. Lawrence C. Dodd and Bruce I. Oppenheimer (Washington, D.C.: CQ Press, 1989).

32. See Palazzolo, *The Speaker and the Budget*, 177-186.

33. Elizabeth Wehr, "Southern Democrats Dislike Tax-Welfare Mix," *Congressional Quarterly Weekly Report*, Oct. 17, 1987, 2505.

34. The appropriations bill passed 209 to 208, with Democrats voting 116 to 128 and Republicans voting 93 to 80. The reconciliation bill passed 237 to 181, with Democrats voting 193 to 51 and Republicans voting 44 to 130.

35. Michael Oreskes, "Foley's Law," *New York Times Magazine*, Nov. 11, 1990, 70.

36. Ibid., 70.

37. Jackie Calmes, "Democrats Labor to Meet Targets for 1991 Deficit Reduction," *Congressional Quarterly Weekly Report*, April 7, 1990, 1051.

38. Alan Murray and Jackie Calmes, "The Great Debate: How the Democrats with Cunning, Won the Budget War," *Wall Street Journal*, Nov. 5, 1990, A1, A4.

39. Ibid., A4.

40. "President's Budget Proposal Stirs Reaction on the Hill," *Congressional Quarterly Weekly Report*, June 30, 1990, 2095.

41. Both Bush and Foley quoted in George Hager, "Defiant House Rebukes Leaders; New Round of Fights Begins," *Congressional Quarterly Weekly Report*, Oct. 6, 1990, 3186.

42. U.S. Congress, House, *Congressional Record*, daily ed., 101st Congress, 2d sess., Oct. 4, 1990, H8996.

43. Thomas H. Edsall and Tom Kenworthy, "Democrats Bowed to 'Scorched Earth' Fear," *Washington Post*, Oct. 6, 1990, A6.

44. See Janet Hook, "Conference Without Walls," *Congressional Quarterly Weekly Report*, Aug. 7, 1993, 2128; George Hager and David S. Cloud, "Democrats Tie Their Fate to Clinton's Budget Bill," *Congressional Quarterly Weekly Report*, Aug. 7, 1993,

2122-2129; and David Rogers and John Harwood, "No Reasonable Offers Refused as Administration Bargains to Nail Down Deficit Package in House," *Wall Street Journal,* Aug. 6, 1993, A12.

45. See Hager and Cloud, "Democrats Tie Their Fate to Clinton's Budget Bill," 2111-2129.

46. In 1979, Speaker O'Neill directly challenged President Carter's proposals to cut spending in domestic programs, stating: "I'm not going to allow people to go to bed hungry for an austerity program. . . ." Alan Berlow, "Coalitions Forming in Congress to Fight for Restoration of Social Program Spending," *Congressional Quarterly Weekly Report,* Jan. 27, 1979, 126.

6 The Speaker and Foreign Policy

Steven S. Smith and Mark Watts

In this chapter the changing behavior of recent Speakers is explained as a response to the evolving context of foreign and defense policy decision making.[1] Our focus is on the last six Speakers—Sam Rayburn, John McCormack, Carl Albert, Thomas P. "Tip" O'Neill, Jr., Jim Wright, and Thomas S. Foley— all Democrats. We will demonstrate that Speakers have adopted more assertive patterns of support and opposition for presidential positions in foreign policy, assumed more prominent roles as party spokespersons in foreign policy, evolved more partisan patterns of consultation with presidents, and more frequently sought to mobilize colleagues in foreign policy.

Conditions Shaping the Role of Speakers in Foreign Affairs

Several factors must be a part of any account of the changes in the strategies of Speakers in any field of public policy, including foreign and defense policy. These include the expectations of party colleagues, the Speaker's formal powers, alternative sources of leadership in the House, the president, public opinion, and the institutional position of the House.

The Speaker is, first and foremost, an elected party leader who requires the support of most, if not the vast majority, of his or her party colleagues to achieve personal or party goals. This sets parameters on the policy agenda and direction taken by the Speaker. Every Speaker inherits formal powers granted by House and party rules and precedents that may empower or constrain his or her involvement in foreign policy. A Speaker who has a reserve of formal powers is more likely to be subject to demands from colleagues to use those powers than a Speaker who lacks authority to act. In the 1890s Speaker Thomas Brackett Reed could unilaterally block foreign policy resolutions to which he was opposed; in the 1970s Speaker Albert could not prevent Majority Whip O'Neill from offering resolutions to end the war in Vietnam.

There often are other members, such as committee and subcommittee chairs, who are more capable than the Speaker of taking the lead in devising policy proposals and generating support on specific issues. The Speaker will typically defer to key committee or subcommittee chairs but may have to step in at times to assume personal responsibility for an issue when a chair is unfit for a leading role for personal or political reasons.

Whether the Speaker is of the same party as the president, the compatibility of the president's views with those of the Speaker and the majority party, and perhaps even the competence of the president and the administration, will influence the strategies pursued by a Speaker. The president's formal powers are superior to the Speaker's, and so the president is often able to mold the foreign policy agenda.

Because public opinion, measured in polls, mail, and many other means, influences the judgments of presidents and many members, it is a major factor in the Speaker's calculations. Whether to be bold or cautious may turn on which party's position is favored by the public, the popularity of the president, and the mix of views in the party's electoral coalition.

The strategies of the Speaker are constrained by the formal powers of the institution.[2] In some areas, perhaps those in which the president has been granted or assumes great discretion, there is little that Congress can do, at least in the short run, to affect the direction of policy. Moreover, in areas involving treaties or nominations the direct formal powers of the House are limited. And the resources available to the Speaker through committees, congressional support agencies, or leadership staffs may determine the Speaker's ability to pursue an independent course of action.

All Speakers come to office with issues and priorities of personal interest and long-established views on major issues. The compatibility of their personal priorities and views with those of their party, along with their skills, health, and other personal considerations, are likely to play a major role in shaping the policy-making role of Speakers.

These factors make plain that explaining the behavior of just six Speakers over four decades is a precarious business. Nevertheless, several widely accepted generalizations about the changing context of policy making in the foreign policy arena would lead us to predict that Speakers' approaches to their jobs should have changed in important ways. The generalizations constitute a loosely structured story about the "resurgent Congress."[3]

• As television became the major source of news for Americans in the 1950s and 1960s, it brought the world into American living rooms, making the politicization of international affairs easier, if not inevitable.

- In the same period, foreign policy attitudes in the mass public and policy elite began to align with domestic policy attitudes, which gave foreign policy divisions a more partisan cast.
- Technological advances in transportation and communication furthered the integration of domestic and international affairs.
- The number of organized interests with international agendas grew, which enhanced the priority of international affairs in Washington, D.C. Local party organizations withered and legislators became more independent of party bosses—increasing legislators' dependence on interest groups and encouraging legislators to pursue individually defined legislative agendas.
- The democratization of Congress in the early 1970s— primarily a result of the weakening of the autonomy of full committee chairs—gave rank-and-file members the opportunities to pursue their own policy agendas.
- The increasing demands of foreign policy on presidents, the increasing importance of foreign policy to presidents, and presidents' distrust of the foreign policy bureaucracy have led to a centralization of foreign policy decision making within the executive branch.
- Prolonged divided government—a Democratic Congress with Republican presidents—intensified partisan motivations in foreign affairs and stimulated congressional activity.
- Foreign policy developed as more regulatory and less diplomatic and treaty-oriented, as economic and arms trade as well as human rights and environmental concerns became more central to American relations with foreign governments.
- The end of the cold war reduced the threat to national security and eliminated the major force shaping American foreign policy and public and elite views about foreign and defense policy.

These developments altered the strategic context confronted by Speakers. Within the House, much of the power flowed to subcommittee chairs and rank-and-file committee members, but they could not mobilize the same resources and exercise the same agenda control that full committee chairs once did. Little help could be found in the White House, which was controlled by the opposite party for all but four years between 1969 and 1992. The power vacuum created opportunities for the majority party leaders to exercise greater influence over policy outcomes. Enhancing the Speaker's control over committee assignments, bill referral, and the Rules Committee strengthened the majority party leadership's capacity to act.

Beyond new opportunities and capacity, the Speaker gained additional motivation to be assertive as congressional partisanship intensified in the late 1970s and 1980s. What theory we have about congressional leadership suggests that salient, highly partisan issues tend to generate strong party leadership.[4] Cohesive parties are more inclined to empower their leaders to act on their behalf. As leaders become more assertive and partisan, further polarization of the parties occurs.

The larger institutional context in which some foreign policy is made changed as well. As Congress sought to respond to executive excesses and opposition presidents, it forced into law new constraints on executive action in international affairs. Most noteworthy were requirements for congressional approval of certain kinds of action (arms sales, use of military force, and so forth), which limited the president's ability to manipulate the policy status quo. Requests for congressional approval from the president gave congressional party leaders, as gatekeepers for Congress's agenda, a source of leverage with the president that they often lacked in the past. These developments gave the House a formal role in policy making, which created new opportunities and burdens for the Speaker in foreign policy.

The new circumstances created greater need for a strong speakership, greater demand from Democratic liberals for strong Speakers, greater freedom for Speakers to meet those needs and demands, and more opportunities for influence to be exercised by the Speaker. In the foreign policy, Speakers became increasingly partisan in their attitudes toward presidential *policy positions,* more active as *policy leaders,* more active as *opinion leaders,* and more partisan in their services as *intermediaries* between the White House and their Hill colleagues.

Leaders' Policy Positions

Congressional presidential relationships of the 1950s remain the modern standard by which foreign policy decision making is judged. Profound anxiety about the threat of communism from the Soviet Union and China helped to eliminate the remnants of the isolationist wing of the Republican party and served to forge a new consensus about American internationalism. The consensus was reflected in relationships between the branches and the parties in world affairs. The national consensus about the threat to the nation, divided party control of the branches, and President Dwight Eisenhower's status as a hero of World War II provided ideal ingredients for the emergence of a norm of congressional deference to the president in world affairs. Small differences over tactics and regional matters were often suppressed in the interest of maintaining a solid front in the fight against world communism.

The Rayburn Standard

Speaker Rayburn, who was Speaker from 1940 to 1960 with the exception of two Congresses, seldom differed with President Eisenhower on world affairs and always chose to avoid publicly criticizing the president when detectable differences emerged. Rayburn supported the administration much less frequently in the domestic arena than in the foreign arena, creating a sharp and often-noted contrast. Rayburn even took the lead in promoting Eisenhower's policies when House Republicans refused to support the president. For example, Rayburn appeared to be pivotal to House approval of the 1955 reciprocal trade bill. As the House was about to vote on a closed rule to protect the bill from crippling amendment, Rayburn went to the floor and made a speech that was described by one reporter as "spine-tingling." [5] Rayburn's efforts managed to sway enough members to gain a one-vote victory for the rule.[6]

Rayburn's commitment to bipartisanship was more than skin-deep. On more than one occasion he found himself supporting Eisenhower's position in opposition to the rest of his party. On the Mutual Security Act of 1956, Rayburn sided with Eisenhower in the president's attempt to restore foreign aid funding that had been slashed by the House Foreign Affairs Committee. Rayburn joined with Minority Leader Joseph Martin in support of a floor amendment to get some of the president's request restored. Again Rayburn took to the floor, this time declaring, "We just have one President of the United States at a time. He is the voice of America or America has no voice. And, I have said that for thirty years in this House, it mattered not who was the President of the United States." James Richards (D-S.C.), chair of the Foreign Affairs Committee, responded:

Here they are, the former Speaker of the House and the present Speaker of the House, who have said time after time how they loved this House and how they would fight to serve the integrity of this House, leading this fight to repudiate what a committee, an arm of this House, has done. . . . [Y]et these distinguished gentlemen . . . are themselves helping to destroy one of the checks essential to the preservation of democratic government, and they are doing it in their own House.[7]

The amendment, and Rayburn, lost on a 112 to 192 teller vote.

The episode is enlightening. In the conflict between the norm of deference to the president in world affairs, on the one hand, and the norm of deference to committees, on the other, it appeared that Rayburn chose deference to the president. And this was an era in which standing committees were as powerful as at any time in history and the norm of committee deference nearly defined the decision-making process of the House.[8] As his biographers note, Rayburn spoke about bipartisanship on many occasions. His commitment to bipartisanship in foreign policy was genuine and deeply felt. In 1956 Rayburn went so far as to make several public statements to warn presidential and congressional candidates of both parties not to politicize foreign policy. To be sure, Rayburn's policy views were quite close to Eisenhower's views, so that deference to the president generally served his policy goals as well. Nevertheless, it seems fair to say, Rayburn was truly committed to the principle; Rayburn, even more than Eisenhower, symbolized bipartisanship.

The Albert-O'Neill Transition

In the 1960s, Speaker McCormack, who was as much of a Cold War hawk as any member of Congress, supported President Lyndon B. Johnson's Vietnam war policies and refused to support the efforts of Democratic war opponents during the Nixon years. His majority leader and successor, Carl Albert, also supported Johnson and Nixon Vietnam policies. Albert was elected Speaker in 1971, and, despite the fact that sentiment against the war was growing among congressional Democrats, he continued to give deference to the Republican administration's war policy. Indeed, Albert, more than any other member, was responsible for defeating a number of "end-the-war" resolutions and amendments in his party caucus and on the floor.

Albert's awkward situation became clear early in his term as Speaker. In June 1971, an amendment that would stop funding for the war at the end of the year was proposed to a defense authorization bill. Albert, as with McCormack, very seldom spoke from the floor, but he did so on this occasion. Albert simply said, "I do not believe we should undertake by legislative fiat to settle the war at a time certain to tie the hands of the President in any way." [9] While the amendment lost by a vote of 158 to 254, Democrats supported the amendment by a vote of 135 to 105.

Democratic opposition to the war intensified over the next year. In April 1972, under pressure from party colleagues, Albert finally allowed an end-the-war resolution, co-sponsored by his party whip Thomas P. "Tip" O'Neill, Jr., to be given serious consideration in a meeting of the caucus. Previously, Albert had allowed committees to meet during the caucus meetings, which ensured that a quorum would not be present at the caucus meetings to take formal action. This time he asked, at O'Neill's request, that committees not meet during the caucus so that a vote on the war could take place. Albert first opposed, and the caucus rejected, the original version of O'Neill's resolution, but then he and the caucus accepted an amended version that criticized North Vietnam's role in the war. The resolution passed 144 to 58. In response to the caucus resolution, the House Foreign Affairs Committee attached an end-the-war provision to a foreign military aid bill. But when the bill came to the floor, Albert voted to knock out the provision and, indeed, the provision was removed by a 229 to 177 vote, with the Democrats voting 80 to 154.[10] Thus, as the balance in the party was shifting more against the war, Albert showed a willingness to allow the caucus and the House to address the issue, although, for the time being, he was not yet willing to bind the president.

A year later in May 1973, the House went on record in opposition to the war for the first time. It approved an amendment that would prevent the Pentagon from transferring funds between accounts to pay for the bombing in Cambodia. The amendment, which had been defeated in committee by a 14 to 31 vote, was endorsed by the party's Steering and Policy Committee, 18 to 3, and was approved by the House on a 219 to 188 vote. The amendment received Albert's quiet support.[11] To do otherwise would have put Albert in a rapidly shrinking minority within his party. The balance among Democrats had shifted even further by this time—they voted 184 to 45 in favor of the amendment.

In contrast, Albert's majority leader and successor as Speaker, Tip O'Neill, led the charge against the war as Democratic whip and majority leader in the early 1970s. This marked an important transition in the views of House Democratic leaders about world affairs and their relationship with Republican presidents. The decline of bipartisanship was an often-repeated theme and presidents began to assume, correctly, that cooperation from congressional leaders of the opposite party was problematic.

Substantial differences between presidents and opposition congressional leaders continued in the Carter and Reagan administrations. Nevertheless, bipartisanship continued to be a theme in leaders' rhetoric. Even O'Neill noted the importance of bipartisanship from time to time. When President Reagan sent marines to Lebanon as part of a "peace-keeping" effort on September 28, 1983, O'Neill negotiated a compromise agreement that allowed Reagan to keep the troops in place for eighteen months in exchange for Reagan's implicit acceptance of Congress's right to invoke the War Powers Resolution. Only with O'Neill's effort did the compromise agreement pass the House; a slim majority of Democrats opposed it.

Eleven months later, the U.S. Marine Corps barracks in Lebanon was bombed, and O'Neill quickly came under fire by Democrats who opposed the initial agreement. Many Democrats were also very critical of O'Neill's silence in the days following the invasion of Grenada. O'Neill defended himself at a meeting of the Democratic Caucus in what was described as "his most emotional and eloquent speech in years." He claimed that there was a need for national unity in times of foreign crises and closed his speech by asserting that he was standing by the president because he was "a patriot." [12]

O'Neill eventually adopted a far more critical view of President Reagan's policies. In early 1984, O'Neill set up a Lebanon monitoring group designed to press the Reagan administration into justifying the Marine Corps' mission. After the first meeting of the Lebanon group, O'Neill declared that he would "join with many others in Congress in reconsidering congressional authorization for Marine presence in Lebanon" unless there was more rapid diplomatic progress.[13] At a January White House meeting, O'Neill complained to Reagan that his policy was being handled in a "simplistic manner" and that people everywhere were saying that the Marines should be withdrawn. Rep. Richard Cheney, (R-Wyo.) responded that Lebanon was "increasingly becoming a partisan issue" and that O'Neill was "functioning more and more as a party leader and less as a Speaker." [14] O'Neill soon had reversed completely his position. He pushed a resolution through the Democratic Caucus that called for the "prompt and orderly withdrawal" of U.S. Marines from Lebanon and sharply criticized Reagan's Lebanon policy.[15] It is hard to avoid the conclusion that O'Neill could not resist the pressure, or perhaps the persuasiveness, of the majority of his party colleagues. O'Neill's new position stimulated an angry response from President Reagan, who, in a *Wall Street Journal* interview, accused O'Neill of surrendering Lebanon and claimed that removing troops from Lebanon would be the end of that country. Four days later, Reagan announced that the U.S. Marines were going to be re-deployed to offshore ships.

The New Partisanship

O'Neill's successors, Jim Wright and Foley, also took highly visible positions in opposition to Republican presidents. Wright's most visible dispute with President Reagan concerned support for the Nicaraguan Contras. We will discuss Wright's efforts again later, but Foley's opposition to President Bush's request for authorization for the use of force to expel

Iraq from Kuwait in 1991 deserves special notice.

Wright's resignation and Foley's ascension to the speakership in 1989 were widely recognized as an important change in style—from the confrontational, personalistic, and sharply partisan style of Wright to the more accommodating, managerial, and much less partisan style of Foley. In some important respects, Foley's style looked much like Rayburn's. Yet, as Foley's position on the Persian Gulf resolutions demonstrated, Foley shared with Wright a belief about the importance of Congress exercising independent judgment in matters of national security policy. He made his views plain when he spoke on the floor of the House:

This debate is not about who supports the President of the United States and who does not. I honor and respect the President. I know his determination and I also know the awful loneliness and terrible consequence of the decisions that he must make.

In a letter to Thomas Jefferson, James Madison wrote: "The Constitution supposes what the history of all governments demonstrate, that the Executive is the branch . . . most interested in war, and most prone to it. It has accordingly . . . vested the question of war in the legislature."

I do not believe that the President wants war. I believe that he devoutly wishes peace and will continue to hope and work for it. But it is wrong to suggest that we who have taken our own oath can burden him further by giving to him alone the responsibility that also must be ours today. We must share in this decision. We have been elected to do it. The Constitution mandates it, and we would shirk our duty if we easily acquiesce in what the President decides. That is unfair to him, as it is to our constituents and to our responsibilities. . . . [16]

Plainly, whatever the stylistic similarities between Rayburn and Foley, their attitudes about deference to the president and the location of their policy positions relative to the president were quite different. Foley believes not only that Congress has independent powers to be exercised in foreign policy, but also that its members have an affirmative obligation to exercise their own judgment. In Foley's view, doubt and uncertainty about the consequences of the use of force at that time were sufficient reason to vote against the position of the president. Foley's position appeared to be shared by most of his party colleagues. Democrats voted with Foley 179 to 86, although Bush's resolution was adopted by the House on a 250 to 183 vote.

The Roll-Call Record

Systematic evidence on Speakers' levels of agreement with presidents is difficult to muster because Speakers seldom cast roll-call votes. One way to ap-

Figure 6-1 House Leaders' Support for the President (percent on roll-call votes) on Foreign and Domestic Issues: 1953–1988

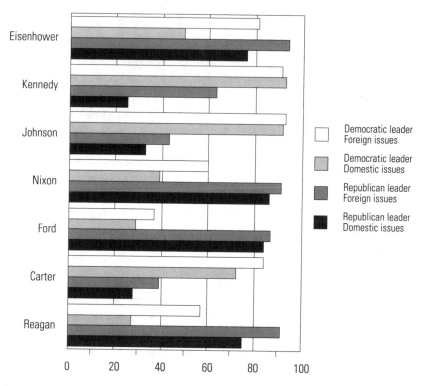

Source: Jon R. Bond and Richard Fleisher, *The President in the Legislative Arena* (Chicago: University of Chicago Press, 1990), 166–167.

proach the problem is to make the reasonable assumption that the Speaker and the majority leader usually take very similar positions and use the majority leader's vote as a measure of the Speaker's position. Some caution must be exercised for the Albert-O'Neill team, although by the time O'Neill became majority leader in 1973 following the death of Hale Boggs (D-La.), Albert had shifted ground on Vietnam. Bond and Fleisher have calculated, for the 1953 to 1988 period, the frequency of floor leaders' support for the president on roll-call votes when the president's position was known to *Congressional Quarterly*.[17] Figure 6-1 shows their presidential support scores for the House majority leader and minority leader.

The figure demonstrates that leaders of the president's congressional party consistently provided more support than the opposition party's leaders in both foreign and domestic policy since the Eisenhower administration. However, during the Eisenhower administration, the difference between the two sets of leaders was quite small in the foreign policy arena. During no subsequent presidency was the difference between the two floor leaders nearly so small as it was during the Eisenhower years. And the difference between the two leaders was usually much greater in the foreign policy arena than in domestic affairs. The difference was greater in foreign policy than in domestic policy in only the Carter administration—and then only by a trivial amount.

A similar pattern of change occurred on a small set of major foreign policy issues. General agreement with the president changed to substantial disagreement with the president during the 1960s, particularly among leaders of the opposite party. The contrasts are stark: whereas Rayburn agreed with Eisenhower on five of the six issues on which they had discernible views in 1959 to 1960, O'Neill agreed with President Ronald Reagan on only two of six major issues in 1983 to 1984, and Wright agreed with Reagan on only one of five issues for which the Speaker had discernible views. Speaker Foley's 3 to 1 agreement disagreement ratio with President Bush in 1991 to 1992 is notable.[18]

Service as Policy Leaders

In the 1950s, party leaders, including Speakers, were characterized as middlemen, managers, negotiators, and facilitators.[19] Their chief function was to service the real policy leaders who were found in the standing committees. Such a leadership style was not adopted by all leaders on all issues, but it does seem to have been the modal pattern. The pattern was consistent with a decentralized legislative process, one with weak parties and a dependence on specialists. To be sure, leaders could be critical, even decisive, players. But their influence was at the margins—finding a crucial compromise and rounding up a few pivotal votes. The basic direction of policy was determined by others.

Scrutiny of journalistic and biographical accounts indicates that the last three Speakers have been much more active players in the foreign policy arena than their immediate predecessors.[20] A summary count is shown in Figure 6-2, which displays the frequency with which leaders sponsored legislation or amendments, led the effort to attract votes, or negotiated legislative compromises. It is not surprising that McCormack and Wright mark the two extremes of Speakers' foreign policy activism. The last three Speakers have been more active than their immediate predecessors.[21]

Figure 6-2 Frequency of Significant Activity by House Speakers and Senate Majority Leaders on Major Foreign Policy Issues: 1955–1992

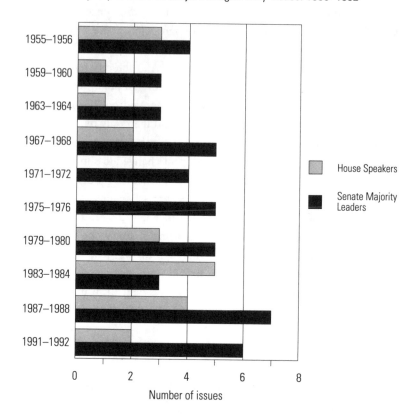

Speaker Wright's policy leadership on Central American issues deserves special notice. (It is discussed from the Republican point of view in Chapter 4 and by Speaker Wright himself in Chapter 11.) Wright assumed the speakership in 1987 with more expertise on Central American affairs than nearly any other Speaker has had about any Third World region. He had traveled to Central America frequently and was reasonably fluent in Spanish. As majority leader, Wright led the opposition against aid for Nicaraguan rebels—the Contras—which angered White House officials, and yet he supported aid to the government of El Salvador, which upset many liberal Democrats. In fact, Wright was the only House Democratic leader to support an increase of military aid for El Salvador during the early Reagan years. In appreciation of his stance on Salvadoran aid, the Reagan administration asked Wright to lead the U.S. delegation sent to observe the 1984 elections in that country.

Wright became Speaker just as conditions were reaching a critical point for the Nicaraguan Contras. The Iran Contra conspiracy—in which the Reagan White House used funds from secret arms sales to Iran to support the Contras, thus circumventing a congressional ban on military aid to the Contras—had become public in December 1986. As a result, several administration officials who managed Central American policy were dismissed, resigned, or became so distrusted by Congress that they handicapped the president's effort to get new aid approved. The public had turned against continued aid and the House Democratic Caucus was overwhelmingly opposed to it. Indeed, it was highly unlikely that the House would support any extension of military aid. Wright himself had rewarded the House's leading opponent to continued aid, David Bonior (D-Mich.) with a top leadership post, chief deputy whip.

In this context, the Reagan administration approached Wright to see if he would be willing to join with the president in offering a peace plan to end the war in Nicaragua. Reagan's emissary argued for Wright's cooperation by noting what it would mean for the speakership by exclaiming, "It would be precedent-setting, enormously important—it would involve the Speaker of the House in foreign policy in a new way. What significance for the speakership! The importance to our allies, to the Soviets, to the world, of seeing the United States united in foreign policy—it would be just tremendous!" [22] Wright heard from the Sandinistas and others in the region that the idea might help the peace process. Yet Wright was suspicious of the administration's sincerity, and Bonior, who still led the Speaker's task force on Contra aid, feared a trap. If the administration could gain bipartisan support for a peace plan that was then rejected by the Sandinista government of Nicaragua, it could use the Sandinistas' refusal to seriously discuss peace as an argument for more aid. Despite his concerns, over the opposition of other Democratic leaders, and knowing that his caucus would be outraged if his fears were realized, Wright agreed to the administration's offer. [23]

The Wright-Reagan plan—which set some conditions on the Sandinistas, established a reconciliation commission, and set a deadline for peace negotiations—succeeded in breaking the stalemate. The nations in the region agreed to accept a variation of the plan worked out under the guidance of Costa Rican president Oscar Arias Sanchez. Wright, who had maintained better relationships with Arias, was informed of the agreement and announced it to the press before the White House or State Department had a chance to do so. [24]

Wright soon became unhappy with the progress of the negotiations. Three months after the Arias plan was announced, Wright accepted Nicaraguan president Daniel Ortega's request to meet to help the peace process along. The Sandinistas wanted to negotiate directly with the U.S. government but it refused, the Contras wanted to negotiate directly with the Sandinistas but they refused, and, it appeared to Wright, the Reagan administration was eager to have the negotiations fail so that it could justify more military aid for the Contras. The Sandinistas suggested that Wright serve as an intermediary between themselves and the Contras, but Wright demurred, saying that "the State Department resents my involvement already.... We don't need any more hostility from there." [25] Wright convinced the Sandinistas to accept Nicaraguan Cardinal Miguel Obando y Bravo as an intermediary for negotiations between the Sandinistas and the Contras. Ortega reluctantly agreed but wanted to meet with Wright before making it official.[26]

Wright met with Ortega without notifying the administration. He reviewed the Sandinista proposals for peace and suggested ways to change them in order to make them more palatable for the Contras. Only after a second session with Ortega did Wright inform Secretary of State George Shultz of his meetings or Ortega's request for an intermediary. Despite Shultz's advice to stay out of it, Wright proceeded with a meeting with the Contra leadership and later with Ortega and Obando. Through the press, the State Department learned of these follow-up meetings; both the meetings and the way they learned about them outraged State Department officials. Wright explained to the Contra leaders that Congress would no longer support aid requests, which left the Contras little choice but to seek a negotiated solution to their conflict with the Sandinistas. Cardinal Obando was accepted as an intermediary.[27]

A tidal wave of protest followed the news of Wright's activities. Even the traditionally liberal *Washington Post* accused Wright of overextending his role as Speaker. *Post* editors said, "Mr. Wright appears to have gone way over the line that separates opposition from interference." [28] At the White House, Wright was scolded for his activities by Reagan's aides and cabinet officials. Wright was unrepentant. On PBS's *MacNeil/Lehrer Newshour*, Wright declared:

> I must uphold the legislative branch as co-equal with the executive.... The people who wrote the Constitution never intended Congress to be subservient.... My job is to work with whomever is president and I shall do that. But also my job is to represent the people of the United States as expressed by their elected representatives.[29]

Later Wright and Secretary of State Shultz made amends and jointly read a six-point statement of cooperation, which did not deny the Speaker the right to meet with any Central American working on the peace plan. The Democratic Caucus rallied behind Wright and voted unanimously to commend the Speaker for his peace-making efforts.[30]

Within just a few years following the events of 1987, a consensus seemed to develop that Wright went too far in conducting "congressional diplomacy." The view is shared even by many liberal Democrats, perhaps because many of them eventually became quite frustrated with Wright's aggressiveness on many issues. In this case, his critics contend, Wright went far beyond exercising influence over the use of congressional powers and moved into the executive realm of diplomacy. Wright's defenders correctly point out the exceptional circumstances that drew Wright into the role that he played. Wright was first invited into the peace-making process by the administration, and his subsequent involvement was in response to requests by the Contras and Sandinistas after it became clear that the administration did not intend to live up to its commitment to the Wright-Reagan plan. Even critics could not deny the efficacy of Wright's effort to get a peace treaty among the Central American governments.

The events of 1987 indicate the potential power of the Speaker in foreign policy. To be sure, the mix of political circumstances and personal factors that generated the events of that year are unlikely to be repeated in the near future. Necessary, but not sufficient, conditions for Wright's diplomacy included the following: the president had failed to actively pursue diplomacy when the public expected it; party control of government was divided; sharp partisan divisions and a fairly cohesive majority party were present on a salient foreign policy issue; and the House was in a position to affect policy by its use of the power of the purse. Also critical were Wright's personal familiarity with, and intense interest in, the region. And even then it appears that Wright came very close to backing away from direct personal involvement.[31]

Service As Opinion Leaders

Only since the 1970s have House Speakers made interaction with the press an important part of their leadership activities. The increasing importance of television as a medium of political communication, presidents' domination of television news, and the increasing number of news programs increased the demand for telegenic leaders. Since the mid-1960s, opposition congressional leaders sought and have been granted time on the television networks to re-

Figure 6-3 Number of *New York Times* Stories Mentioning Leaders that Concern Foreign Policy Matters: 1955–1991

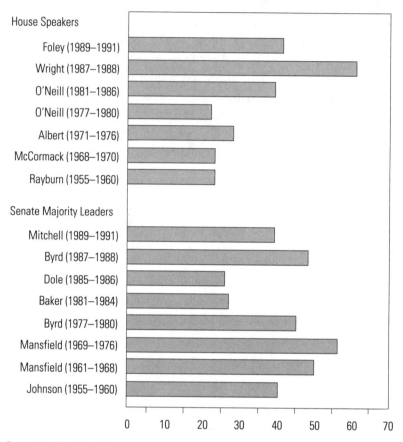

Source: *New York Times* Index.

Note: Each entry is based on policy-related stories that mention the leader. Each entry is the annual average for the years indicated.

spond to presidential addresses.[32]

By the early 1980s the spokesperson's role had become so prominent it warranted listing among leaders' primary responsibilities.[33] Speakers O'Neill and Wright accepted invitations to appear on television but did so selectively. Speaker Foley has more frequently appeared on television interview programs than any of his predecessors. More frequently Speakers began to address foreign policy issues through the media.

Figures 6-3 and 6-4 illustrate the extent of coverage of Speakers and, for comparison, Senate majority leaders in the *New York Times* and in the network

Figure 6-4 Percent of Television Evening News Stories Mentioning Leaders that Concern Foreign Policy Matters: 1968–1991

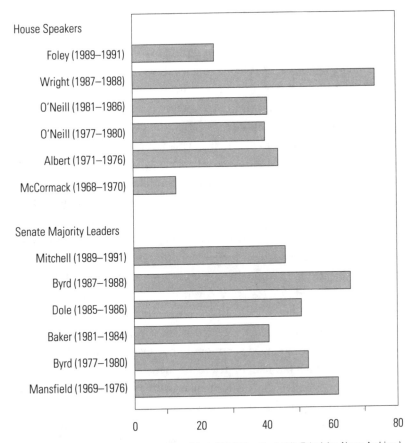

Source: Television News Index and Abstracts (Nashville, Tenn.: Vanderbilt Television News Archives).
Note: Each entry is based on policy-related stories that mention the leader. Each entry is the annual average for the years indicated.

evening news programs related to world affairs.[34] The volume of coverage reflects leaders' efforts and newsworthiness, as well as the judgments of reporters, editors, and news directors about what is newsworthy. It paints a picture of the attention given to leaders and the policy content of the coverage.

In the main, the pattern of media coverage reflects the influence of the leaders in foreign policy.[35] Prior to the late 1970s, the proportion of mentions in the *Times* involving foreign policy was higher for Senate majority leaders than House Speakers, consistent with the traditional foreign policy roles of the two chambers. It was common for a majority of Senate leaders' coverage to be related to foreign policy, while House leaders' foreign policy coverage seldom exceeded one-third of their coverage on policy matters. Of course, leaders show great variation, with Sen. Mike Mansfield (D-Mont.) forging the way for other leaders in their emphasis on foreign policy.

Not until the late 1970s did a Speaker regularly exceed a Senate leader in foreign policy emphasis. O'Neill exceeded both Senators Robert Byrd (D-W.Va.) and Howard Baker (R-Tenn.) in the proportion of stories devoted to foreign policy issues. O'Neill attracted coverage on a number of issues: legislation to implement the Panama Canal treaties, the deployment of troops to Lebanon, aid to El Salvador and to the Nicaraguan Contras, and others. Nearly all of the coverage concerned House legislative activity. But Speaker Wright stands out. Wright took charge of Central American issues for his party and, primarily as a result of Central American issues, Wright surpassed his Senate counterpart in the proportion of *Times* coverage involving foreign policy.

The pattern of coverage on network news programs is not quite so clear. Until Senator Baker's emphasis on foreign policy dipped during the first Reagan term in the early 1980s, both Senate leaders outpaced House leaders in their foreign policy emphasis. Newscast coverage of O'Neill and Baker showed nearly equal emphasis on foreign affairs during the early 1980s. Speaker Wright's foreign policy efforts are reflected in his appearances and mentions on the network news programs. Even more impressive is the fact that during the 1980s the absolute number of television news stories mentioning the Speaker in a foreign policy context exploded. Until 1981, Speakers averaged about thirty mentions per year related to foreign policy in the *New York Times*; since then, the number of mentions has doubled. When House activity on a variety of Middle East and Central American issues was salient in the mid-1980s, House leaders gained a significant presence on the network news programs.

Speaker Foley has not been as aggressive in some respects. In the *Times*, where there is more foreign affairs coverage than on the television newscasts, Foley has maintained a high foreign affairs emphasis. But on the newscasts, which tend to be devoted to only the very most important world events, Foley has fallen back to a point below his predecessors and the Senate's majority leader in both the absolute number and percentage of stories devoted to foreign affairs. Only in 1991, the year of the U.S. action in the Persian Gulf, did the newscast coverage of Foley show a foreign affairs emphasis as strong as that of the other Speakers of the 1980s.

In sum, House Speakers began to challenge Senate leaders' distinctive positions as opinion leaders in foreign affairs during the 1980s when the role of the House and the partisan character of policy alignments dictated an intensified role for the Speaker. If the Foley speakership is any indication, the end of the Cold War may lead to somewhat lesser prominence for the Speaker on television in foreign affairs.

Service as Intermediaries

One of the special responsibilities of the House Speaker is to serve as an intermediary between Capitol Hill and the White House. The job has both institutional and partisan elements. Each modern Speaker has taken seriously his role as the only constitutional officer and elected leader of the House. In this capacity, the Speaker is the official conduit for communications between the branches and the two houses and performs certain essential and ceremonial functions on behalf of the institution.

Nonetheless, the working relationship between Speakers and presidents usually turns on partisan considerations. The specific nature of the relationship between presidents and Speakers is a function of choices made by each participant. No Speaker has been unwilling to consult with the president, although presidents sometimes have preferred to avoid or ignore the Speaker. But presidents have often found little use in making the Speaker a confidant on policy matters, particularly in the field of world affairs.

A convenient standard by which to gauge the working relationship between Speakers and presidents is Rayburn's relationship with Eisenhower. As we have seen, it is often touted as the model of bipartisan cooperation—a close and even personal relationship developed in an era of divided party control of government. This relationship, however, must be viewed in the context of Eisenhower's sometimes poor relationship with leaders of his own party. During Eisenhower's two terms in the White House, about 200 weekly breakfast meetings were held between the president and his party's leaders while Congress was in session. The agenda usually involved both domestic and foreign policy matters, with 75 percent of the meetings including discussion of at least one foreign policy issue.[36] Frank discussion often took place at these meetings, but the quality of the discussion declined over the years. Eisenhower grew tired of listening to Senate Republican leader William Knowland lecture him, particularly on policy toward communist China. By the time Knowland left the Senate in 1958, according to one historian, Eisenhower turned many of these meetings into "pep talks on holding down spending." [37]

Between early 1954, after Robert A. Taft (R-Ohio) died and Knowland took over, and the end of his second term in 1960, Eisenhower called nineteen formal bipartisan leadership meetings.[38] The first of these meetings was called by Eisenhower to stem sharp partisan exchanges about China policy and the administration's leaking of the Yalta papers. The bipartisan meetings were devoted almost exclusively to foreign and defense policy matters. Little genuine consultation occurred at these meetings. The meetings took place over lunch and the usual format was a briefing, normally by cabinet officers, followed by legislators' comments and questions. More than twenty members of Congress were usually in attendance. It was the norm that the leaders of the Appropriations, Foreign Policy, and Armed Services Committees, as well as top party leaders, were invited.

After House and Senate Democrats regained majority status in 1955, Eisenhower began to cultivate the good will of Majority Leader Johnson and Speaker Rayburn in evening get-togethers over cocktails. The threesome eventually met this way at least once a month, according to one report.[39] Additional meetings that included foreign policy committee leaders, particularly Senators Walter George (D-Ga.) and William Fulbright (D-Ark.) were sometimes held as well. Genuine consultation appeared to occur at these meetings, and there is evidence that Eisenhower was influenced by what he learned from time to time.

Beginning in 1957, a series of foreign developments occasioned privately communicated objections to Eisenhower's policies from the otherwise deferential Rayburn.[40] Middle East policy was the most important sticking point, but policies concerning the Soviet Union and its actions also were subject to disagreement. A biographer noted that "whenever Rayburn offered objections in foreign matters, Eisenhower showed displeasure as if he was violating the rules." [41] By late 1958, the relationship between Eisenhower and the Democratic leaders Rayburn and Johnson had lost much of its warmth, and the number of personal meetings declined. In fact, Eisenhower contributed to the deterioration by becoming more partisan in the 1958 election campaign. Despite Eisenhower's and Johnson's rhetoric about reestablishing bipartisanship in foreign policy, Eisenhower appeared to become more assertive and partisan during the next two years, when he called only one formal bipartisan leadership meeting. [42]

The cooling of relationships in the last two years of the Eisenhower administration is instructive. It appears that partisanship was the root cause. In the

1958 election, Democrats gained a net of forty-eight House seats and fifteen Senate seats. Many of the new Democrats were liberals who believed that their leaders had been too uncritical of the administration. And members of both parties sharpened their rhetoric in preparation for the 1960 elections. Indeed, the Eisenhower administration ended with partisan rhetoric and a partisan pattern of consultation, even in foreign policy. Rayburn's successor, McCormack, served most of his tenure as Speaker under Democratic presidents and so did not have to overcome a partisan divide. In fact, at least for a brief period, McCormack had a most unusual experience for a modern Speaker. From November 1963 to November 1964, when there was no vice president and the Speaker was next in line for the presidency, McCormack attended National Security Council (NSC) and other foreign policy meetings and had rare access to classified information. Even after Hubert Humphrey was elected, McCormack attended some NSC meetings on Vietnam. McCormack appears not to have taken an active role during these meetings, but he did eagerly support each step Johnson took in escalating the war. [43] Articulating the norm he inherited from Rayburn in a meeting with Johnson about the need for the Gulf of Tonkin Resolution, McCormack said, "I think the Congress has a responsibility and should show a united front to the world." [44] And at a later meeting discussing an escalation to the war, McCormack asserted that "the President will have the support of all true Americans." [45] McCormack's participation faded after the 1964 elections.

All presidents since the 1950s have scheduled weekly meetings, usually breakfast meetings, with leaders of their own party while Congress is in session. These weekly meetings generally concerned legislation currently before Congress and so tended to emphasize domestic policy. These meetings remain a well-established norm, the violation of which would risk the wrath of congressional leaders whose support is vital to the success of the president's legislative program. The nature of the weekly meetings has varied, as has the frequency of special meetings and telephone conversations with party leaders.

Meetings with opposition leaders, usually jointly with leaders of their own party, also are regular features in presidents' schedules in recent decades, although there is great variation in the frequency of these meetings. But as with Eisenhower, Johnson, and Rayburn, the relationship between presidents and Speakers of the opposition party often has turned on more private and informal relationships. It is in this area that the decline of bipartisan consultation is most notable.

After Eisenhower, the next president to deal with a Speaker of the opposite party was Republican Richard Nixon, who maintained quite cool relationships with congressional leaders of both parties. He began in the usual pattern by conducting weekly meetings with his party's leaders, but little consultation appears to have taken place in these sessions. [46] Nixon held about as many bipartisan leadership meetings proportionately as did Kennedy and Johnson. As for his predecessors, these dealt with foreign policy almost exclusively. However, Nixon's meetings appear to have been more superficial, often just briefings following one of his international trips. As the 1972 election approached and the Watergate affair unfolded, Nixon's legislative agenda shrunk and the increasing emphasis on vetoes led Nixon to operate more and more without consulting Hill leaders of either party.

President Gerald Ford reestablished relationships with his party's elected congressional leaders as his primary conduit to the Hill and kept his commitment to hold weekly meetings with them. He, too, held many bipartisan leadership meetings—at least twenty-five during his thirty months in office—most of which were devoted to foreign policy. [47] Democratic leaders were pleased with the turnaround in their relationships with Republican presidents, although Ford did not have special private rendezvous with any opposition leader as his four predecessors did. Moreover, Ford shared Nixon's views about the obstructionist Congress in international affairs and the inappropriateness of consulting congressional leaders prior to making certain military decisions. [48] Thus, even with a president who had strong personal relationships with members of Congress, the institutional and partisan divide prevented meaningful consultation between the president and the Speaker.

President Jimmy Carter's first-year problems with his own party's congressional leaders stemmed from a lack of advance consultation, distrust of Washington insiders, inattentiveness to the courtesies usually extended to members of Congress, and weak White House support for leaders' efforts to enact Carter's legislation. [49] Relationships improved considerably during Carter's term in office, but unfortunately, as Speaker O'Neill saw it, Carter spent far too much of the leadership breakfasts on foreign policy matters at the expense of pressing domestic issues. [50]

There was only one major military deployment about which Carter could have consulted with Hill leaders in advance—the hostage rescue in Iran. The general subject was discussed at one or two leadership breakfasts, but Carter did not advise congressional leaders of his plans. He apparently intended to inform them after the rescue team was positioned in Iran. Just before the operation took place, Carter consulted with Senate leader Byrd about who should be notified, telling Byrd that a rescue attempt was imminent. No member, including Byrd and Speaker O'Neill, was advised about the actual plan before the results were known. [51]

President Reagan maintained the established pattern of occasional meetings with opposition leaders. As usual, the sessions concerning world affairs took the form of briefings. However, the IranContra investigations exposed a pattern of deliberately misleading briefings and other communications from executive officials to the Congress.

Since the Nixon administration presidential relationships with opposition leaders have been more circumscribed and formal. The private bonds that Eisenhower, Kennedy, and Johnson shared with at least some opposition leaders were not present in subsequent administrations. Relative dependence on formal meetings increased and the frequency of meaningful consultation, including consultation on foreign affairs, was much lower after the Johnson administration.

Speakers in a New Era

The substantial changes in the role of Speakers in world affairs are plain: Speakers have shown increasingly partisan patterns in their support for presidents' policies and in their service as intermediaries between the Hill and the White House, and they have demonstrated increasing activism as party spokespersons and policy leaders. In conclusion, three observations must be made about this pattern of change.

First, the pattern of change in the arena of foreign affairs by Speakers is closely connected, indeed inseparable, from the pattern of change found in domestic affairs. [52] Many of the same party and institutional conditions that promoted strong leadership in the foreign affairs political arena—divided control, partisan policy alignments on salient issues, a pivotal role for the House, institutional weaknesses that only a Speaker can overcome, rank-and-file demand for media-oriented leaders—are shared with the domestic political arena. The enhancement of the Speakers formal control over the Rules Committee, bill referral, committee assignments, and other elements of the legislative process, which are largely the product of developments in domestic affairs, have had important spillover effects in foreign affairs. It is fair to conclude that the presence of mutually reinforcing conditions in domestic and world affairs during the 1980s made it even easier for Speakers to forge a new path in world affairs, an arena in which they were disadvantaged historically.

Second, great care must be exercised in gauging the degree of Speakers' independent influence in foreign policy. Committees remain the center of congressional action on most foreign policy matters. In most cases, committee members are the effective policy leaders and committees are the point of origin for the vast majority of legislative measures shaping foreign policy. Perhaps more important, rank-and-file members are far more active in both domestic and foreign policy making. One leadership response has been to channel the energies of rank-and-file members into party committees and task forces. House Speakers have relied on task forces to devise party policy proposals and tactics. House Democrats have used task forces on arms control, Central America, and Lebanon, among many other issues. More generally, the House is now characterized by highly flexible policy-making processes that are adapted by the Speaker and his party to the conditions it faces on particular issues. Power is more widely dispersed, particularly within the majority party, and is only sometimes funneled successfully by the Speaker on behalf of party causes.

Third, it is important to note how rapidly the Speaker's role in foreign affairs may change. Differences between Foley and his immediate predecessors already are obvious. The demise of the Cold War has diminished the salience and partisanship of national security issues. Trade issues have split the Democratic party. The election of President Bill Clinton shifted the foreign policy initiative to the White House for Democrats. Clearly, the Speaker's role in foreign affairs, while greatly enhanced in comparison with the mid-twentieth century, will remained highly conditioned by institutional and partisan factors beyond the Speaker's control.

Nevertheless, partisan and institutional factors are likely to give Speaker Foley and future Speakers a higher profile in world affairs than Speakers of the mid-twentieth century. Partisanship spawned by regional problems is likely to be rekindled periodically into the indefinite future. The use of force as a tool of national security and foreign policy in regional politics continues to divide the parties. Republicans are more likely to support the use of force to protect American economic or political interests abroad. Democrats resist such uses of military power but are more likely to endorse the use of U.S. military personnel in United Nations' peacekeeping forces and for humanitarian purposes.

On the institutional side, the House and its Speaker have gained a lasting foothold in foreign policy making because of the requirements for congressional approval and executive reporting of presidential foreign policy choices that have been adopted in the past two decades. Even when they want to do so, Speakers will not be able to distance themselves from world affairs as much as mid-century Speakers could. They frequently will be drawn into disputes by competing factions. Even presidents will demand that Speakers use their substantial formal powers to ensure swift and favorable House action. In short, the institutional role of the House will compel Speakers of the near future to play a significant role in foreign policy.

Notes

1. Unless otherwise noted, references to foreign policy include defense and national security policy as well.

2. Joseph Cooper and David W. Brady, "Institutional Context and Leadership Style: The House from Cannon to Rayburn," *American Political Science Review* 75 (June 1981): 424.

3. For a useful summary of these developments and references to other literature, see Thomas E. Mann, "Making Foreign Policy: President and Congress," in *A Question of Balance: The President, the Congress, and Foreign Policy,* ed. Thomas E. Mann (Washington, D.C.: Brookings Institution, 1990), 134.

4. Cooper and Brady, "Institutional Context and Leadership Style," 411-425.

5. Richard Stout, "Tariff Program a Bipartisan Victory," *Christian Science Monitor,* Feb. 18, 1955, 3.

6. *Congressional Quarterly Almanac* 11 (Washington, D.C.: Congressional Quarterly), 293.

7. U.S. Congress, House of Representatives, *Congressional Record,* 84th Cong., 2d sess., June 7, 1956, 9830-9831.

8. Roger Davidson and Walter Oleszek, *Congress against Itself* (Bloomington: Indiana Univ. Press, 1977).

9. "House Passes Defense Bill: Vietnam Debated Extensively," *Congressional Quarterly Weekly Report,* June 25, 1971, 1365.

10. Mary Russell, "End-War Move in House Fought," *Washington Post,* April 19, 1972, A1, A12; Mary Russell, "House Democrats Vote to Seek Bill to End U.S. Role in War," *Washington Post,* April 21, 1972, A1, A12; Roland Evans and Robert Novak, "Doves Jump the Gun," *Washington Post,* April 26, 1972, A17; and "Nixon's Performance: The Voters Will Decide," *Congressional Quarterly Weekly Report,* Aug. 12, 1972, 2033.

11. "House Votes Fund Cutoff for U.S. Bombing of Cambodia," *Congressional Quarterly Weekly Report,* May 12, 1973, 1170-1171, 1183-1184.

12. John Felton, "Congress Reels under Impact of Marine Deaths in Beirut, U.S. Invasion of Grenada," *Congressional Quarterly Weekly Report,* Oct. 29, 1983, 2217.

13. Michael Glennon, "Lebanon Policy Is Questioned as Support Wavers on Hill," *Congressional Quarterly Weekly Report,* Jan. 7, 1984, 3.

14. John Felton, "Reagan Lobbies a Restive Congress on Lebanon," *Congressional Quarterly Weekly Report,* Jan. 28, 1984, 127.

15. John Felton, "Democrats Step up Pressure for Beirut Pullout," *Congressional*

Quarterly Weekly Report, Feb. 4, 1984, 227.

16. U.S. Congress, House, *Congressional Record,* daily ed., 97th Cong., 1st sess., Jan. 12, 1981, H437.

17. Jon R. Bond and Richard Fleisher, *The President in the Legislative Arena* (Chicago: University of Chicago Press, 1990), 166-167. The Speaker is excluded because the Speaker seldom votes.

18. Similar results are obtained when attention is limited to the most contested and "key" votes, as identified by Congressional Quarterly (data not shown). We thank Professors John Bond and Richard Fleisher for sharing their data with us.

19. David B. Truman, *The Congressional Party: A Case Study* (New York: John Wiley & Sons, 1959), 104-106.

20. Several sources have been searched for evidence on leaders' activity: *Congressional Quarterly Weekly Report,* the *New York Times,* several book-length treatments of congressional foreign policy activity, the most useful of which is John Rourke's extensive book on Congress and foreign policy, *Congress and the Presidency in U.S. Foreign Policymaking* (Boulder, Colo.: Westview, 1983), and leaders' and presidents' biographies. The search was restricted to the fifteen or sixteen top foreign and defense policy issues for the Congresses examined. The top issues were selected on the basis of the subjects most frequently discussed in the *Department of State Bulletin* and the subjects highlighted in the *Congressional Quarterly Almanac,* an annual review of Congress and public policy. This approach is necessarily biased against the inclusion of issues that did not become public. For example, in 1956 congressional leaders' opposition to a loan to Egypt for construction of the Aswan dam helped to convince President Eisenhower not to request formally legislation from Congress. And in 1963 and 1964 congressional leaders' views played a role in President Johnson's decision not to pursue a multinational nuclear force with NATO allies, but the issue was not subject to much public discussion and it is not addressed in the *Department of State Bulletin.*

21. Steven S. Smith, "Congressional Leaders and Foreign Policy," in *Congress and the Making of Foreign Policy,* ed. Paul E. Peterson (Norman: University of Oklahoma Press, 1994).

22. Thomas Loeffler, quoted in John Barry, *The Ambition and the Power* (New York: Penguin Books, 1989), 312. The sequence of events in this section has been taken mostly from John Barry's book. However, another good source is Speaker Wright's recent book, *Worth It All* (Washington, D.C.: Brassey's, 1993), which provides an equally detailed account and agrees with the sequence of events as described in this chapter.

23. Barry, *The Ambition and the Power,* 309-323, 327-340.

24. Ibid., 340-361; Pat Towell, "The Issue Ahead: Will Peace Plans Head Off Fight over New Contra Aid?" *Congressional Quarterly Weekly Report,* Sept. 8, 1987, 17831784.

25. Ibid., 495.

26. Ibid., 493-496.

27. Ibid., 497-505; John Felton, "Nicaragua Peace Process Moves to Capitol Hill," *Congressional Quarterly Weekly Report,* Nov. 14, 1987, 27892791.

28. "What Is Jim Wright Doing?" *Washington Post,* Nov. 16, 1987, A12,

29. Barry, *The Ambition and the Power,* 513.

30. Ibid., 509515; John Felton, "Schultz, Wright: A Truce on Contra Diplomacy," *Congressional Quarterly Weekly Report,* Nov. 21, 1987, 2867-2868.

31. Barry, *The Ambition and the Power,* 332-345.

32. Joe S. Foote, *Television Access and Political Power: The Networks, the Presidency, and the "Loyal Opposition"* (New York: Praeger, 1990), 33ff.

33. Barbara Sinclair, *Majority Leadership in the U.S. House* (Baltimore: Johns Hopkins University Press, 1983), 40-41; Roger H. Davidson, "Senate Leaders: Janitors for an Untidy Chamber?" in *Congress Reconsidered,* 3d ed., ed. Lawrence C. Dodd and Bruce I. Oppenheimer (Washington, D.C.: CQ Press, 1985), 236.

34. The *New York Times* is the only national newspaper with a quality index for the entire period under study. It has the additional advantage of giving substantial emphasis to foreign policy issues. The shortcoming of the *Times* as an indicator of change is that it altered its reporting practices in the late 1970s so that it included fewer but larger stories on Congress, reducing the number of stories in which leaders could be mentioned. We thank Stephen Hess, Steven Roberts, and Martin Tolchin for pointing out that in the past five years or so the *Times* has reduced the number of stories providing daily updates on developments and substituted fewer but larger stories. The Vanderbilt News Archive has assembled indexes and abstracts of the television evening news programs of the three television broadcast networks since 1968. Systematic data on newscasts other than the evening news, television interview programs, news specials, and documentaries are not available.

35. On this general theme, see Stephen Hess, *The Ultimate Insiders: U.S. Senators in the National Media* (Washington, D.C.: Brookings Institution, 1986).

36. See *President Eisenhower's Meetings with Legislative Leaders, 1953-1961* (Frederick, Md.: University Publications of America, 1986), taken from a file at the Eisenhower Library, which includes memoranda on Eisenhower's formal meetings with leaders drafted by a professional historian, L. Arthur Minnich, who served as assistant staff secretary. Burns notes that weekly meetings with one's own party leaders had become an "institution" by the time Eisenhower was president. See James MacGregor Burns, *The Deadlock of Democracy: Four-Party Politics in America* (Englewood Cliffs, N.J.: Prentice-Hall, 1963), 255. According to Eisenhower, inviting more than just the top two Republican leaders of each house was an innovation necessary to providing an early warning system. Truman apparently invited only the "Big Four." See Fred I. Greenstein, *Hidden-Hand Presidency: Eisenhower as Leader* (New York: Basic Books, 1982), 112.

37. Stephen E. Ambrose, *Eisenhower: The President* (New York: Simon & Schuster, 1984), 549.

38. See President Eisenhower's Meetings with Legislative Leaders, 1953-1961 .

39. Roland Evans and Robert Novak, *Lyndon B. Johnson: The Exercise of Power* (New York: New American Library, 1966), 168-169.

40. On Rayburn, see Alfred Steinberg, *Sam Rayburn: A Biography* (New York: Hawthorn Books, 1975), 318-321.

41. Ibid., 318.

42. Some observers attribute at least part of the responsibility for the cooling of Eisenhower's feelings about Johnson and Rayburn to the absence of John Foster Dulles in the last two years of Eisenhower's presidency. Dulles, as secretary of state, courted Congress and organized many of the bipartisan leadership meetings. It also has been noted that Senator Walter George's departure from the Senate and the chair of the Committee on Foreign Relations at the end of 1956 eliminated a moderating influence on Johnson.

43. Lyndon Baines Johnson, *The Vantage Point: Perspectives of the Presidency, 1963-*

1969 (New York: Holt, Rinehart, & Winston, 1971), 65n, 116n, 124n, 128; William Conrad Gibbons, *The U.S. Government and the Vietnam War: Executive and Legislative Roles and Relationships, Part II (1961-1964)* (Princeton, N.J.: Princeton University Press), 294-295; William Conrad Gibbons, *The U.S. Government and the Vietnam War: Executive and Legislative Roles and Relationships, Part III (Jan.-July, 1965)* (Princeton, N.J.: Princeton University Press, 1989), 40n, 62, 79, 427-428, 430.

44. Johnson, *The Vantage Point*, 117; Gibbons, *The U.S. Government and the Vietnam War Part II*, 295.

45. Johnson, *The Vantage Point*, 151; Gibbons, *The U.S. Government and the Vietnam War, Part III*, 430.

46. John Erlichman reports that the Republican leaders "rarely were given a chance to say anything" at the weekly breakfast sessions. See *Witness to Power* (New York: Simon & Schuster, 1982), 204.

47. Walter Kravitz, "Relations between the Senate and the House of Representatives: The Party Leadership," *Policymaking Role of Leadership in the Senate*, a compilation of papers prepared for the Commission on the Operation of the Senate (Washington, D.C.: Government Printing Office, 1977), 129. Also see Gerald R. Ford, *A Time to Heal* (New York: Harper & Row, 1979), 140.

48. In the case of the *Mayaguez* incident, Ford briefed congressional leaders after issuing orders for the use of force to free the captured Marines. See Ford, *A Time to Heal*, 280-281, 283.

49. Charles O. Jones, "Congress and the Presidency," in Mann and Ornstein, *The New Congress*, 240; Robert L. Peabody, "Senate Party Leadership: From the 1950s to the 1980s," in *Understanding Congressional Leadership*, ed. Frank H. Mackaman (Washington, D.C.: CQ Press, 1981), 94-95.

50. Tip O'Neill, with William Novak, *Man of the House* (New York: Random House, 1987), 316.

51. See Jimmy Carter, *Keeping Faith: Memoirs of a President* (New York: Bantam Books, 1982), 513-514, 518; O'Neill, *Man of the House*, 328.

52. Barbara Sinclair, "The Emergence of Strong Leadership in the 1980s House of Representatives," *Journal of Politics* 54 (1992): 658-684.

7 The Speaker and the Media

Joe S. Foote

Presidents since Franklin D. Roosevelt have used the broadcast media as a means to go directly to the people to marshal support on issues they consider important. This proactive use of media has become a key strategic weapon in the presidential arsenal. In many cases, presidents have used their access to national television to gain advantage over Congress on a particular issue. The image framed is usually that of an activist president against an obstructionist Congress.

Congress is placed at a severe disadvantage in these media battles. The president can speak with one voice; Congress cannot. The president presents a single focal point on which the media can focus; Congress presents multiple focal points. The modern president comes to the office with highly developed media skills; congressional leaders often do not. Presidents place a high priority on mobilizing a national constituency; Speakers traditionally do not. A Speaker's power base springs from the internal constituency that elected him or her. There is little utility in developing an external base unless it satisfies some need among the internal constituency.

Nowhere has the contrast in philosophy toward the use of media been more apparent than between presidents and Speakers of the House. In the thirty years after World War II, the media role of the presidency expanded greatly while the limited public role of the Speaker remained passive. Presidents developed numerous outlets for public persuasion while Speakers spurned any serious attempt to develop an external role as a counterpoint to the president. Thus, presidents gained access to a grand national forum without having to worry about a comparable voice of opposition. In some cases, the opposition role was taken by the media themselves, with the three commercial television networks serving as a de facto "loyal opposition" to the president.

Political scientists only recently have focused on the external role of the speakership, concentrating almost exclusively on the internal dynamics. Barbara Sinclair, in 1983, was one of the first political scientists to discuss the Speaker's role as spokesperson for both the House and the majority party.[1] Since the mid-1970s, the public role of the speakership has been slowly changing, becoming more responsive to external publics and using the media proactively to further legislative goals. Speakers have devoted more time to relations with media and have surrounded themselves with more specialized staff.

The intensity and scope of the external role of the speakership has fluctuated widely during the past half century depending on the national media climate and public interest in the Congress. Relations with the media is a task that few Speakers have relished and most have actively avoided, preferring the cloistered environment of the House to the unpredictable world of public opinion and national media. Yet, a more demanding press and an anxious internal constituency have been agents for change, forcing Speakers to develop an outside as well as inside strategy and adding the role of national spokesperson to their repertoires. Because the postwar Speaker's relationship with the media has very much been an evolutionary one, with each speakership bringing greater sophistication and a higher priority to the role, this chapter will examine Speakers' relations with the media chronologically, from Sam Rayburn to Tom Foley.

Speaker Rayburn

To understand how and why the speakership remained largely aloof from the swirling media trends during the postwar years, one must examine Speakers' attitudes toward the media beginning with Speaker Rayburn, who had a profound effect in defining the external role of the speakership during an emerging media age. Throughout his long tenure, Speaker Rayburn actively avoided contact with much of the national media, especially network television, and resented their distractive intrusion into the business of the House.

Speaker Rayburn rarely gave priority to the media except with his favored inner circle of reporters, and viewed media activity as largely extraneous to his duties as Speaker. A telling example of Speaker Rayburn's suspicion of the national media came in a letter he wrote in 1957 to Lawrence Spivak, the producer and moderator of NBC's "Meet the Press":

I do appreciate your wanting me to be on "Meet the Press," but I never go on programs such as yours because some twenty or more years ago I did go on a panel program on the radio and all the folks on the panel got in such an argument that I had enough. The trouble about my going on one program is then I would have no excuse to say to others that I could not go on their program. It is a chore that I have never relished and one that I doubt if I would be very good. So, at the present I will have to tell you what I tell all of the others, and that is that I do not go on these programs.[2]

While Speaker Rayburn was actively spurning national media exposure, many senators were clamoring for access to programs that helped set the political agenda in Washington, D.C., and made newspaper headlines. Legislators who wanted to raise their Washington profile or push a particular point of view saw the Sunday interview programs as ideal opportunities for reaching opinion leaders. During the Rayburn era, senators were much more likely to be seen on the national media than their counterparts in the House, especially since the House leadership essentially had defaulted its opportunity for access.

In retrospect, Speaker Rayburn's avoidance of the media seems misplaced, but his behavior was totally in harmony with the wishes of most of his colleagues. Speaker Rayburn once characterized members as either "showhorses" or "workhorses," a characterization that was one appreciated by most of the House. Members generally wanted leadership that was fair, impartial, and sensitive to their needs. The system was geared for media attention to be focused on committee chairs whose job was to move legislation through the legislative labyrinth. The Speaker was a facilitator who worked quietly behind the scenes to help the committees realize their goals. If a Speaker during this era had taken center stage in the media, there would no doubt have been repercussions among the venerable committee chairs.

Speaker Rayburn's media contact was limited to a small group of favored reporters who covered the House of Representatives. A few veteran wire and magazine reporters even became part of the Rayburn inner circle and were invited to participate in the "Board of Education"—the Speaker's end-of-the-day reflection and drinking sessions held in his Capitol hideaway.[3] In Rayburn's mind, these trusted reporters were different from the rest of the national press; they understood and appreciated the work of the House of Representatives. They also understood the importance of longstanding personal relationships as Rayburn did and would not sacrifice those relationships for a single story. It was a true symbiotic relationship.

Speaker Rayburn's close friendships with veteran House reporters fit with his broader philosophy toward relationships that formed the cornerstone of his success. As Anthony Champagne wrote, the foundation of Rayburn's power was "his ability to use information networks to build personal loyalties."[4] Reporters were a valuable part of the Rayburn information network; they knew the House and its members well and helped the Speaker keep his hand on the pulse of his colleagues.

Ironically, Speaker Rayburn, who had strong antipathy toward the national media as a whole, had closer personal relationships with a few members of the press than did any of his successors. Reporters who were not favored would frown on chosen colleagues being invited to the inner sanctum of the "Board of Education," and eyebrows would be raised at the way Rayburn's inner circle of press friends protected him repeatedly from publication of damaging remarks during his daily press briefings. It is unlikely that this would be tolerated today.

Speaker Rayburn perceived relationships with reporters as an advantage internally within the House rather than a conduit to a national constituency. He was far more concerned with what his colleagues read than with what the general public read. There is little evidence that Speaker Rayburn gave much attention at all to his external role as spokesperson for the House or the Democratic party. Even during the Eisenhower administration, when he was the highest ranking Democrat in Congress, the Speaker showed little inclination to assume the role of national spokesperson. If one wanted to get Speaker Rayburn involved with the media, the best strategy was to frame the request as a personal favor to another member of Congress. The Speaker was more likely to accept an unpleasant task with the dreaded media if it originated from his House environment.

Speaker Rayburn's principal access to the media came during his daily five-minute news conferences just before the House's noon session. These conferences took place in the Speaker's formal office just off the House floor. A few minutes before the session started, the press was ushered into the Speaker's office where Rayburn would outline the day's agenda and answer a few questions about that day's work of the House. Most of the faces around the Speaker's desk were old friends, the regulars from the gallery whom Rayburn trusted. It was customary for the senior wire service reporter, nearly always a Rayburn intimate, to start the questioning.

It was purely an insider's game. Questions focused on arcane procedure or mundane scheduling of business. Today's reporters would hardly call it a press conference. Observers not initiated to the process would have a difficult time understanding what was going on. House jargon and parliamentary shorthand punctuated answers. It was the odd day that a reporter asked a particularly penetrating question or one that did not deal specifically with that day's work in the House.

If a question emerged that the Speaker did not like, an aide would call, "Time, Mr. Speaker," and Rayburn would stand up and quickly make his way through the door on his way to the House floor. Rayburn intimates in the press corps were also careful to warn the Speaker when a new face was in the crowd and would frequently tell the newcomer that the Speaker's press conferences were off-the-record.[5] Through this protection by the gallery "regulars," Speaker Rayburn was never burned by questions during these daily press briefings.

While the press conferences were highly constrained and lacking in news value by today's standards, they provided daily access to the Speaker of the House of Representatives. On good days and bad, the Speaker had to endure at least a few minutes with the press corps. If nothing else, the ritualistic conferences served as a daily reminder of the presence of the press and their importance as a conduit to the public.

On the negative side, the daily conferences gave Speakers a false sense of accomplishment, a feeling that they had spent more than adequate time with the press and that nothing else would be required. This illusion of proper treatment would plague some of Rayburn's successors, leading them away from a robust media agenda, especially with the broadcast media. Television cameras were barred from the daily press briefings. If the Speaker wanted to make a statement for the cameras, he had to go to the Radio-Television Correspondents Gallery on the third floor of the Capitol above the Appropriations Committee room. Because Rayburn had no inclination to be on television, trips to the gallery were not part of his ritual.

Not only did the media have to contend with Speaker Rayburn's reticence toward the press personally, but they had to deal with his dictates concerning coverage of the House as well. As television emerged, there was a natural bid for access to the House chamber, committees, and Capitol grounds by the three commercial television networks, ABC, CBS, and NBC. In virtually every case, Speaker Rayburn closed the door to access.

On the opening day of the 80th Congress, Speaker Joseph Martin, who had just taken the chair from Speaker Rayburn for the first time after the Republicans captured the House in the 1946 elections, allowed television to cover the swearing-in ceremony. It was a television first and almost a last. It was thirty-two years later before the House floor would be opened to cameras again. In the chamber to be sworn in that day in 1947 were two first-term members,

John F. Kennedy and Richard Nixon, both of whom learned to master television as well as any two presidents in the twentieth century and both of whom would aggressively use its power to promote their agendas. Also being sworn in was Carl Albert, who as Speaker would eschew many of the advantages television provided to follow in the steps of his mentor, Speaker Rayburn.

The television networks, used to getting access wherever they wanted it, became increasingly frustrated with Speaker Rayburn's inhospitable treatment. They clashed with a Speaker whose singular commitment was to protect the members of the House from embarrassment and to preserve the decorum and traditions of the House. Access to the television networks figured far below those priorities. Requests from the media were a nuisance with no intrinsic value.

One of Speaker Rayburn's most controversial rulings was his 1952 decision to ban radio and television broadcasts of House committee hearings. Rayburn reasoned that because the House did not allow broadcasts, the ban should extend to committees as well. The Speaker said he was "not going to let this thing deteriorate into a sideshow, however good the performance" and firmly believed that he was not trampling on the rights of the broadcast media.[6]

Because Senate committees were accessible to cameras, the ban further isolated the already uncovered House and enraged some committee chairs who saw the ruling as a one-person edict. The Chair of the House Committee on Un-American Activities challenged the ban on cameras in committees in 1957 by allowing a field hearing in San Francisco to be televised. Speaker Rayburn immediately summoned the recalcitrant chair to his office, and no other chair ever tried to circumvent Rayburn's ruling.[7]

Proactive media exposure did not fit the Rayburn concept of leadership based on personal relationships. Only in dealing with the Texas media did the Speaker show sparks of enlightened media relations. As with any House member, Speaker Rayburn saw the correlation between positive treatment in the local media and electoral success. The Speaker saw no such connection with the national media. In fact, Speaker Rayburn genuinely could not understand why members of the House would actively seek media exposure. His showhorse/workhorse characterizations were mutually exclusive; in Speaker Rayburn's mind, it would have been impossible to be a highly productive member of the House and be highly visible at the same time. Only senators would attempt that. Rayburn once said, "When a man has to run for reelection every two years the temptation to make headlines is strong enough without giving him a chance to become an actor on television."[8]

It is interesting to note that Speaker Rayburn owed much of his national visibility to network television. It was presiding hour after hour over the 1952 Democratic convention on national television that lifted the Speaker from obscurity and made him a recognized public figure for the first time. Network television also greatly boosted his image as a powerful Speaker. Rayburn biographer D. B. Hardeman claimed that the Speaker "owed much to television" for the "dramatic" change in his personal and political status brought about by the national exposure.[9] It is ironic that Rayburn's flirtation with fame did not spring from the House he loved (where he had banned cameras), but from a party gathering outside Washington where the cameras were more than welcome.

While Speaker Rayburn at times seemed to enjoy his new public persona and his title of "Mr. Democrat," the rise of his own star nationally never influenced his attitudes toward the media in general. The Speaker never made the connection between national media visibility and legislative effectiveness, and neither did most of his colleagues. The Speaker and his supporters saw only the threat from media exposure, never the promise. Rayburn was a person from another age making a quiet exit before the storms of change approached. The Rayburn media doctrine became a way of life in the House that would be felt long after his years as Speaker.

Speaker McCormack

Speaker Rayburn's legacy of avoiding the national media influenced at least two of his protégés, John McCormack and Carl Albert. As David Halberstam unflatteringly portrayed McCormack and Albert, "It was Rayburnism without Rayburn."[10] The McCormack years would be among the most important in the history of television and its involvement in politics, but nearly all of the action would be at the other end of Pennsylvania Avenue. Both the presidency and the television networks grew in stature and visibility during the 1960s while Congress stood silently in the background.

President Kennedy provided the media with more access than they could ever dream. The media were enchanted with Camelot and used it to increase their own prestige and power. It was during the Kennedy and Johnson years that television began to eclipse newspapers as the primary media players on the Washington scene. In 1963, two of the networks expanded their evening news to a half-hour. It was such an important event on CBS that the president inaugurated the broadcast. Prime time presidential speeches drew as many as sixty million Americans to their television sets.[11] During the decade, news events such as the space race, the Kennedy and King assassinations, the civil rights struggle, and the Vietnam War captivated the American people and promoted television as their main source of information.

With both the White House and the Congress controlled by Democrats, the president took center stage. The Speaker appeared to be little more than a pale, aging backdrop for presidential speeches to joint sessions of Congress. Speaker McCormack never became a public figure and never achieved a singular identity in the way Rayburn did. With the spotlight so firmly focused on the White House, it is doubtful that any leadership initiatives would have been noticed.

When Nixon took office in 1969, the Speaker and the Senate majority leader once again became the chief spokespersons for the opposition. They were almost singularly unsuccessful in their efforts to secure network airtime to rebut President Nixon. It was the beginning of an airtime drought that would continue for more than a decade. One bright spot for media coverage during the McCormack speakership was the lifting of the Rayburn ban on televising committee hearings. Under the Legislative Reorganization Act of 1970, committees could decide for themselves whether they wanted to let cameras into their proceedings.[12]

One of the most important media precedents set during the McCormack period involved the minority leadership. The dominance of the Democrats during the early 1960s sent the media scurrying to find a counterpart within the opposition. What emerged was the "Ev and Charlie Show," as *New York Times* columnist Tom Wicker dubbed it, a series of sixty-four news conferences by Senate Majority Leader Everett Dirksen and House Minority Leader Charles Halleck.[13] When Gerald Ford replaced Halleck as Minority Leader, the news conferences became known as the "Ev and Jerry" show.

Early on, congressional Republicans realized that they had to mount a visible opposition to the highly visible Kennedy. The outcome was a joint leadership strategy session followed by a news conference. In the early days, the "Ev and Charlie Show" drew as many as one hundred reporters, and usually produced news even if it paled in comparison to Kennedy's dominant coverage. Although Dirksen and Halleck often came across as "harsh, pedestrian, and graceless" compared to the charismatic Kennedy, the initiative was important because it was the first calculated maneuver by the congressional leadership to assert itself in the national media arena.[14] The Republicans realized that the leadership had an important role to perform externally and would be judged in part by the way it carried out that role.

Speaker Albert

As with McCormack, Speaker Albert was a Rayburn protégé who developed his attitudes toward media at Speaker Rayburn's side. Albert's lack of interest in national media attention was reinforced by his own experience. After Rayburn's death in 1962, Albert prided himself on winning the majority leader's race against Richard Bolling of Missouri by pursuing an internal strategy. Albert quietly concentrated on personal contact with House members while Bolling waged a national media offensive. Albert later said:

I never once got on television. The sum total of my national publicity was a [press] release when I got into the race and a [press] release when I got up to Washington saying I thought I had enough votes to win. I refused to go on television although I was invited to go on most of the news and panel shows.[15]

Albert's resounding victory only reinforced his beliefs that the business of the House was an internal affair and that the media played a largely intrusive role. Despite Albert's having attitudes similar to his predecessors, there was great expectation in the media when he became Speaker. Here was a younger and more open-minded person, a widely traveled and well-read Rhodes scholar who had the capacity to move the speakership farther into the twentieth century. Before becoming Speaker, Albert received memos from Democratic operatives exhorting him to become a national spokesperson for the party, give priority to media, and organize an infrastructure in which the "loyal opposition" would have a much more powerful voice. Albert was the first Speaker to hire a press secretary; he used the Democratic Steering and Policy Committee as a vehicle to launch high profile economic initiatives, he was far more attentive to the broadcast media, and he was open-minded to initiatives that provided a strong opposition voice. Yet, as with Rayburn and McCormack, he viewed the media as largely irrelevant to the running of the House of Representatives.

Albert's tenure as Speaker was spent entirely as a member of the opposition during two Republican administrations. With Majority Leader Mike Mansfield, Albert consistently petitioned the television networks for time to rebut Presidents Nixon and Ford. Mansfield and Albert almost always failed to get time comparable to the president's. The networks had developed a double standard by which the president's requests for time were granted automatically, but congressional requests for time were judged according to their "newsworthiness." This usually meant that the leadership was either denied time altogether, given time by one network, or given access at different times by the three networks. Even in the best circumstances, the leadership never received time comparable to the president's. The opposition received its best shot after presidential State of the Union messages, when it became almost habit to let the opposition have a few minutes for a rebuttal after the president spoke.[16]

In 1976, Speaker Albert commissioned the Congressional Research Service of the Library of Congress to do a study comparing the presidents' and opposition's coverage. The study clearly showed the networks' double standard and the access drought the Democrats in Congress had endured. President Nixon received simultaneous airtime every time he asked for it while the opposition had nearly always been turned away.[17] While Albert and Mansfield's persistent petitioning of the networks did not always help their immediate cause, it laid a foundation that would greatly help succeeding Democratic leaders during the Reagan and Bush administrations to receive rebuttal time comparable to a president's for the first time.

Throughout the television age, the Senate with its smaller number of members and its greater hunger for publicity had routinely dominated the House in exposure. A handful of senators had extensive visibility while few, if any, House members were household names. This changed temporarily at the end of the Watergate investigation when the eyes of the nation turned to the House of Representatives after the Senate had completed the Ervin committee hearings. The obscure House Judiciary Committee sustained intense national media attention for months, climaxing with the hearings that led to the Committee voting articles of impeachment out of committee.

While uneasy about the carnival atmosphere that was developing around the Judiciary Committee hearings, Speaker Albert tried hard to accommodate the television networks and the rest of the media. When the Judiciary Committee had completed its work, Speaker Albert authorized his staff to make plans for the televising of impeachment proceedings in the House. This was a key decision because it represented a turnaround from Rayburn's strict ban on television in the House, which had been in effect since the day Albert came to Congress in 1947. Speaker Albert's willingness to open the House to television during this crucial moment in history paved the way for permanent access to the House five years later.

With Speaker Albert twice next in line to the presidency during the Watergate period, the speakership attracted unprecedented media attention.

The Speaker's daily news conference for a handful of regulars would sometimes swell to nearly a hundred reporters from around the world. Television cameras were still barred from the Speaker's conferences, but Albert made a special effort to go to the Radio-Television Gallery to repeat important statements.

By the mid-1970s, few could escape the call for better communication initiatives by the Congress and its leaders. In 1970, Senator James Fulbright held hearings showing the dominance of the president in political communications.[18] In 1973, Minow, Martin, and Mitchell punctuated that point with the book *Presidential Television.*[19] In 1974, the Joint Committee on Congressional Operations exposed congressional communication deficiencies in their report *Congress and Mass Communications.*[20] No longer was Congress hiding its head in the sand. It had finally discovered the liabilities of its self-imposed exile from the media mainstream and the inherent constraints to be faced in trying to communicate on a par with presidents.

The importance of the communications issue was reinforced by a large group of young Democrats swept into the House in 1974 by the public reaction to Watergate; they created an ambitious new set of expectations for the leadership. This new generation of Democratic congressional representatives, many serving traditionally Republican districts, were well-schooled in the latest campaign technologies and strategies. They understood the importance of media and public relations far better than their predecessors. When the "Watergate babies" came to power, they computerized their office mail systems; produced a blizzard of attractive, substantive newsletters; established mobile district offices; and produced regular radio, television, and cable programs for their districts. It was only natural that they would expect the same type of proactive, external role for their leaders. These first-term members galvanized the issues that had been percolating up through the institution for the previous decade.

While Speaker Albert had taken far more positive initiatives with the media and external publics than Rayburn and McCormack combined, his actions paled against the burgeoning expectations of the new members. Speaker Albert was still one of the old school in their minds—part of the problem, not the solution. In response to pressure from new members, the Speaker appointed a task force on information to be chaired by the chief deputy whip, John Brademas of Indiana. Brademas's grouped outlined a number of media initiatives that would be fully implemented during subsequent speakerships.

Changing attitudes among new members emphasized the importance of a Speaker's external role compared to the traditional internal role. No longer could a Speaker rely exclusively on knowledge of the institution, personal relationships with members, ability to mediate conflicts, and ability to move legislation through the system. As Timothy Cook wrote, "Making news and making laws are not contradictory." [21] Speakers would have to take a more active role in developing their party's agenda and in promoting it to the American people. There would have to be a dedicated communications apparatus in the leadership that concerned itself primarily with the media and other external constituencies. The Speaker would have to begin framing the leadership message with much more sophistication and intensity than had ever been contemplated.

Speaker O'Neill

With the presidency and Congress both coming under Democratic control in 1977, the pressure on the leadership to communicate a national message was temporarily off, but the message from the first-term members of 1974 was not lost on the new Speaker, Tip O'Neill. Speaker O'Neill expanded his daily press briefing, strengthened the role of the Democratic Steering and Policy Committee, expanded the leadership's communications staff, and provided members with the technology to support the leadership's communications initiatives in their districts. Speaker O'Neill shared many of the reservations toward the media held by Rayburn, McCormack, and Albert, but his public persona offered a more open, media-minded speakership.

Speaker O'Neill's most significant media initiative was the opening of the House to cameras in 1979, which he would later say was one of the best decisions he ever made.[22] Distrust of the media lingered long past Speaker Rayburn's death, but by 1979 many of the older members had retired and the large and active class of 1974 was making its influence felt. A proposal to let the networks handle broadcasting of the House nearly made it to the floor in 1976, but Albert and O'Neill stopped it in the Rules Committee because it gave the networks exclusive control of the system.

The feature of the 1979 resolution that appealed to Speaker O'Neill was that the House controlled its own system; the Speaker was in charge. The system, which began as a ninety-day test and was then made permanent, forbade the cameras to focus on any area of the chamber except the person speaking. There were no reaction shots of members on the House floor. The distribution problem that had made previous proposals unworkable was solved by satellite technology. The cable television industry created an organization called C-SPAN (Cable Satellite Public Affairs Television) that would provide an outlet in thousands of communities nationwide. It is ironic that Washington, D.C., was one of the last cities in the United States to get access to House proceedings. Although many of the people most vitally interested in the workings of the House are in Washington, D.C., the city was not wired for cable until the late 1980s.

The House of Representatives wired its own premises with closed circuit television, allowing members and their staffs to watch House proceedings from their offices. This may have changed significantly the corporate culture of the House. In the past, there had always been a strong incentive to go to the House floor to learn what was going on. Speaker Albert, for example, credited his initial success and his promotion to the leadership ladder to the many hours he spent on the House floor and in the cloakrooms. Members spending time in the chamber also contributed to the traditional camaraderie of the House and helped to overcome the problems of 435 disparate persons working together as a legislative body.

With the advent of television, it was far easier for members to stay in their offices and rush back and forth to the House floor briefly to vote. The lack of members in the chamber kept the leadership, including the Speaker, from forming many of the personal relationships with newer members that characterized previous generations. Backbench members looked to television coverage more, both C-SPAN and network coverage, for cues from the leadership. Some members' views of O'Neill may have come from the same perspective as the little old lady in Des Moines watching C-SPAN at home. If a Speaker was impressive on television and was carrying the party message forward, he might be perceived in the same way on Capitol Hill. This was particularly true of congressional staff who rarely had personal contact with the Speaker, but had ample opportunity to watch him on television.

During the early years of televising the House, the minority took greater initiative than the Democrats to spread its message via C-SPAN. A group of young activist Republicans, led by Newt Gingrich of Georgia, turned the seldom-used prerogative of addressing the House for an hour at the end of a session into an effective forum that received considerable national attention. The Republicans orchestrated daily speeches attacking the Democratic leadership and its policies that were broadcast to a minuscule C-SPAN audience, but an audience that included a significant number of opinion leaders and the media.

This televising of "special orders" eventually became a thorn in the Speaker's side. The practice was not only interfering with the running of the House, delaying adjournment and causing hundreds of staff to work overtime just to let one or two members hold forth in an empty chamber, but the Republican speeches were also starting to have an impact. Members of Congress received mail from constituents, editorial writers picked up Republican themes, and the Washington media started watching the conservative attacks. Soon Gingrich became a force to be reckoned with in the House and around the country. Eventually, the Democrats would also have to use one-minute speeches at the beginning of the session and special orders at the end to balance the Republican offensive.

Speaker O'Neill's patience with the Republicans finally ran out in 1985 when he watched Gingrich give a special order after the close of business. Gingrich attacked the voting record of O'Neill's good friend Eddie Boland, pausing occasionally as if Boland were in the chamber and could answer him. As was discussed in Chapter 3, when Rep. Robert Walker of Pennsylvania used a similar tactic the next day, Speaker O'Neill ordered the cameras to pan the empty chamber.[23]

The Republicans, naturally, were furious that the Speaker arbitrarily had changed the rules of the game without consulting them. It is ironic that the Democrats had imposed the rule limiting shots to closeups in order to protect members from embarrassment, but it was the Democrats who were being embarrassed by the Republicans' special orders. Panning an empty chamber exposed the conservatives' ploy as an exercise in deceptive posturing rather than a serious legislative initiative.

By the mid-1980s, the momentum for visibility lay with the House rather than the Senate. C-SPAN had attracted a small, but loyal, following. The national broadcast media gravitated toward the real time coverage of the House floor. Local television stations around the nation found it much easier and cheaper to pick up a sound bite from their representative on the House floor than to arrange a special interview with the senator.

When a major legislative issue came to Congress, C-SPAN captured the drama of the moment in the House, making the previously reclusive body more appealing. Having a ten-year head start on the Senate in televising proceedings no doubt helped the House of Representatives on a number of fronts. By the time C-SPAN II (providing Senate coverage) was established, channel space on local cable systems was very tight and carriage of C-SPAN II was limited. C-SPAN I remained the dominant channel, giving the House a permanent edge.

The Democratic leadership during the Reagan administration was more successful in gaining time to rebut presidential addresses than ever before. The Republicans opposing Jimmy Carter not once received airtime to oppose the president on all three networks simultaneously; the Democrats opposing Reagan had nine opportunities. During the Reagan administration, the congressional leadership received three-network access (not necessarily simultaneous) 91 percent of the time they asked for it compared to 30 percent during the Carter administration, 40 percent during the Ford administration, and 43 percent during the Nixon administration.[24]

After twenty years of using a double standard to deny congressional access to rebut presidential speeches, leaders of the three major networks finally decided that giving time to the opposition was the prudent thing to do. The House and Senate leadership helped promote the improved treatment by aggressively petitioning the networks, improving the quality of the congressional replies, and tailoring the format to fit the time constraints of the networks. For the first time, the leadership had a proper platform on which it consistently could be seen nationally as the "loyal opposition."

The move toward more network rebuttal time was one of a package of media initiatives begun during the O'Neill speakership. An office was formed to handle communications for the leadership and to help rank-and-file members get their views on the evening news via satellite. The Speaker also upgraded his own press office. Speaker O'Neill was the first Speaker to have an activist press secretary. Chris Matthews, a former speech writer in the Carter White House, was given a wide-ranging portfolio to deal with the media.

Eventually, Matthews's quotes of the day were featured as prominently in the media as the Speaker's, making him one of the few leadership aides ever to veer from the longstanding staff norm of anonymity. Matthews's autonomy gave the Speaker's office a two-pronged press attack: the more stately official remarks of the Speaker and the more outrageous, witty, and partisan remarks of Matthews. There were certain situations in which it was much more effective for Matthews to launch an attack rather than the Speaker, and it was always easier for Matthews to retract a statement than it was for the Speaker. Matthews's elevation to the role of Speaker's spokesperson came during a highly partisan period when the Reagan Republicans controlled the White House. Speaker O'Neill felt comfortable with the surrogate spokesperson arrangement that provided a barrage of media initiatives unthinkable during the Rayburn era. It is quite possible, however, that Speaker O'Neill would have given his press secretary less free reign during less partisan times.

As with Speaker Albert, Speaker O'Neill became caught in a game of rising expectations within his own party. While the Speaker had taken unprecedented action to develop an external strategy for the leadership, he was perceived as relatively passive during the height of the Reagan economic assault by some partisan Democrats.[25] The Democrats were being clobbered by the "Great Communicator" without having the ability to fight back. Speaker O'Neill was seen by some as the source of the problem. A younger, more media-savvy Speaker, they reasoned, would have been better-suited to launch a proper offensive.

Regardless of how personally skilled Speaker O'Neill was in dealing with the media, it was his fate to be thrust onto a giant media stage with the president. For a few brief moments, the president and Speaker stood face to face on the same level. Both Reagan and O'Neill presented a compelling set of personal comparisons and contrasts (two gregarious people of Irish decent, of the same generation, with polarized views of the world). They became perfect media bookends, symbolic media caricatures representing two boldly contrasting views of America. Eventually, the message could not be separated from the stereotypes of the leaders. For several months, a broad range of media (print and electronic) feasted on the Reagan-O'Neill battles, placing a Speaker on the same media platform as the president for the first time in the television age. It was as close as a twentieth-century Speaker would get to parity with a president.

Although Speaker O'Neill held many of the same reservations concerning the media that Rayburn, McCormack, and Albert had before him, and was not particularly comfortable with television, the course of events and good staff work made O'Neill a highly visible public figure. That Speaker O'Neill's autobiography was a best seller and that he received contracts for a variety of high profile commercial endorsements after leaving office showed just how high a Speaker's visibility could climb in the television age.

Speaker Wright

As this book has already discussed, Jim Wright was the most activist Speaker in the postwar era, giving high priority to shaping his own legislative agenda and pushing it through the Congress. Such an ambitious legislative goal could not be accomplished without an equally ambitious external plan of attack. No modern Speaker had ever tried a simultaneous inside-outside strategy. As Wright biographer John Barry said, "To win required the ability to manipulate the media, read polls, and play the outside game with the public, and also required the inside game, the mastery of each detail, each comma on a piece of paper, and a sensitivity subtle enough to read a handshake or a nod." [26]

There had been frustration with Speakers whose sole interest was with the internal workings of the institution, who shunned the media, who did not understand the mechanics of sophisticated, proactive public relations, and who failed to seize the moment as spokesperson for the House. Now the House had a Speaker more than willing to use every weapon in his arsenal to attempt to govern from the House of Representatives. No doubt the House wanted a Speaker capable of strong, focused leadership, but whether they wanted a Speaker bent on exercising that prerogative was questionable. Perhaps the institution did not want to be led, after all, but merely guided as its most skilled Speakers in the past had done.

Speaker Wright was an orator ready-made for the big stage where he could captivate an audience with his intense, emotional, eloquent delivery. By no means was Speaker Wright naturally suited to the relaxed, low key, "cool" medium of television. Yet, he tried very hard to be successful on television. Speaker Wright personally wrote his nationally televised replies to the State of the Union message and was willing to let handlers coach him for hours on his delivery.[27]

Speaker Wright courted the media aggressively and was more available for television appearances than any of his predecessors. His ambitious legislative agenda demanded it. Yet, he also had a more contentious relationship with journalists than previous Speakers, once calling them "enemies of government." [28] Partly because of his combative personality and partly because of his activist speakership, Wright often found himself battling with reporters. According to Barry, Wright "patronized" the media and often sounded "sanctimonious, disingenuous." [29]

Before Speaker Wright could push his legislative agenda to conclusion, he became the target of an ethics investigation that led to his resignation after less than three years in office. His speakership offered a prototype of an activist Speaker complete with the requisite external strategy one would need to push an ambitious legislative agenda. It would demand immense energy and political dexterity and require a Speaker committed to taking his message directly to the most influential media of the day.

Members who had demanded a more activist speakership got a taste of strong leadership with all its distinct advantages and disadvantages. For the first time in the television age, there would be no charges of weak and ineffective outside leadership, of reticent response to the opposition, of reluctance to act as partisan spokesperson for the majority. On the contrary, there was a yearning for the less partisan, more conciliatory coalition-builders of old.

Speaker Foley

Speaker Foley, who came to power six months into the 101st Congress in June 1990, was a kinder, gentler Speaker than his predecessor. There were no sharp edges, no manic rush to push a legislative agenda, no combative tendencies. Yet, Speaker Foley, in a quieter way, placed an equally high priority on improving the leadership's communications abilities. As majority leader, Foley was responsible for organizing a leadership counterpoint to President Bush. He understood and appreciated the challenge he faced as Speaker in trying to communicate effectively in the national media.

Under Speaker Wright, Majority Leader Foley and Majority Whip Tony Coelho had developed a "message of the day" system similar to the one that had worked so well for the Republicans for years. Each House Democrat received daily communication from the leadership stating what themes the Speaker would stress that day and urging members to support that theme through one-minute speeches on the House floor, interviews with district media, and so forth. The leadership also arranged satellite hookups for members to have easier access to television stations in their districts.

The success of the system varied greatly with the times. When there was a hot, partisan topic swirling above Washington that captivated the press, the Democratic communications staff could ride the wave, arranging appearances on high profile interview programs, getting quotable statements to the galleries quickly, coordinating all leadership responses, and arranging a chorus of backbench response. During fallow periods, however, all the initiative the leadership could muster failed to make a ripple in the tide of the media agenda. During the Gulf War, for example, there was no need or opportunity to launch a Democratic media offensive; the majority party simply had to wait out the storm.

Despite his broad-based media initiatives, Speaker Foley, as with his predecessors, was criticized for being too passive in his dealings with the White House. He rarely landed the kind of partisan blows characteristic of O'Neill and Wright. Speaker Foley was sophisticated in his understanding of the media, but frequently he chose to use the media in a less partisan way.

It had been assumed that during the Rayburn, McCormack, and Albert eras the ineffectiveness of Speakers in executing an external role was a result of their lack of skill in dealing with the media: if only these Speakers had been more willing to engage the press proactively, they would have been far more successful as spokespersons for their party and more successful Speakers overall, so the criticism went. In Speaker Foley's case, the issue was not media sophistication, but willingness to embrace partisanship.

As with other speakerships, the tenor changed significantly when the White House changed parties. With Democrat Bill Clinton in the White House, no longer was the pressure on a Speaker to launch a media offensive. Yet, with media-savvy leaders at both ends of Pennsylvania Avenue, expectations naturally rose concerning the ability of the Democrats to communicate their message. The Speaker was an important complement to the White House strategy. When the president's economic plans hit snags on Capitol Hill in 1993, it was the Speaker and Senate majority leader who were supposed to provide a loud echo to the Clinton media machine to rejuvenate Democratic support on Capitol Hill. As during the 1960s, Democratic control also shifted the spotlight on Congress to the Republicans who were more primed than ever to play the role of "loyal opposition."

Toward a Television-Age Speaker

During the past thirty-five years, the speakership has been in transition from a strictly inside speakership to an inside-outside speakership. Each Speaker since Rayburn has contributed to the transition, but Newt Gingrich may be the first television-age Speaker, one who feels as much at home on national television as in the Speaker's chair.

It took a minimum of three speakerships to erase the Rayburn legacy and create positive attitudes toward dealing with the media. In many ways, this linear progression toward more enlightened use of media was the easy part of the task. Once the transition period ends, a much more difficult challenge will be to strike a balance between the inside and outside strategies. How will Speakers use the tools they have acquired to capitalize effectively on their public platform without alienating the internal constituency that elected them and to which they are beholden? How visible does the House want its Speaker to be? When does the House want its Speaker to be seen and heard? How does external effectiveness translate into power and influence within the House?

Unlike the president, whose advocacy role and visibility goals remain constant, a Speaker's external role changes radically according to changes in the White House. Members must choose a Speaker who can be a highly visible, activist opposition spokesperson one year and a relatively passive water carrier for the president the next. Invariably, the external persona of a Speaker will be better suited for one environment than another.

The majority in the House may one day want to use the speakership as a platform for its party leader. Because there is no requirement that the Speaker be a member of the House, a party could install its most promising standard bearer in the office primarily as a high profile leader for the party. While this unlikely maneuver would turn the history of the House on its head, it would be the quickest and easiest way for an opposition party to provide a high visibility platform and power base for a party leader.

Despite the advances made by recent Speakers in developing the role of external spokesperson by using the national media, the traditional "inside" duties of the Speaker clearly anchor the office. As John Barry wrote, the leadership, however much it talks about media, is geared toward "the most prosaic, least visually attractive, most internal elements of policy making." [30] Media prowess will always be a modest complement to the traditional skills and abilities the institution has always sought in its Speakers. Yet, future Speakers, weaned on television, will face a job requirement that Speakers Rayburn, Mc-Cormack, and Albert never faced and may not have met—the ability and willingness to develop an active external communications strategy that promotes the Speaker of the House as the chief spokesperson for the institution in the national media.

While modern Speakers realize the positive potential of the national news media as a vehicle for legislative momentum, most Speakers have experienced the negative thrust of the media firsthand and have felt the personal pain of being overwhelmed with bad press at their most vulnerable moments. House Parliamentarian William Brown, who has served under Speakers from Rayburn to Foley. Rayburn, recalls a common thread of the postwar speakership being the deep personal wounds each Speaker has received at the hands of the media. These stressful times, according to Brown, have been defining moments in shaping the Speakers' attitudes toward the media.[31]

Unlike the constant attention they give the president, the national media focus on the speakership only sporadically, usually in times of crises. During these periods, media attention increases geometrically; the collegial press conference balloons to a mob of strangers. Speakers find themselves constantly on the defensive, unable to assert their normal control on the process. It is not surprising that some former Speakers reflexively think of the media as scandalmongers who robbed them of a particular part of their career, or in Speaker Wright's case, the speakership itself.

Notes

1. Barbara Sinclair, *Majority Leadership in the U.S. House* (Baltimore: Johns Hopkins University Press, 1983), 40-41.

2. H. G. Dulaney and Edward Hake Phillips, ed., *Speak, Mr. Speaker* (Bonham, Texas: Sam Rayburn Foundation, 1978), 325.

3. D. B. Hardeman and Donald C. Bacon, *Rayburn* (Austin: Texas Monthly Press, 1987), 304.

4. Anthony Champagne, *Congressman Sam Rayburn* (New Brunswick, N.J.: Rutgers University Press, 1984), 156.

5. Hardeman, *Rayburn*, 415.

6. Dulaney and Phillips, *Speak, Mr. Speaker*, 459.

7. Hardeman, *Rayburn*, 424.

8. Dulaney and Phillips, *Speak, Mr. Speaker*, 458.

9. Hardeman, *Rayburn*, 363.

10. David Halberstam, *The Powers That Be* (New York: Alfred Knopf, 1979), 249.

11. Newton Minow, John Bartlow Martin, and Lee Mitchell, *Presidential Television* (New York: Basic Books, 1973), 56.

12. Joint Committee on Congressional Operations, *Congress and Mass Communication: An Institutional Perspective*, 93d Cong., 2d sess., 1974.

13. Henry Z. Scheele, "Response to the Kennedy Administration: The Joint Senate-House Republican Leadership Press Conference," *Presidential Studies Quarterly* (Fall 1989): 825.

14. Ibid., 842.

15. Robert L. Peabody, *Leadership in Congress: Stability, Succession, and Change* (Boston: Little, Brown, 1976), 77.

16. Joe S. Foote, *Television Access and Political Power: The Networks, the President, and the "Loyal Opposition"* (New York: Praeger, 1990), 50-54.

17. Denis S. Rutkus, "A Report on Simultaneous Television Network Coverage of Presidential Addresses to the Nation" (Washington, D.C.: Congressional Research Service, 1976).

18. Senate Committee on Commerce, Communications Subcommittee, *Public Service Time for the Legislative Branch*, S. Doc. 91-74, 1970, 40.

19. Minow, Martin, and Mitchell, *Presidential Television*.

20. Joint Committee on Congressional Operations, *Congress and Mass Communications*, 93d Cong., 2d sess., 1974.

21. Timothy Cook, *Making Laws, Making News* (Washington, D.C.: Brookings Institution, 1989), 9.

22. Thomas P. O'Neill, with William Novack, *Man of the House* (New York: Random House, 1987), 288.

23. Ibid., 354.

24. Foote, *Television Access and Political Power,* 114.

25. O'Neill, *Man of the House,* 350.

26. John Barry, *The Ambition and the Power* (New York: Viking, 1989), 92.

27. Ibid., 105.

28. Ibid., 251.

29. Ibid., 250.

30. Ibid., 252.

31. William Brown, interview by author, July 12, 1993.

8 The Speaker and Institutional Change

Roger H. Davidson

A ll institutions must innovate in order to survive and fulfill their social functions. The U.S. House of Representatives faces the same pressures to adapt and change as any other organization. Whether those changes respond sufficiently to the challenges of the time or whether they are ineffective can spell the difference between an institution's growth or attrition, or even its life or death.[1]

Despite its unflattering public image, the contemporary House of Representatives has undergone profound changes. Self-examination and structural tinkering are by no means infrequent. Since World War II there have been three joint House-Senate reorganization committees; the House has sponsored two extensive studies of its committee system, a wide-ranging administrative commission (and several minor ones), and numerous *ad hoc* study committees. Few Congresses convene without adopting at least a few rules changes. The 1970s brought such rapid and extensive innovations that those years are referred to as the reform era; more recent changes have been less sweeping but nonetheless noteworthy.

No one is better positioned to affect Congress's responses to pressures for change than the Speaker of the House. Emerging out of reform politics and shifting partisan alliances, the new speakership dates only from the 1970s. After decades of eclipse following the 1910 revolt against the inordinate power of Speaker Joseph Cannon, the office acquired new procedural and structural tools to shape the House's agenda, allocate its resources, and manage floor proceedings. Inasmuch as Senate leaders fall far short of matching these powers, today's Speakers are truly unique in their resources for helping Congress to adapt to changing conditions.

Yet Speakers, like other congressional leaders, are "middle people" who occupy the modal point of their parties and are acceptable to most of their component factions.[2] Whether from conviction or from constituency tolerance, they must be free to vote as a "mainstream Democrat" or a "regular

Republican"; they must voice the concerns of a majority of their colleagues while maintaining open lines of communication to deviant factions. Speakers are products of a weeding-out process that begins when they arrive in Congress. Not only must they gain seniority and serve an apprenticeship that normally requires the indulgence of a safe constituency and the time to devote to chamber matters while on Capitol Hill, they must normally pass muster with previous cadres of leaders, sometimes enjoying mentorship from them. Successful leaders practice "the politics of inclusion"—reaching out to all segments of their parties.[3]

In light of the continuing pressures for change, it is an opportune moment to consider the paradoxical role of Speakers in the politics of institutional change. This requires an examination of the part played by successive Speakers in major innovations from the reform era to the present. The underlying assumption is that authentic leadership implies not only understanding the external and internal forces that define the institution or group being led, but also responding creatively to move the institution or group closer to common goals.[4]

Pressures for Institutional Change

As with all organizations, the House of Representatives is challenged to survive and maximize its competitive position. Mere survival is not the issue: periodic crises of confidence come and go, and accommodations are made. But will the House's effectiveness suffer as a result? Will it be able to preserve its autonomy, its control over its own decisions? Will it maintain its scope of operations and its sphere of influence?

In order to maintain its autonomy and scope of influence, the House must adjust to *external demands* while at the same time coping with *internal stresses*. The Constitution sets forth baseline legal requirements and influences public expectations for congressional performance. Developments outside the chamber—social, economic, political—generate demands that the legislature enact laws or take other actions to further the general welfare. Such forces also redistribute the resources held by contending factions and interest groups. Among the external forces that exert direct pressures for change are partisan or factional shifts, long-term social changes, domestic crises or scandals, and wartime mobilizations.

Another set of pressures for change emanates from forces within Congress—primarily the goals and careers of individual members. Often internal stresses are caused by shifts in the House's external environment—as when a ballooning workload (external demand) produces personal or committee scrambles for jurisdiction (internal stress). Other tensions flow from membership turnover, agenda or workload shifts, factional balances in committees or caucuses, and members' attitudes and norms.

Innovations may be initiated by the leaders themselves or by various factions; or they may be articulated by outside groups, media commentators, executive agencies, or even the president. Sometimes Speakers play the role of *resistor*, marshalling their formal and informal powers to thwart the proposed innovation. In other cases, speakers serve as *managers* for innovations pressed by others, using their superior procedural and informational resources to broker between the reformers and the resistors. Occasionally Speakers actually *sponsor* innovations designed to enhance their own prerogatives, solve particular institutional problems, or protect the institution's integrity.

The New Speakership

Vigorous central leadership is one of the features of the postreform Congress—a term generally applied to Congress since the end of the reform era in the late 1970s.[5] After the revolt against Speaker Cannon, the term "House leadership" was regarded by many as an oxymoron. Although Sam Rayburn is cited as a possible exception, he "was not an institutionally powerful speaker."[6] His influence rested more on his extraordinary combination of personal skills—which included integrity, persuasiveness, and mastery of parliamentary procedure. His formal powers were constricted, and he had to contend with the powerful "barons," seniority leaders who dominated key House committees and shaped domestic policy to the specifications of the conservative coalition of southern Democrats and "Old Guard" Republicans. For a half century or more after the fall of Speaker Cannon, leadership in the House remained "in commission"[7]—that is, dispersed among a circle of powerful members and committees.

Reforms of the 1960s and 1970s embraced, paradoxically, centralizing as well as decentralizing elements. The powers of the Speaker and the majority party caucus were enlarged. The targets of the reform movement were, after all, not the elective party leaders but rather the committees' "old bulls." Many House insurgents (Rayburn protégé Richard Bolling, for example) believed in encouraging party responsibility as well as in expanding opportunities for all members. So the reform-era legacy not only dispersed opportunities for influence but also enhanced central guidance. The rank-and-file members gained at the expense of the committee chairs, but the party leaders and especially the Speaker gained also.[8]

The Reform Era: McCormack and Albert

Reform politics of the 1960s and early 1970s focused on giving more legislators a "piece of the action." At its core the reform movement was a power struggle pitting liberal activists against senior conservatives. Although the national Democratic party's center of gravity was increasingly with its non-southern liberals and moderates, key House committees remained in the grip of mostly southern, mostly cautious scions of the conservative coalition. In 1965, the Great Society's zenith, southerners still chaired two-thirds of all House committees—including Appropriations, Armed Services, Commerce, Rules, and Ways and Means.

Agitation for change emanated from the Democratic Study Group (DSG), which since its founding in 1959 was the closest equivalent in the House to an "executive committee of the proletariat." Following the 1964 elections, DSG reformers appealed to Majority Whip Hale Boggs (La.) for tactical advice and mediation with Speaker John McCormack.[9] Eventually McCormack acceded to a series of reformers and demands, especially creation of a Joint Committee on the Organization of Congress. True to his word, the Speaker designated Democrat Ray Madden of Indiana—a "safe" liberal who also sat on the Rules Committee—to carry the proposal in the House and subsequently appointed a balanced delegation, led by Madden, to serve on the body.

The 1970 Reorganization Act

After ten months of deliberation throughout 1965, the joint reorganization committees—co-chaired by Madden and Senator A. S. Mike Monroney (D-Okla.)—produced an omnibus reorganization package consisting of sixty-six proposals that had garnered unanimous support within the panel. The heart of the report was a "committee bill of rights" designed to regularize committee procedures, prevent chairs from exercising arbitrary powers, and protect minority-party rights. Included were such items as the majority's right to call meetings and report bills in the event that the chair refused to act; more open hearings; broadcasting and telecasting of hearings at a committee's discretion; participation of all committee members in preparing reports; elimination of proxy voting; and designated staff for the minority party. Although they did not strike directly at the seniority system, these provisions would have democratized committee proceedings while preserving the organizational integrity of the full committees.

Even these centrist proposals faced stiff opposition from entrenched committee leaders. After the Senate approved the reform package, Speaker McCormack referred it to the House Rules Committee (rather than a special panel composed of the chamber's members of the joint committee, as the Senate had done). Even with Senate modifications, the committee bill of rights was too radical for McCormack and his close circle of senior committee leaders. He would not, if he could prevent it, allow the bill to go to the House floor until the offending provisions had been diluted drastically. As one Rules Committee member confided, McCormack "put the bill in the refrigerator,"[10] where it remained for more than three years.

Altered political conditions eventually thawed the reorganization bill from the Rules Committee's freezer. The 1968 elections brought Republican Richard Nixon to the White House to face a divided, demoralized Democratic party. Many Democrats concluded that McCormack, at age seventy-seven, was not the compelling spokesperson the party needed. A long-shot challenge by Arizona's Morris Udall uncovered a surprising level of discontent—virtually one-third of the House Democrats gave McCormack a "no confidence" vote. "Congressional reform has become a symbolic thing to many members, and it's awfully difficult to resist it under these circumstances," one of McCormack's associates confessed. "I think the Speaker has become reconciled to having a bill."[11]

The bill (H.R. 17654), crafted by a Rules Committee task force headed by California's B. F. Sisk, struck a careful compromise between committee leaders' fears and reformers' determination to have a bill of some kind. A coalition of DSG activists and a GOP counterpart, "Rumsfeld's Raiders" (reform-minded members associated with Illinois's Donald Rumsfeld), pushed the Rules Committee to report the bill and then put together a series of ten floor amendments designed to strengthen the measure.

McCormack, who by this time had announced his retirement, turned negotiations over to his heir-apparent, Majority Leader Carl Albert of Oklahoma. Although scrupulously loyal to McCormack, Albert stood midway between the reformers and the committee barons. As Albert related,

I became the intermediary between the established leadership and the young reformers. The former never doubted my loyalty; the latter always expected my sympathy. Both were correct, and because they were, I became the conciliator working behind the scenes to maintain public harmony while carefully weighing and quietly promoting the allowable measures of change.[12]

Negotiating privately but sympathetically, Albert facilitated the reformers' objectives. "I gladly let others lay claim to making the footprints," he explained, "and I never let a single one fall on the toes of my friend the Speaker."[13] McCormack shunned the floor debate. When asked for his views on one of the floor amendments, the recorded teller vote, he told a reporter, " 'It's all right with me. It would have been all right twenty years ago.' Then, spreading his arms wide, he added with disbelief, 'Why, it's the great utopia.' "[14]

The Legislative Reorganization Act (P.L. 91-510) was adopted, complete with the reformers' package of floor amendments. The key floor amendment, providing for recorded teller votes, was co-sponsored by future Speaker Tip O'Neill (Mass.) and advocated by Albert ("... I used every single lever I had available").[15] It had an immediate impact on House floor proceedings. Yet the "committee bill of rights"—a modest set of guarantees by today's standards—had been so watered down that it fell short of satisfying the demands of junior members. It is ironic to note that the failure of this effort forced reformers to seek another forum for change—the Democratic Caucus, where they had the votes to win and where leaders were elected rather than chosen by seniority.

The Democratic Caucus Reforms, 1969-1975

Even as deliberations on the reorganization plan reached their climax, the liberal reformers also pressed for a series of changes to strengthen the Democratic Caucus's role in committee assignments, committee procedures, leadership prerogatives, and floor business. The opening gambit was to push for regular monthly caucus meetings, a proposal adopted in 1969. The next year the DSG proposed a caucus committee to investigate the seniority question: the insurgents were seeking an orderly way of exploring changes rather than pressing a frontal assault on seniority. The result was the Committee on Organization, Study, and Review—at first known as the Hansen Committee (after its chair, Washington Democrat Julia Butler Hansen) but now referred to simply as "OSR." Majority Leader Albert and Democratic Caucus Chair Dan Rostenkowski (Ill.) made sure the panel was carefully balanced among all segments of the party. It was an unwieldy group ("a real circus," one member called it), but it worked because its members represented virtually every segment of the caucus, including the leadership.

The initial set of Hansen Committee reforms, adopted by the Democratic Caucus in early 1971, had two effects. First, they regularized caucus procedures for approving committee assignments and chairs—to create a way to circumvent the seniority system. Second, they institutionalized the subcommittees and their autonomy by spreading subcommittee chairs more widely and providing subcommittee staffs. The seniority provisions caused sharp debate in the caucus and, once adopted, almost succeeded in ousting one chair, archconservative John McMillan (S.C.) of the District of Columbia Committee, who used his post to dominate the nation's capital and its disenfranchised residents. Only a last-minute intervention by Albert and Ways and Means Chair Wilbur Mills (Ark.) saved McMillan's post, though it did not halt his arbitrary rule.

The second aspect of the Hansen report, subcommittee reform, aroused less controversy but proved more consequential. In the short run, the provisions created at least sixteen new subcommittee chairs, spreading power to less senior members and especially to liberal non-southerners.[16] Two years later, in 1973, the Democratic Caucus strengthened subcommittees by adopting the so-called subcommittee bill of rights, empowering majority party caucuses within each standing committee to determine their subcommittees' membership, size, jurisdiction, and budget—formerly prerogatives of the committee chairs. The DSG liberals also succeeded in gaining automatic caucus votes on committee chairs. These reforms, like the earlier ones, were initiated by DSG liberals, refined by the Hansen Committee, and generally supported by party leaders. Once the proposals reached the caucus, Albert (aided by Majority Leader O'Neill and caucus chair Olin Teague) fought to prevent them from being watered down, in the process fighting off some resistance from senior committee leaders.

Speaker Albert also supported moves that promised to enlarge the leadership's own authority. As Peters explains, "he found it necessary to walk a fine line in maintaining his relationships with the senior committee chairs and providing the kind of forceful party leadership that many younger members would demand."[17] Along with other leaders, Albert enthusiastically backed creation of the Steering and Policy Committee (which included the Speaker and other top leaders) and its later expansion to include members chosen by the Speaker. The same was true of the 1975 innovation authorizing the Speaker to nominate all Democratic members of the Rules Committee, subject to caucus ratification. Two years later, in 1975, the reform movement completed its cycle. The formidable Mills having departed, the caucus enlarged the Ways and Means committee and required it to establish subcommittees; committee assignment recommendations were transferred from Ways and Means to Steering and Policy. That year, three committee chairs were actually removed from their posts by caucus vote.

In these innovations, extended over four Congresses, McCormack and Albert played reactive roles. Both Speakers resisted direct challenges to the seniority system, working to forestall challenges to incumbent chairs such as McMillan. Neither Speaker originated any of the caucus reforms (nor, for that matter, did any other elected party leaders). That was true even for those innovations that enhanced leadership authority, such as the Steering and Policy Committee and the Speaker's nomination of Rules Committee Democrats.

Yet there were important differences between the two Speakers. McCormack saw no need for change and had little patience with the reformers; his reactions ranged from resigned tolerance to ill-concealed anger. Albert was more flexible in dealing with reformers' demands. A true border-state moderate, he sensed the shifting power balance in the caucus, willingly and sometimes enthusiastically supporting the changes. Once the new procedures were in place, he implemented them with care and sensitivity.

Taken together, the Caucus-sponsored reforms of 1971, 1973, and 1975 had the effect of weakening House committees and their traditional deliberative processes. First, by making committee leaders answer to the party caucus, the new rules obliged leaders to seek intra-party rather than inter-party coalitions on key issues separating the parties and their supporting factions. This helped to intensify partisanship in the House, at the very time that party loyalty was fading at the grassroots level. Second, the reforms bypassed the full committees in favor of greater subcommittee autonomy—a development that encouraged subcommittees to take charge of legislation and undermined the integrity and strength of the full committees. The effects of the new rules varied from committee to committee, of course, but the ultimate impact was widespread and by no means benign.

More flexible House leaders might very well have altered the course of these changes. The earlier, more modest proposals to improve committee responsiveness by amending the House rules had been met with hostility and obstruction—the latter abetted by the leadership. A more positive response would have brought changes more extensive than those embodied in the 1970

Act; further, such adjustments might have made unnecessary the later, caucus-driven changes.

In retrospect, the defenders of the old order would have been well advised to abandon such chairs as McMillan and give more thought to adjusting committee procedures to meet the new political demands. Instead, they seemed so concerned about frontal attacks on seniority that they gave little thought to the long-range fate of the committee system.

Committee Realignment

By the early 1970s the House committee system was in serious disarray. Especially troublesome were the outmoded and unwieldy committee jurisdictions, last codified in 1946. Decentralizing the committee system, intended to equalize participation, led to a new generation of problems. By the 93rd Congress (1973-1974), the House had 27 standing and select committees and 132 subcommittees, not to mention 9 joint committees (and their 16 subcommittees)—a total of 184 work groups for 435 legislators.[18] With so many assignments, members were hard-pressed to manage their crowded schedules; meetings competed with one another, committee quorums were harder to achieve, and members' attention was dissipated. In a 1973 survey of 101 House and Senate members, a foreign policy study commission discovered that 81 percent were dissatisfied with "committee jurisdictions and the way they are defined in Congress."[19]

The committee realignment effort, unlike most innovative efforts, was actually a leadership creation. It grew out of conversations among Speaker Albert, Minority Leader Gerald Ford, and Rep. Richard Bolling (Mo.), a senior Rules Democrat and long-time reform advocate. They agreed that the time was ripe for reevaluating House committees. Although as leaders they were held publicly accountable for congressional performance, they lacked the tools to coordinate or schedule the legislative programs. The leadership, Albert complained, was "at the mercy of the committees in planning floor schedules and in disposing of the critical business of the House."[20]

The resulting study committee, chaired by Bolling and co-chaired by Dave Martin (R-Neb.) labored for almost a year before reporting a wide-ranging realignment plan that soon stirred up resistance from affected members, staffs, and their allied outside lobbies. Speaker Albert later described the opponents as an "otherwise inexplicable alliance of such strange bedfellows as the DSG, organized business, and organized labor in a single mighty bloc."[21] In the Democratic Caucus, the opponents ganged up and sent the Bolling Plan to the

Hansen Committee. That group might well have scuttled the plan altogether, except for a drumbeat of pressure from Republicans, outside pro-reform groups, and a host of newspaper editorial writers.

Thus the Hansen panel hastily drew up its own reorganization package, which was essentially the Bolling Plan with its more controversial features excised. Following acrimonious debate in the Rules Committee and on the floor, the Hansen substitute was adopted over the Bolling Plan by a 203 to 165 vote. "The name of the game is power, and the boys don't want to give it up," explained Majority Leader O'Neill.[22]

As an instigator of the realignment effort, Albert opened the Bolling Panel's hearings, expressing strong support for several proposed changes. Throughout the panel's deliberations, he was kept informed, although he made few concrete suggestions. Once the controversial reorganization plan surfaced, he made no move to sponsor the delicate negotiations between Bolling's group and the affected interests. Still, Albert bravely continued to support the Bolling Plan. On the eve of the floor debate he made a series of telephone calls, and he used his procedural powers to steer the House toward a final vote. But among top Democratic leaders he was alone: Majority Leader O'Neill, Majority Whip John McFall (Calif.), and all of the deputy whips voted against the Bolling reforms.

The Post-Reform Years: O'Neill and Wright

The post-reform Congress witnessed not a concerted reform effort but a gradual adaptation to changing political and legislative agendas. Confronted by a lagging economy, debates over the efficacy of government programs, and intermittent periods of divided partisan control, Congress gradually changed the way it approached its legislative work load, in the process adapting its procedures and habits to conform to the decentralized system implanted by the reforms of the 1960s and 1970s. "I intend to be a strong speaker," O'Neill declared. "I hope to make some innovative changes around here."[23]

Recurring Entanglements over Committee Jurisdictions

The 1974 innovations were insufficient to cure the ills of the House committee system. Especially troublesome was the scramble for control over energy jurisdiction, scattered among some eighty-three House committees and subcommittees. Two efforts to coordinate energy policy making—a caucus committee (94th Congress) and an ad hoc committee (95th Congress)—had proved helpful but had not resolved the basic jurisdictional confusion. The latter panel was instigated by Speaker O'Neill using authority granted by a Bolling proposal that had been adopted by the House. The purpose was to process President Carter's omnibus energy bill. Under the Speaker's scheme, the bill was first divided and sent to the respective committees of jurisdiction, which then sent it back to the ad hoc committee chaired by O'Neill's friend, Thomas "Lud" Ashley of Ohio. With O'Neill's prodding and Ashley's skillful liaison, the various committees processed their portions of the measure while retaining their jurisdictional claims. The procedure was only a temporary palliative for the jurisdictional problem, but it enabled the Speaker to expedite one of the president's major initiatives. "To me, it was survival," O'Neill later explained. "I *had* to get that bill through—and quickly, so that Congress could move ahead on other fronts." [24]

Members themselves continued to complain about the committee system's unwieldiness and inefficiency. In January 1979 both the Democratic Caucus and the Republican Conference voted in favor of a new Select Committee on Committees. Approved two months later, the panel was directed to study committee structures, jurisdictions, rules and procedures, media coverage of meetings, staffing, and facilities. The resolution creating the panel (H. Res. 118) was approved by a narrow margin of 208 to 200, and its funding by a 212 to 180 vote—hardly a resounding sendoff.

"Without strong leadership backing," Indiana Democrat Lee Hamilton predicted, "there won't be major changes." [25] In fact, neither Speaker O'Neill nor his key deputies—Majority Leader Jim Wright (Texas) and Chief Whip John Brademas (Ind.)—had backed the earlier Bolling Plan or identified themselves with broadscale change. Wright was quoted as remarking that restructuring committees was "taking things from one box and putting them in another. I never thought it made much difference." [26]

Despite their ambivalence, O'Neill and his associates had a stake in the committee inquiry. Jurisdictional overlaps remained troublesome, especially in the energy field. And if the problem was to be addressed, a special committee would be more easily controllable than was the Rules Committee, which Bolling chaired, or the Hansen Committee, chaired by the fiery and unpredictable Phillip Burton of California. To head the new effort, O'Neill chose Jerry Patterson (Calif.), an amiable, low-key three termer.

Speaker O'Neill kept in touch with the Patterson Committee's work. Rather than risking a full-scale realignment plan, the panel decided to concentrate on consolidating energy jurisdiction. At least four influential House Democrats were vying for advantage: Morris Udall (Interior), Don Fuqua (Science and Technology), John Dingell (Commerce's Subcommittee on Energy and Power), and Thomas "Lud" Ashley, who had chaired the ad hoc energy panel. Ashley made a forceful case for a new, separate energy committee; his proposal seemed to have the backing of his friend O'Neill. Subsequently, O'Neill helped to reverse a tentative Patterson Committee decision giving the new committee environmental jurisdiction, a move that had angered environmental lobbyists and foes of nuclear power.

The modest plan for a new energy panel stirred up fierce opposition among the committees that stood to lose jurisdiction. A parade of committee leaders beseeched the Rules Committee to scrap the plan. The affected committee leaders all rushed to embrace a conciliatory plan of Jonathan Bingham (D-N.Y.) designed to apportion the jurisdiction carefully among the committees already exercising authority. The Bingham substitute, cemented by an elaborate series of agreements signed by all the relevant chairs, was adopted eventually by the House, 274 to 134. On the eve of the floor vote, O'Neill told reporters that "the cardinals of the House," had rallied behind the Bingham compromise to give Commerce more jurisdiction and leave everything else alone. O'Neill claimed to favor a separate energy panel. He remarked that a Republican plan, endorsed by Patterson at the last minute, to give the proposed committee jurisdiction over nuclear power and the outer continental shelf, would probably be the best solution. However, because the plan was to be offered by a Republican motion to recommit with instructions, he felt he could not support it.[27]

In essence, O'Neill walked away from the energy jurisdiction plan. The Speaker, observers noted, was conspicuously absent from the floor during debate on the question. Bereft of leadership support, Ashley declined to speak out for the separate committee—even though he was the presumed beneficiary. The abandonment was not lost on House observers. The most bitter criticism came from Toby Moffett (D-Conn.) who declared that "maybe nothing is the answer today until we get the leadership and everyone else who is interested in a regular energy committee to come forward, to get behind somebody to put an energy committee together and to offer it as an alternative."[28] Once O'Neill abandoned the energy committee plan, chairs were free to carve up the existing jurisdiction as they wished. Their solution, the Bingham substitute, was adopted by a 300 to 111 vote and gained the support of every Democratic leader except Bolling, Brademas, and one other. The motion to recommit, embodying the stronger energy committee plan, received no votes at all from Democratic leaders. On the final vote, the only "nay" from a high-ranking Democrat came from Bolling, who must have had a sense of déjà vu as he saw committee realignment once gain fall victim to entrenched interests.

Pay Raise/Ethics Code Deal

Leaders' sponsorship was the determining factor in the ethics code passed by the House in 1977. Earlier that year, Speaker O'Neill, along with Senate Majority Leader Robert Byrd (W. Va.), successfully defended a controversial congressional pay raise, which was politically hazardous and unlikely to be approved in an open vote. A variety of legislative maneuvers was employed to gain additional time and forestall a vote of disapproval within the prescribed thirty-day period. Thus the pay adjustments went into effect in February 1977.

In allowing the president's pay recommendations to take effect, House and Senate leaders repeatedly promised strict ethic codes as the "price" of the pay raises. O'Neill, along with Senate Majority Leader Byrd, kept his word. Within a month after the pay raise took effect, the House adopted its new code of ethics (H. Res. 287). Although the code embraced a variety of provisions, its chief feature was to limit members' outside income to 15 percent of their official salary. Because unearned income was exempted, many members, especially those of modest means, argued passionately that the code discriminated in favor of the wealthy. Responding that the limit on outside income was "the heart and soul of the entire package," O'Neill whipped his troops in line and won the passage of the measure. The critical vote, on a "modified closed rule" for debating the measure, was 267 to 153—a party-line vote with only fifteen Democrats in opposition.[29] The Senate soon followed suit.

Exploiting the Powers of the New Speakership

The O'Neill speakership was built on a combination of "assertiveness on procedure and distance from policy."[30] O'Neill made the most of the parliamentary tools bequeathed by the reform era without alienating the policy protagonists. His successor, Wright, in contrast, exploited the full range of his powers to advance specific policy goals.

The advent of multiple-referred legislation—a "sleeper" in the Bolling reforms that found its way into the House rules in 1975—has added immeasurably to the Speaker's prerogatives. Originally the device was intended to spread the action on legislation to more committees and more members; more importantly, it enlarges the Speaker's fundamental power of scheduling. The Speaker may assign bills or resolutions to two or more committees—jointly, sequentially, or in split fashion. In sequential referrals, the Speaker routinely sets deadlines for consideration by all but the initial committee—an impressive power for today's House to bequeath to its chief officer. This authority involves the Speaker more directly in committee decision making than perhaps at any time since the days of "Uncle Joe" Cannon.

The Speaker can employ multiple referrals to accomplish a variety of objectives. Referrals can be used to build credits among colleagues, to impose deadlines on committees, to coordinate fragmented committee deliberations, and to expedite or delay action on certain measures.[31] For example, the 1986 Democratic trade bill came from six committees; an omnibus drug package was made up of portions from twelve committees. In both instances, Speaker O'Neill decreed a legislative goal for partisan purposes and assigned Majority Leader Wright to coordinate it.

To expedite the trade bill in the 100th Congress, Speaker Wright delegated coordinating duties to his leadership colleagues, eventually producing lopsided floor votes for passage and again for overriding President Reagan's veto (the Senate, however, eventually sustained the veto).

Building on his experience, Speaker Wright exploited his scheduling powers, especially over sequential referrals. Although comprising only a tiny portion of all multiple referrals, they are almost always employed for important leadership packages. Moreover, of those multiply referred bills that reach the House floor, one-third are considered under special rules crafted in the Rules Committee (compared with one-tenth of all other bills). Thus, such legislative packages can directly involve the Speaker from referral through committee deadlines to floor scheduling and final voting.

Speaker Wright's activism, independence, and risk-taking made him controversial. When he took office, Wright unveiled an ambitious list of legislative goals, including highway improvement, clean air, trade, and catastrophic health insurance. Two years later, nearly all those bills had passed the House and many had been signed into law. His tight control over scheduling, including aggressive use of the Rules Committee to shape alternatives during floor deliberations, embittered minority members (one GOP leader accused him of making "minority status more painful") and even some members in his own party.[32]

Speaker Wright exploited his prerogatives so aggressively that his enemies determined to destroy him. "If Wright consolidates his power, he will be a very, very formidable man," declared Rep. Newt Gingrich (R-Ga.). "We have to take him on early to prevent that."[33] Republican foes raised ethical charges against Wright, and eventually the Committee on Standards of Official Conduct charged him with several violations of House rules. Wright did not survive these ethical and political challenges and resigned from the House in 1989.

The fall of Speaker Wright, like that of Cannon eighty years earlier, demonstrates that the broad prerogatives of the speakership rest fundamentally on party, institutional, and public consensus. The Speaker's management of the House is based on the premise that the office is essential for realizing members' objectives—leaders and followers, majority and minority. "Members of the House will always prefer a fair speaker to a powerful one," Peters writes, "and the speaker who forgets this places himself in harm's way."[34] When a Speaker pushes the entire array of prerogatives to the limit, the members' stake in the office is placed at risk. In the cases of both Cannon and Wright, objections were couched in the rhetoric of ethics: the call for broader participation in 1910 and the demand for stricter ethical standards in 1989. But while the Cannon revolt eclipsed the speakership, the Wright case left the office and its prerogatives essentially intact.

Foley and the "Civic Temper Tantrum"

The 1990s brought to Capitol Hill a new wave of public criticism and reformist pressure. One lawmaker called it a massive "civic temper tantrum."[35] Although few institutions were spared, Congress bore more than its share of the public's anger. As a veteran journalist observed, "Congress—which gets trivial television attention, has no sense of news management and cannot speak with a clear voice—tended to get the brunt of the blame for mutual inaction."[36] In spring 1992 only 17 percent of those questioned in a national survey approved of the way Congress was doing its job, whereas 54 percent approved of their own representative's performance. Both figures were all-time lows.[37] Although triggered by scandals (some grave, others trivial), the public outcry was intensified by growing pessimism concerning the current health and future direction of the nation. Many elite observers and members themselves shared the public's antipathies.

Scandals fanned the public's anger. In late 1991, what turned into a seven-month furor erupted over House members' penalty-free overdrafts at their Capitol "bank" (actually, an old-fashioned payroll office). Although no public funds were lost in the transactions, average citizens—who know all too well what happens when their own checks "bounce"—reacted furiously to this seeming evidence of special privilege. A special prosecutor was named to investigate the affair, and the numbers and amounts of overdrafts were published. Members became panicky. Half a dozen of those with overdrafts were dumped in primary elections and another nineteen in the general elections. Still more decided to retire rather than face the voters. Other reports probed members' unpaid bills at House restaurants and employee thefts and drug deals at its post office.

House leaders were at first slow to discern and counteract the damage done by the scandals. Eventually, the House Sergeant at Arms, the official in charge of the bank, resigned, as did the House postmaster. Several postal employees pleaded guilty to various crimes, while a federal grand jury subpoenaed expense account records of three Democratic members as part of a long-running inquiry. Finally, a retired Army lieutenant general was hired as House administrator, or "director of nonlegislative and financial services."

Speaker Thomas S. Foley's (D-Wash.) leadership came under fire from other quarters. Although his low-key style brought Republicans some relief from Wright's tense partisanship, Foley faced criticism within his own party. Many Democrats faulted his tepid partisanship, his cautious approach, and, during the Bush years, his reluctance to define and promote a clearcut partisan agenda. Foley himself admitted that:

> [O]ne of the things that I'm criticized for personally is not being political enough, not being enough of an opposition leader, not taking political opportunities when they come with sufficient aggressivity and toughness, to be the political attacker of the president.[38]

Nervous Democrats turned against Foley's understated leadership; one of them (John Bryant of Texas) stood on the House floor and urged him to resign. Rumors circulated throughout 1992 that his speakership was in peril.[39]

Foley succeeded in surviving the travail through an adroit two-pronged leadership campaign that bolstered support among senior Democrats (chairs who might have challenged him directly) and that won significant backing from the sixty-four new Democrats elected in November 1992. Immediately after the election the Speaker and other top leaders held three regional meetings (in Chicago, Los Angeles, and Atlanta) with the newly elected Democrats. Large numbers of these newcomers pledged their support to Foley during these "get acquainted" sessions. Agenda planning for the new Congress was also discussed during the meetings. Moreover, with a Democratic presidency, Foley's instincts for conciliation became an asset in fostering harmony among House Democrats and supportive relations with the Clinton White House.

As for the larger institutional crisis, Foley's leadership was even less consistent. He campaigned publicly against the more extreme remedies being urged—for example, term limits, the balanced budget amendment, and across-the-board cuts in congressional staffs. He was willing to employ a wide range of techniques, from parliamentary prerogatives to speeches and press conferences and even court litigation (to verify that term limits for federal officeholders could be instituted only by amending the constitution). Other proposals were resisted or stalled until public pressure demanded their acceptance—for example, leadership responses to the House scandals, campaign finance reforms, demands that the House apply to itself all federal laws, and the proposed Joint Committee on the Organization of Congress. With regard to the Joint Committee, the Speaker finally agreed to its creation and appeared at its opening session to offer general support but few concrete proposals. He appointed emissaries to the committee who opposed broadscale reforms and offered little encouragement to the panel's more reform-minded members (mostly Republicans). The Committee's Senate and House contingents eventually went their own separate ways, and the more far-reaching reform topics fell victim to partisan and bicameral hostilities. A similar fate befell campaign finance reform, as House Democrats produced a partisan package that had little chance of gaining widespread acceptance.

The 1990s crisis was distinctive because initially it lacked a clear or compelling political, partisan, factional, or even institutional agenda. Complaints about structures and procedures were legion. House Republicans, frustrated after four decades of minority status, had an exhaustive list of complaints about how Democrats were managing the chamber. Sponsors of the Joint Committee cited overstaffing, committee overlaps, budget strife, breakdowns in communication between the chambers and among the branches, lack of policy integration, and too much partisanship. Representative Hamilton, who co-chaired the Joint Committee, declared that "Congress increasingly seems bogged down and unable to tackle the main issues that Americans are concerned about—from jobs and crime to health care reform." [40] Yet little consensus was reached on the desired direction of the changes. Equally unclear was the extent to which institutional defects had caused, or contributed to, public or elite discontent with Congress's performance.

Can Speakers Orchestrate Change?

House Speakers played critical roles in institutional innovations during the reform era and in the post-reform years since then. They rarely played the leading roles in major innovations. Most often, they served as managers or brokers of proposals made by others, mediating between reform factions and those members defending the status quo. Successful brokerage meant that the Speaker was able to satisfy the reformers' core demands while protecting the interests of those who stood to lose by the change. Not infrequently Speakers resisted change, siding with senior colleagues against junior insurgents, defending traditional arrangements against radical revision.

On rare occasions Speakers have moved out front on structural issues to take on the role of sponsors or advocates. This occurred when they perceived threats to their own ability to fulfill their roles or threats to the integrity and reputation of Congress itself. Thus Rayburn led the fight to enlarge the Rules Committee because his ability to process a Democratic president's program was at stake. Albert launched an investigation of House committees when the jurisdictional inefficiencies and power imbalances threatened his management of the House. O'Neill maneuvered to gain adoption of the 1977 pay raise and ethics codes—tandem innovations designed to cope with sensitive issues threatening Congress's public image. Foley waged war on the term limit movement, which he viewed as a threat to democratic values and the institutional strength of Congress.

Because they typically serve as mediators or managers, House and Senate leaders generally enter innovative politics in midstream at the coalition-building stage rather than earlier. When leaders sponsor innovations, they are usually in on formulating the innovation and even preparing the agenda. For all innovations that are adopted, Speakers play an indispensable role in implementing them. They are not always enthusiastic or even faithful in putting into practice the changes on which they agreed. Noncompliance can erase a negotiated innovation—for example, the ambivalence of successive Speakers toward appointing ad hoc committees to untangle competing jurisdictional claims over major legislation.

No mystery surrounds past Speakers' mixed record regarding institutional innovation. When one remembers who these leaders are, how they attain their positions, and what constituencies they must serve, it is clear why they are not reformers. And yet, leaders need to serve on occasion as agents of change, acting decisively to overcome, or at least rechannel, the dysfunctional organizational tendencies of Congress. Such leadership is difficult but not impossible. Indeed, it has arisen periodically in western parliaments, in state legislatures, and even on Capitol Hill.

On what foundations would such a leadership stand? The traditional answer is party discipline—of the type inherent in the innovations of Thomas B. Reed and other post-Civil War Speakers. Indeed, the House's increasingly ideologically cohesive parties underlie the power of the modern Speakers and animate the harsh partisanship that has marked the chamber in recent years. (This Capitol Hill partisanship contrasts dramatically with the electorate's fading party loyalties, and even with officeholders' self-reliant tendencies.) A dramatic partisan takeover—with new members claiming policy "mandates" that require expediting procedures—is the most likely impetus for leadership commitment to major institutional innovations. The 1994 elections created a unique historical opportunity for Speaker Newt Gingrich to lead his Republican colleagues in adopting a wide array of structural and procedural changes.

Other resources may provide cornerstones for such leadership. The power of personality, media and public attention, or intellectual force could provide leverage for vigorous, innovative leadership. The very decentralization of the contemporary Congress has set in motion counter-trends that may stimulate innovative and change-oriented leadership. Already there is widespread acceptance of the strong speakership, which in fact commands impressive powers, especially in scheduling. Further developments depend on the correct combination of personality, agenda, and circumstance.

Notes

1. Harold F. Gortner, Julianne Mahler, and Jeanne Bell Nicholson, *Organization Theory: A Public Perspective* (Chicago: Dorsey, 1987), 390.

2. Robert L. Peabody, *Leadership in Congress: Stability, Succession, and Change* (Boston: Little, Brown, 1976), 470.

3. This phrase was first applied to Speaker Thomas P. O'Neill. See Paul Houston, "O'Neill Putting the Nation's House in Order," *Los Angeles Times*, Aug. 28, 1978, 1.

4. This is similar to the notion of "transforming leadership" advanced by James MacGregor Burns in *Leadership* (New York: Harper & Row, 1978).

5. There is a growing literature that treats the post-reform era. See Roger H. Davidson, ed., *The Postreform Congress* (New York: St. Martin's, 1992).

6. Ronald M. Peters, Jr., *The American Speakership: The Office in Historical Perspective* (Baltimore: Johns Hopkins University Press, 1990), 294.

7. Paul D. Hasbrouck, *Party Government in the House of Representatives* (New York: Macmillan, 1927). For a positive account of Rayburn's powers, see D. B. Hardeman and Donald C. Bacon, *Rayburn: A Biography* (Austin: Texas Monthly Press,

1987), 343-347.

8. Barbara Sinclair, "House Majority Party Leadership in an Era of Legislative Constraint," in *The Postreform Congress*, ed. Roger H. Davidson, 91-111.

9. The story of the Legislative Reorganization Act of 1970 is recounted in John F. Bibby and Roger H. Davidson, *On Capitol Hill*, 2d ed. (Hinsdale, Ill.: Dryden, 1972), chap. 8.

10. Ibid., 259.

11. Norman C. Miller, "Updating Congress," *Wall Street Journal* (March 27, 1969), 1.

12. Carl Albert with Danny Goble, *Little Giant: The Life and Times of Speaker Carl Albert* (Norman: University of Oklahoma Press, 1990), 311.

13. Ibid., 312. See also Peters, *The American Speakership*, 153-155.

14. Andrew J. Glass, "Congressional Report: Legislative Reform Effort Builds New Alliances among House Members," *National Journal*, July 25, 1970, 1607-1614.

15. Albert with Goble, *Little Giant*, 312.

16. On the House Democratic Caucus changes of the reform era, see Norman J. Ornstein, "Causes and Consequences of Congressional Change: Subcommittee Reforms in the House of Representatives, 1970-1973," *Congress in Change*, ed. Norman J. Ornstein (New York: Praeger, 1975), 88-114; and David W. Rohde, "Committee Reform in the House of Representatives and the Subcommittee Bill of Rights," *Annals of the American Academy of Political and Social Science* 411 (January 1974): 39-47.

17. Peters, *The American Speakership*, 156.

18. House Select Committee on Committees, *Committee Reform Amendments of 1974*, H.R. 93-916, 1974, 11.

19. Commission on the Organization of the Government for the Conduct of Foreign Policy, *Report* (Washington, D.C.: Government Printing Office, 1976), Appendix Volume V (Appendix M).

20. House Select Committee on Committees, *Committee Organization in the House*, 93d Cong., 1st sess., 1993, Part I, 5.

21. Albert with Goble, *Little Giant*, 346.

22. Quoted in *New York Times*, May 10, 1974, 45.

23. Quoted in Peters, *The American Speakership*, 215.

24. Thomas P. O'Neill with William Novak, *Man of the House: The Life and Political Memoirs of Speaker Tip O'Neill* (New York: Random House, 1987), 384.

25. Quoted in Richard E. Cohen, "Tinkering with House Rules," *National Journal*, August 25, 1979, 1417.

26. Quoted by Richard L. Lyons in "On Capitol Hill," *Washington Post*, April 25, 1979.

27. Ibid., March 25, 1980.

28. U.S. Congress, House of Representatives, *Congressional Record*, daily ed., 96th Cong., 2d sess., March 25, 1980, H2152.

29. "House, Senate Adopt New Code of Ethics," *1977 Congressional Quarterly Almanac* (Washington, D.C.: CQ Press, 1978), 767.

30. Peters, *The American Speakership*, 217.

31. On the Speaker's use of multiple referrals to manage the committee system, see Roger H. Davidson and Walter J. Oleszek, "From Monopoly to Management: Changing Patterns of Committee Deliberation" in *The Postreform Congress*, 129-141.

32. Tom Kenworthy, "House GOP Signals It's in a Fighting Mood," *Washington*

Post, Dec. 26, 1988, A8.

33. John M. Barry, *The Ambition and the Power: The Fall of Jim Wright* (New York: Viking, 1989), 6.

34. Peters, *The American Speakership*, 279.

35. Cited by Lawrence N. Hansen, "Our Turn: Politicians Talk about Themselves, Politics, the Public, the Press, and Reform," Centel Public Accountability Project (March 1992), 5.

36. Adam Clymer, "The Gridlock Congress," *New York Times*, Oct. 11, 1992, 1, 30.

37. Richard Morin and Helen Dewar, "Approval of Congress Hits All-Time Low, Poll Finds," *Washington Post*, March 20, 1992, A16.

38. Bill Whalen, "Mr. Nice Guy Under Fire," *Insight*, August 19, 1991, 34.

39. See, for example, Adam Clymer, "Foley in a Harsher Light," *New York Times*, March 14, 1992, 1; David Rogers, "Angry Democrats in a House Divided by Scandal Speak of Mutiny and Turn Their Fury on Foley," *Wall Street Journal*, April 3, 1992, A12.

40. House Committee on Rules, *To Establish a Joint Committee on the Organization of Congress*, 102d Cong., 2d sess., May 21, 1992, 98-104.

9 The Speakership in My Time

Carl Albert

It sometimes is sobering to consider how few advantages my longevity now provides me. Eighty-five years old, I already have lived far longer than either of my parents and many of my friends. The one inestimable benefit that my many years bestow on me is that they provide a rare backdrop for thinking about the many changes that my own eyes have witnessed. Born within a year of my state's (Oklahoma) admission to the Union, I grew up among people who still spoke fondly of the Indian Territory and the Choctaw Nation. I have no trouble at all recalling life in a small, rural Oklahoma community known as Bug Tussle, including the arrival of the community's very first automobile. Beholding it, I never imagined that I would one day play a role in building my country's interstate highway system. I can easily remember Charles Lindbergh's solo flight to Paris—never dreaming that I would one day be responsible for the legislation that put Americans on the moon. I recall, too, my first visit to Washington, D.C., (it happened in the very week that Lucky Lindy touched down in France) and the awe with which I first beheld the United States Capitol—not knowing that that magnificent building would be my workshop for thirty wonderful years.

Not least of my memories are those of my first days and weeks there: my wonder as I moved into my first congressional office, the first time I stood on the floor of the House of Representatives, and my haste to meet the legendary Sam Rayburn, only to be turned aside by his secretary, who told me that Mr. Rayburn did not have time to waste on pages!

In some respects, the House of Representatives that I first entered in 1947 is as far removed from the contemporary House as is Lindbergh's "Spirit of St. Louis" from a modern space shuttle. For one thing, the Republicans held a majority of seats in the first post-World War II Congress. That circumstance (as with their equally brief majority of 1953-1954) proved to be temporary—all the more so given the four unbroken decades of Democratic rule in Congress. Much longer lasting was the nature of the Democratic party, the distribution of power within the Congress, and the role of its formal leadership, including the Speaker.

My party still bore the marks of the process that had created its modern form and provided its normal congressional majorities. We Democrats remained the beneficiaries of the so-called Roosevelt Coalition that already had outlived Franklin Roosevelt and had much life left within it. During the Great Depression, President Roosevelt had assembled and polished that coalition, which consisted of groups long left out of the political mainstream.

Southerners made up one such group. If it were true that the South entered the twentieth century as a "Solid South" of certain Democratic success, it also had been true that the South was one of the few dependable sources of Democratic influence in Washington during the century's early decades. In fact, the South provided the great majority of those who represented the minority party in the halls of Congress through the 1920s. After Roosevelt's 1932 presidential landslide and his party's sweep of Congress, southern Democrats found themselves part of the new majority.

With them in that new status were the representatives of the still sturdy urban political machines, primarily of the industrial northeast and midwest. Some (such as New York City's Tammany Hall) dated to the nineteenth century. Others (such as the Pendergast machine of Kansas City and the Crump machine of Memphis) were of more recent vintage. All were Democratic. The difference after 1932 was that their local power now had national implications.

To those earlier elements of Democratic strength, the Roosevelt Coalition added others—enough others to assure Democrats a normal majority in both presidential and congressional contests. Working men and women, already blaming the Republicans for the loss of jobs and income, moved over into the Democratic electoral column. A bundle of favorable laws kept them there. Ethnic groups, the so-called "hyphenates," such as German-Americans and Jewish-Americans, left the GOP in favor of the choice long made by Irish-Americans. The most conspicuous of those shifting voting blocs were the African-Americans. Although still disfranchised in the South, they had voted for the party of Lincoln whenever and wherever they could vote—increasingly, in the great northern cities. In the 1930s, they turned Lincoln's picture to the wall and became a dependable source of Democratic ballots.

The glue that held all of those groups together had been the "bread-and-butter" programs that began with Roosevelt's New Deal. As representatives of these habitual political outsiders became insiders, they rewarded their constituents with concrete economic benefits: jobs programs for those able to work, a new welfare system for those who could not, federal sponsorship of unions for workers, price supports for farmers, regional development for the South and West, and the like.

Once in Congress, I saw the consequences on every side. Southerners busily hurried down the corridors, rushing off to direct committee sessions. People such as Tom O'Brien, leader of Chicago's machine Democrats, lounged along the House chamber's back rail, his voice rarely heard but his pockets crammed with Democratic votes. Union leaders conferred with their representatives all over the Capitol. The accents of blacks and white ethnics echoed in the Democratic cloakroom.

Except for the two-year aberrations after 1946 and 1952, these were the groups that gave us our congressional majorities. That was one form of power. Another form—keenly felt within the House—had other historical roots and other historical consequences. "Congress at work," Woodrow Wilson had written in the 1880s, "is Congress in committee." So it was, and so it remained. And Congress in committee usually meant southern Democrats in power.

The reason was one of the unintended effects of the great reform of the House of Representatives that occurred early in this century. Disgusted with Republican Speaker Joseph Cannon's high-handed ways, House Democrats and insurgent Republicans had revolted in 1910 to break the worst forms of the Speaker's arbitrary powers. One was his ability to appoint all members—both majority and minority members—of all committees. Another was his power to designate all committee chairs.

After the revolt against Cannon, each party adopted its own mechanism to fill committee assignments. Mine assigned the task to the Democrats who sat on the House Ways and Means Committee, renaming them for that purpose the Democratic Committee on Committees. On each committee, seniority—the length of time that a member had served on the committee—would determine its chair. The results were visible another half-century and longer.

Well into the 1960s, southern election laws still disfranchised a good portion of the region's potential electorate: the huge numbers of blacks. Moreover, lower income southern whites lacked the electoral discipline imposed elsewhere by labor unions and ethnic organizations. Instead they shared a political culture that discouraged their own political participation except when it was necessary to hold the racial lines intact. Over the years, a conservative southern oligarchy of planters, merchants, and small industrialists had perfected the technique of political power in Washington: find a candidate faithful to their interests, send him to the Capitol as a young man, keep returning him, and let seniority have its natural effect. That effect was southern domination of nearly every major House committee.

The Power of the South

By the time that I arrived in Congress, not even a fourth of the American electorate lived in our southern states. But never has such a small minority exercised such disproportionate influence. As long as the House held fast to the absolute rule of seniority in selecting all committee chairs, the South controlled the posts that controlled the Congress. Americans outside the South elected the president and most of the members of Congress, but those who voted in the South (remembering that a good number of southerners either could not or did not vote) provided the chairs of no fewer than fifteen of the House's twenty legislative committees—including every single one of the most important committees—well into the 1950s and beyond.

As chairs, the southerners' power was all but absolute in their committee rooms. They convened the committees, if and when they wanted to. They took up bills and assigned them, if they favored them. They scheduled hearings, if there were to be any. They designated subcommittees, if they decided to have any. They directed mark-ups, if they wanted to. They reported bills out of committee, if they chose to. They directed the floor debate, thereby influencing its outcome.

Subordinate to the chairs were the committee members, many growing restive. Others did not display such impatience, in part because they expected one day to run the committee their own way, in part because the chairs' views tended to coincide closely with their own. After all, Democratic committee assignments came from the Democrats who sat on Ways and Means, and that, too, was a southern-dominated group. Through the 1950s, eight of the fifteen Democrats on Ways and Means were southerners, generally southerners of the old school. In passing out committee assignments, they tended to listen most favorably to those who approached them with their requests uttered in their own regional accent. The result was that marginal committees such as Interior and Insular Affairs only had six southerners in its eighteen Democratic slots. In a powerful committee such as Armed Services, the proportion was fourteen southerners out of twenty-two.

Seniority also played its heavy hand within the committees. Seniority determined everything from where the member sat to when the member could speak. It was, therefore, the nature of things that the safe districts of the South provided the real power within the committees, too. Consider, for example, the committee on which I did most of my work: Agriculture. As I entered my second decade in Congress, the committee's chair was Harold Cooley of North Carolina. Ranking behind Cooley in order were: Bill Poage (Texas), George Grant (Ala.), E. C. Gathings (Ark.), John McMillan (S.C.), Tom Abernathy (Miss.), myself (Okla.), and Watkins Abbitt (Va.). Dixie may have lost The War, but it was winning the peace a hundred years later. It was winning it every time the Congress got ready to legislate.

For a good portion of the time, Congress did not get around to legislating. Southern Democrats held the reins in the committee rooms. On the House floor, they also often occupied the drivers' seats because they had good friends over on the passengers' side. These were the Republicans, with whom they often worked in an informal but powerful alliance. Absent the crisis of a Great Depression, most southern Democrats returned to the conservative ways of the reigning regional oligarchy. On major issues, they stood ready to vote with the Republicans to block public policies—particularly new social and economic policies—that they regarded as hostile to their interests. This was the so-called Conservative Coalition. It was that coalition that had the votes to stop Franklin Roosevelt's New Deal dead in the waters after 1938. It was the coalition that sank Harry Truman's Fair Deal after 1948. For that matter, it was the coalition that ruled Congress after 1958 and for some time to come.

These were the political realities that shaped American politics and the House of Representatives when I arrived in Washington as a first-term member in 1947. I learned quickly that just as important to my understanding of the House and my own ability to succeed within it were its folkways. The young newcomer was forever reminded of his lowly status. His or her office was the farthest from the House floor, the smallest, and the least equipped. (My first office literally lacked a place on which to hang my hat.) He or she had to accept graciously the least desirable committee assignments. (Boldly seeking a place on Ways and Means, I found myself assigned to the Post Office Committee.) The new member had the most menial of tasks. (Making the same assumption as Mr. Rayburn's secretary, a veteran once handed me a set of papers and brusquely charged me to take them to an office—which I did without correction or complaint.) Generally speaking to senior members only when spoken to, a newcomer dared speak before the House for no more than a few minutes, preferably on an inconsequential matter. (My first floor speech took hours to prepare but only minutes to deliver.) Finally, there was the maxim that everyone knew, everyone repeated, and almost everyone respected: "To get along, go along."

Getting Along

That I got along owed something to the early attention I received from the one person who taught me most of what I learned early about the House of Representatives and its Speaker, the great Sam Rayburn. Mr. Rayburn—I never called him Sam—was already an institution when I arrived in Washington. First elected to the House in 1912, he had established a lasting legislative reputation as a chief architect of the New Deal. Author of the bill that brought electric lights to the nation's countryside, conqueror of utility magnates and securities sharks, Mr. Rayburn was the champion of what he liked to call "the real people," people such as the ones who gathered on his front porch in Bonham, Texas. Except for the two brief interludes of Republican House majorities, he also served as Speaker from 1940 until his death in 1961, longer than any person has held that position and more than twice as long as the only Speaker who could contest him either for longevity or for influence, Henry Clay.

My Third District of Oklahoma lay just across the Red River from Mr. Rayburn's Fourth Congressional District of Texas. That made us neighbors. Once I managed to get past his secretary, I made sure that we were friends. When we were home, I usually found a way to visit with him, as often as not while he lounged around a country store or sale barn. In Washington, I nearly burst my buttons when he went out of his way to congratulate me for my brief maiden speech on the floor. I regarded his first invitation to join him and his political buddies in drinking a toast to liberty in his legendary Board of Education a learning experience equal to the Rhodes Scholarship to Oxford.

As he kept inviting me back and began to seek my judgment on how certain members might vote on pending business, my careful study of my colleagues paid off. Loving the House, I had watched its members, talked with them, studied them, and gradually learned how most of them thought and how they were likely to vote. It was that unintended preparation that allowed me tell Speaker Rayburn—usually within a vote or two—how an issue would be decided. Mr. Rayburn gave me the opportunity to use that preparation.

The Path to the Speakership

"Luck," someone once said, "is what happens when preparation meets opportunity." By that definition, I admit that it was luck that put me on my route to the speakership. In 1955, I had returned to Washington with the Capitol buzzing about the need to select a new whip for the Democratic party. Percy Priest, who had been serving in that capacity, had announced that he would relinquish it in order to chair the Interstate and Foreign Commerce Committee. Several names—most belonging to members senior to me—floated through the House corridors. For that reason, I was utterly stunned when Speaker Rayburn called me to Majority Leader John McCormack's office to tell me that I was their choice for the whip position. That is all there was to it—the choice was theirs and theirs alone. Call it luck—but remember the definition.

It was thus that I joined the official leadership of the U.S. House of Representatives. Entering my eighth year in the House, I occupied the third highest rung on the ladder of its Democratic leadership.

The term "whip" derived from "whipper-in," the fellow whose job it was to keep the hounds organized in an English fox hunt. In the U.S. Congress, it emerged as a leadership position under Woodrow Wilson's presidency, when William Bankhead assumed the responsibility of organizing Democratic House majorities behind the president's New Freedom proposals. Later, under President Roosevelt's early New Deal, a system of regional whips expanded the office's authority and tools. By the time that Speaker Rayburn and Majority Leader McCormack named me whip, the job involved being the Democrats' chief vote-counter (if need be, vote-getter) for the party's legislative program.

My office's institutional tools were few. My good friend (and another of Mr. Rayburn's handpicked protégés) Hale Boggs helped out as my deputy whip, and we had a group of regional assistants ready to help with their delegations. That made it relatively easy to know when we had the votes to pass our bills. The problem was that when we did not have the votes, there was little that I (or anybody else) could do to force them our way. Ultimately each member of Congress owed his or her job not to the formal House leadership but to people far removed from Washington. Once in Congress, they could remain there and (through seniority's magic) advance without toeing any party line. As a consequence, I was less a whip for this unruly pack than a persuader, one whose job was to know who to persuade and with what argument. In other words, my powers—such as they were—were less institutional than personal.

In that regard, they were just like those of the other members of the leadership team. McCormack, our majority leader, was a master in that role, but what gave him his mastery was his network of personal friendships and his rare gifts in public debate. Even Mr. Rayburn owed his effectiveness less to the powers of his office than to his qualities as a person.

Sam Rayburn

In formal terms—the powers and privileges attached to the office that he occupied—Sam Rayburn was anything but a powerful Speaker. Lacking the institutional tools to coerce, he had only the personal instruments to persuade. And no one could be more persuasive than Sam Rayburn. Decades of mastering legislative details, years of personal favors and kindnesses that left every member in his debt, the very aura of integrity and fairness that surrounded him—all of these were Speaker Rayburn's tools of office.

There were, however, limits even to Mr. Rayburn's powers of persuasion. Recognizing the divisions that ran through our party, Mr. Rayburn did not dare try to mobilize it as a unified force. The fact was that it was *not* unified. Nothing if not a realist, Mr. Rayburn never pretended it was otherwise. One sign of that was that he deliberately allowed the Democratic Caucus to atrophy as an instrument of party discipline. Previous Speakers, most conspicuously Champ Clark and John Nance Garner, had regularly assembled all Democratic members into caucus to define and mobilize official party positions on major issues. Fearful of eruption between our various factions, Speaker Rayburn limited the caucus to brief biennial assemblies, their only purpose to ratify the party's slate of House leaders.

Lacking the power to select committee chairs and appoint committee members, Speaker Rayburn presided over what amounted to feudal baronies. A word from him might move an obstinate chair, and several words might compel committee action on a particular bill. But Mr. Rayburn knew that such words were effective precisely because they were few. The result was that the committees legislated less under his authority than under his oversight, and even Sam Rayburn knew that he had to overlook many things.

On the floor, Speaker Rayburn had the towering authority of his person, the debating eloquence of his majority leader, and the preliminary work of his whip and my assistants. What he did not have was the ability to break the conservative coalition whenever that coalition was determined to resist. Until the very end of his speakership, he lacked even the power to get bills to the

House floor. That power—perhaps the ultimate power—rested in the very symbol of the conservative coalition's strength: the House Committee on Rules.

The Ultimate Power: The Rules Committee

Until the 1910 revolt against Cannon, the Rules Committee had been known as the Speaker's Committee. Cannon and his predecessors had not only appointed every member of the committee but also had served as its chairs. Breaking Cannon's power, the reformers had made the Rules Committee independent of the Speaker and, in the process, a power unto itself. Over time, it had become the central agency directing, coordinating, and executing southern and conservative control of the entire legislative process. With a few inconsequential exceptions, virtually every bill had to go through the Rules Committee before it could be scheduled for floor debate and final vote. It was reported that the coalition killed no fewer than twenty bills of President Roosevelt and Harry Truman, thereby stalling out the New Deal and destroying the Fair Deal. The coalition frustrated the Democratic leadership of Congress on many occasions thereafter.

The number doubtlessly would have been greater but for the personal influence of Sam Rayburn. A southerner himself, Speaker Rayburn got along well with Gene Cox, the Georgian who led the conservative faction on the committee during much of Rayburn's early tenure in the speakership. In addition, Republican Floor Leader Joseph Martin was often willing to use his influence with the committee's Republicans when Speaker Rayburn and President Eisenhower really needed it.

Those, however, were arrangements made possible only by the Speaker's personal stature. By the late 1950s, even that kind of solution was becoming increasingly problematic. In the same year that I joined the leadership team as Democratic whip, Judge Howard Smith took over the Rules Committee. Every bit as conservative as Cox, Judge Smith (he kept the title after earlier service in the Virginia judiciary) was infinitely smarter. In fact, with the single exception of Rayburn, Smith was the smartest person and most skilled legislator that I ever saw in Congress. Always calm, unfailingly polite, he was the kind of person who could place one hand on your shoulder while the other was cutting out your heart. Most of all, he had a determination such as I have never seen in another human being. To call him a reactionary was to honor him, for reaction was his political religion. Smith was the prophet, the messiah, and the apostle of reaction, all rolled into one talented and un-flinching whole.

Judge Smith controlled the Rules Committee, and the almost equally con-servative Republicans were perfectly happy to see him do so. Particularly after 1959, when Charlie Halleck replaced Joe Martin as the minority leader, Smith and his fellow southerners were in open alliance with the committee's four Republicans. The resulting bloc killed one bill after another, oblivious to the wishes of the legislative committees, the House majority, and the Democratic leadership. As we entered 1961, it was posed to dismantle the legislative pro-gram of John F. Kennedy, our party's first president in eight years.

That was the situation that provoked one of the most famous congressional battles of the twentieth century: the fight to enlarge the Rules Committee and, thereby, break the hold of Howard Smith and his obstructionist gang. It was an intense fight, and it went down to the wire. Sam Rayburn won the fight, beat-ing Judge Smith by exactly five votes. I doubt that any other person alive could have gotten those five votes. Rayburn got them, not because of the powers of his office, but because of the powers of his person. This was Rayburn at his best.

It happened, of course, that it was Rayburn's last fight. Shortly after win-ning it, he returned to his home in Texas, saying that he suffered from lum-bago. He was wrong, for it was cancer, an especially aggressive form, and it rapidly ate away at him. As soon as Congress adjourned, I visited him at his home in Bonham. McCormack, acting Speaker in his absence, was with me. We hardly recognized the withered shell that had become Rayburn's body. Because he was too frail to talk, John and I prepared to leave. As we did, McCormack turned and said, "Sam, do you remember how many votes we beat Judge Smith by?" Too weak to answer, Sam Rayburn smiled and held up the outstretched fingers—all five of them—of his right hand. It was the last time that I ever saw him.

John McCormack

McCormack and I returned to Washington, he as Speaker and I (once I won election in the Democratic Caucus) as majority leader. If most Americans remember McCormack at all now, it is as the tall, gaunt, sepulchral figure who presided impassively over the House during annual State of the Union ad-dresses of the 1960s. They will never know the McCormack that I knew. Fierce champion of scores of legislative measures that built modern America, he was long my party's chief champion and most respected debater on the House floor. This son of Boston's Irish ghetto served his state, his party, and his nation with passion, skill, and brilliance for the long time that began in 1928 when he first came to Congress and ended with his own speakership.

History has unduly slighted and misread his role in the speakership. McCormack had his critics, and many of them had influential pens. Mistaking his legendary privacy for aloofness, many political writers regarded him as ineffectual if not inept. My good friend Dick Bolling hardly helped McCormack's public reputation when he published two books (*House Out of Order*, 1965, and *Power in the House*, 1968) that openly attacked the Speaker's competence. In 1969, Arizona's able young representative Morris Udall launched a rare challenge to John McCormack's reelection as House Speaker. The caucus vote was one-sided (178 to 58), but it was unheard of for a modern Speaker even to have a challenge.

That such was McCormack's fate owed less to his abilities than to circumstances that were transforming the entire American political system, including the House of Representatives. Much of it was generational. Every year the Capitol received more and more young members, all of them ambitious, many of them impatient. For them, the New Deal and Pearl Harbor were items of distant history. Forget that it was members such as McCormack who had crafted the one and responded so successfully to the other. The civil rights movement was transforming the electorate, making Democratic voters of the South's blacks and Republicans of its whites. Forget that it was members such as McCormack that made that happen. A new generation insisted that the hidebound ways of Congress needed reform and needed it now. Forget that it was those ways and the members that had mastered them that made all of those changes happen.

I was McCormack's friend. As majority leader, I was also his chief lieutenant. The difficulties that he faced placed me in an odd position. Journalists freely predicted that younger members were ready to turn McCormack's job over to me. From time to time, some of his younger and brasher critics even approached me about a direct challenge. Probably more would have done so had they not known the futility of it. Having worked with McCormack, I regarded him as the world's chief legislator. If Carl Albert was the only person in Congress who could unseat him, McCormack was going to stay right where he was.

Thus, my role became that of a conciliator instead of a co-conspirator. Generationally and politically in the middle with the Speaker and his allies on one side and the young reformers on the other, I was trusted by both. I respected the traditions of the House and remained loyal to those who had built those traditions. I also knew that the time had come for some of those traditions to be reexamined. With my help, we began that reexamination.

Change

Probably most auspicious for the future was a little noticed change in 1969. For some time, various younger members had hoped to reawaken the Democratic Caucus and make it their instrument for decision making. Rayburn would hear none of that. Neither would McCormack when he became Speaker. Eventually, I arranged a meeting between Speaker McCormack and some determined reformers. With some heat, the reformers indicated that they intended to demand a resolution at the January organizational caucus calling for monthly meetings through the session. McCormack greeted that news with a stony silence that was broken only by my own words. "John," I said, "what would you say if I told you that I was going to introduce that resolution?" Then and there, the impasse was broken. Beginning in January 1969, the Democratic Caucus met in regularly scheduled meetings. In them we cleared the air—sometimes heating it, too—but we had taken the first step toward restoring the ability of the House's majority party to govern itself and the House in a more democratic fashion.

One of the caucus's first substantive decisions was to appoint a Committee on Organization, Study, and Review. Headed by Julia Butler Hansen, a very capable member from Washington, the committee was purely a creation of the House Democrats, charged by us to reexamine many of our party's most crusty ways. One of those ways was included explicitly after my speech in the caucus meeting that defined its responsibilities. Over the united protest of the southern chairs, the caucus voted to accept my recommendation to charge the Hansen committee to study the previously untouchable seniority system by which we awarded committee chairs.

Working with a deliberateness fitted to its assignment, the committee devoted four years to its study. Meanwhile, I worked with my friend Dick Bolling on a more immediate change that would affect the entire House. Close since our days in Mr. Rayburn's Board of Education, Dick kept his friendship with me as his one tie to McCormack's leadership. Bolling's craftsmanship created the Legislative Reorganization Act of 1970, the first proposal to modernize congressional procedures since the La Follette-Monroney Act of 1946. His parliamentary skills got the bill through a hostile Rules Committee and onto the floor. There, I spoke pointedly on behalf of a vital amendment to the already complex bill. That was the amendment to provide for recorded votes on amendments to bills in committee and to measures before the Committee of the Whole House. Thus ended the practice of members concealing their positions on decisive votes with unrecorded decisions. It was a giant step toward opening our decisions to the scrutiny of those who had elected us.

Assuming the Speakership

All of these changes were in motion as I became Speaker in 1971. Still, many things about that office had not changed, including its constitutional status and nature. The speakership is an office explicitly established in the U.S. Constitution. The one who holds it has the first responsibility of presiding over the House of Representatives. That means the entire House of Representatives— the Republicans along with the Democrats, the conservatives along with the liberals, the young along with the old, the restive along with the satisfied. For that reason, a Speaker's first responsibility is to be fair.

Never forgetting those differences, a Speaker has to recall the one thing that he or she shares with all of those people. That is that the Speaker serves with them in a body charged under the Constitution to represent all of the American people. The House of Representatives, after all, is supposed to be precisely that: representative. Ours is the task of representing the American people in all of their conflict, all of their contention, even all of their confusion. Critical to our doing that is another special responsibility of my office: to manage our business in such a way that the deliberative genius of the House can work its way toward effective public policy.

I was determined to manage that business fairly, efficiently, and effectively. I came to the speakership knowing full well that such management would require that I go beyond the roles played by my two immediate predecessors and personal mentors. America and its Congress had changed since the days of Speakers Rayburn and McCormack. Under my management, the House would have to change, too.

Circumstances had forced that role upon me. They also presented me with yet another role. As Speaker of the House, I occupied the highest elective post of any Democrat in the land. Because I was fated to be the first Speaker in modern times to serve entirely with the opposition in the presidency (Jim Wright later had the same fate), I was expected to be something of a national champion for my party. I took that role seriously, but I never forgot its limits. I had no claim to speak for Democratic senators, governors, mayors, or presidential aspirants. For one thing, they displayed no reluctance to speak for themselves. Even in the House of Representatives, I had but one vote in the Democratic Caucus and (by tradition) usually none at all on the floor. When I spoke—as when I led—I had to be sure that there were plenty of others ready to agree and to follow.

The numbers were there. Despite Republican presidential victories in 1968 and 1972 (the latter by a record margin), at no time was our Democratic congressional majority even threatened. The task was to organize those numbers into something that could be led. The Democratic Caucus was my first instrument of choice.

While some members hoped to turn the reborn caucus into a sounding board for their pet notions, my intention was to use it as the vehicle to change the way that we Democrats did our business. By 1973, Hansen's Committee on Organization, Study, and Review had completed its deliberations and filed its recommendations. At their heart was the proposal that the rule of seniority be scrapped in favor of filling all committee chairs by secret-ballot election of the caucus itself. After an angry debate, the caucus agreed to the proposal. The anger outlasted the decision. In fact, a second caucus meeting on the very next day brought impassioned demands to repeal the rule. That might have happened were it not for my own speech that welcomed and embraced the change. The repeal effort failed, and the seniority system—for sixty-two years the path to legislative domination—died that day. It would be some time before the caucus actually voted to oust sitting chairs (that came in 1975, when three were replaced), but from that moment on every chairman knew that power flowed not from personal longevity but from the entire Democratic membership. It was to their colleagues, not to their age, that they were beholden and accountable.

Gone, too, were many of the chairs' more arbitrary privileges. The caucus gave rank-and-file committee members a way to call committee meetings over the chair's opposition. Members also won the right to call up bills and to force them out of committee without the chair's approval. The caucus took from the chair the right to form subcommittees and the right to appoint subcommittee chairs. The caucus itself assumed those powers. In addition, we approved a "subcommittee bill of rights" that ensured the autonomy of each subcommittee and guaranteed to each a staff and budget necessary for its work. The chairs were still important people—make no mistake about it—but the House of

Representatives no longer resembled a feudal barony under their personal fiefdoms.

In a sense, the power that had been so scattered and so arbitrary flowed toward the office that I held. The same caucus that broke the seniority system also finally reined in the Rules Committee by giving the Speaker the power to nominate its chair and its Democratic members (their actual appointment, of course, came from election by the caucus itself). In addition, the Democratic Caucus gave the Speaker his own committee, a new Democratic Steering and Policy Committee designed as an instrument for policy formation and issue analysis. The Speaker would chair the committee and select a majority of its members. The 1973 caucus also placed the Speaker, majority leader, and whip on the Democratic Committee on Committees, which still consisted otherwise of the Democratic members on Ways and Means. Two years later, the Steering and Policy Committee—the Speaker's committee—officially assumed those responsibilities.

In every one of these respects, the speakership gained powers unseen since 1910. My purpose was not to increase the office's power for my own gain. In fact, I had to speak out to defeat the proposal that would most have strengthened my personal power: granting the Speaker the right to bypass completely the Rules Committee in order to place a bill on the House floor, making the Rules Committee irrelevant. It was not power that I sought, certainly not of that kind. Instead, it was responsibility. More accurately, it was a machinery rebuilt so that those who were responsible for legislating had the tools to do the job in a responsible way. The Speaker's responsibility was not to legislate but to see that those who did were responsible to their party, their office, and their nation.

The Committee System

If I had had my way, we would not have stopped there. By changing the way that its Democratic majority did business, the reforms that came through the Democratic Caucus changed the way that the entire House operated. It was still necessary, I believed, to change the fundamental nature of the House itself. That was its committee system.

I believed strongly in that system. After all, it was the one way to ensure that public policy came from mature and expert deliberation, not from momentary passions aroused by ill-considered nostrums. As such, it properly was at the very heart of the Congress's role in government.

The problem was that the particular committee system that I inherited as Speaker was unchanged from that established before I even reached Congress. In the intervening years, the nation had changed, but the system had not. New concerns had arisen, but not new ways to address them. Some of our legislative committees no longer served any useful function at all. Why did we even have a Post Office Committee after its chief functions were assumed by a quasi-independent federal corporation? Others had acquired jurisdiction over matters unsuited to their expertise. Banking and Currency, for example, had authority over mass transit legislation, even though no one could figure out just what that had to do with either banking or currency. In contrast, energy policy—a new issue but one certain never to go away—potentially fell within the jurisdiction of no fewer than eighty-three committees and subcommittees.

Ready to reform our way of doing business so we could get our business done, I picked Bolling, one of my most trusted friends, to head a committee to a recommend thorough-going revision of the entire system. Bolling's committee held six months of hearings, and I was the committee's first witness. It was the first time that a Speaker had appeared before a committee in more than a century.

When the committee's report was ready, it called for a complete restructuring that touched on twenty of our twenty-one committees. Three (Post Office, Internal Security, and Merchant Marine and Fisheries) were to be abolished outright. Every other committee (except for Veterans' Affairs, the one that would see no change) would have altered responsibilities, usually dramatically so.

That was what accounted for the stubborn resistance to the proposals. Every member of every committee slated to lose responsibilities rallied to the old ways of doing business and of exercising their influence. Outside interests sprang to the defense of their well-cultivated friendships in the committee rooms. In the end, an odd coalition of liberals, conservatives, labor lobbyists, and business interests combined to defeat our effort to bring the Congress into the twenty-first century. A weak substitute was passed instead. My consolation was that the reforms that had won had at least (and at last) put the Congress squarely in the twentieth century.

I was not the only one that put it there, but I got less credit for it than I might have deserved. I did not mind that. I had never thought it particularly important for a Speaker to claim personal credit for every change won, especially when there were plenty of people who were perfectly willing to take the credit. What was important was that the changes came.

Looking over them at the time, I often thought back to Mr. Rayburn's discussions of how weak the office of Speaker was when he had first assumed it in 1940. Only gradually and imperfectly did his personal gifts allow him to overcome some of those institutional weaknesses. No one ever confused me with the great Sam Rayburn. But it is a fact that my speakership finally and firmly established the modern era of the House of Representatives. One reason is that I never forgot one of those lessons that Mr. Rayburn liked to pass out in the Board of Education. "You can accomplish almost anything," Sam Rayburn had taught me, "as long as you don't mind who gets the credit."

So, I let others take the credit. I had the reforms. And I had to use them. Richard Nixon saw to that.

The Nixon Years

Richard Nixon had entered Congress with me in 1947. In fact, he had been the very first Republican member to introduce himself to me. Our paths soon parted, but political circumstances eventually brought them together—this time at cross-purposes. In 1969, he moved into the White House. Two years later, I took my place at the Speaker's rostrum. The difference between the two points was much greater than the mile down Pennsylvania Avenue.

Unlike many of my fellow Democrats, I had never harbored any personal ill-feelings toward Nixon. Harry Truman, for one, always referred to him as "that snakey-eyed son-of-a-bitch," and a good number of others overlooked only the snakey-eyed part. For my part, however, I remained on good personal terms with him, and I frankly admired his political skills. All but written off after losing the close presidential race in 1960 and the not-so-close California gubernatorial campaign in 1962, he had restored both himself and his party to respectability after the Goldwater debacle of 1964. No Republican since Lincoln had done more for his party. And no Republican since Lincoln had had to fight longer and harder to win its presidential nomination.

Still, for all my admiration of his skills, I also found something troubling in his personality. Beneath the veneer of friendliness, there ran in Nixon a pettiness rare in such a successful politician. Driven to see his life and career as a series of personal crises, he seemed incapable either of forgetting or of forgiving. Richard Nixon accumulated grudges in the same way that other politicians did favors.

Perhaps that is why he found it so natural to run for something by running against something else. Every one of his successful campaigns was against something or somebody. In 1946, it was against Democratic incumbent Jerry Voorhis, whom he identified with socialists and Communists. He went to the Senate in 1950 after tarring Helen Gahagan Douglas with the label of the "pink lady." As Eisenhower's attack dog, he had lathered up resentment against the entire Democratic party, accusing people such as Truman and Rayburn of what amounted to treason. In 1968, circumstances gave him his best enemies yet: an endless war in Asia, race riots, and student demonstrations at home. For his first midterm congressional election, he invented a new enemy. It was nothing less than the Congress of the United States, a Congress that he depicted as captive to the forces of permissiveness, terrorism, and crime. It did not do him much good—we picked up nine House seats that year—but it did set the tone for much that was to come.

Had I had my way about it, I would have served the Democratic House as Rayburn had under Eisenhower's presidency—looking for cooperation instead of confrontation. With Nixon in the White House, that was never an option. Having baited Congress during the campaign, he was determined to fight it through the rest of his presidency. His favorite weapon was a steady rain of presidential vetoes—twenty of them in my first term as Speaker. Most of the vetoes were directed at our bills necessary to address the economic mismanagement of Nixon himself.

When Nixon had entered the White House, the economy was humming on all eight cylinders. Stock prices and bank deposits both were at record highs. Unemployment was effectively nonexistent. "Nixonomics" (a word as ugly as that which it defined) changed all of that—for the worse. Steadily, the economy dropped into a full-blown recession. By 1970, national production was in actual decline. Unemployment returned. By 1971, the unemployment rate was 80 percent higher than where it was on Nixon's inauguration day. Those with jobs had suffered the first decline in real wages since the 1930s.

It fell to the entire Congress—not to the Speaker of the House—to craft a legislative response. But as Speaker I began to schedule joint press conferences with Senate Majority Leader Mike Mansfield. Such conferences had been rare since the 1930s, but we needed them to lay bare the administration's sorry record. On the House side, I brought the chairs of our legislative committees out of their committee rooms and before floodlights and microphones of other press conferences to discuss our solutions. With the restored tools of leadership, my allies and I coordinated scheduling and rallied every vote we could get. In the end, we got most of our bills—and they got Nixon's vetoes.

Our patient legislating continued, but the economic slide did, too, and the rain of vetoes became a veritable flood after Nixon's reelection in 1972. With a margin large enough to assuage even his monumental insecurities, he escalated the war against Congress. Suddenly "impoundments" accompanied the vetoes. That was the executive's term for refusing to spend the money authorized by the legislative branch. As such, impoundments represented worse than failed economics, worse than bad politics. Impoundments cast a shadow on our entire constitutional structure of government.

Of course, Nixon pretended to see no shadow at all. But the U.S. Constitution clearly assigned to Congress the power to fund all activities of government through "appropriations made by Law." The same Constitution also clearly charged the president to see to it that "the Laws be faithfully executed." Over both principles now lay the shadow of raw presidential power arrogantly displayed.

Some members wanted to fight the president in the federal courts and filed twenty-one lawsuits to overturn the practice in twenty-one specific instances. Twenty-one times the federal judiciary upheld their claims and our reading of the Constitution. Some even talked of turning our appropriations power directly against the White House: choke off the money to run it until its occupants were forced to surrender.

The first method was too cumbersome in its one-to-one response. The president could impound specific funds faster than we could file lawsuits. The latter proposition seemed to me to be as malicious as the impoundments themselves. Substituting congressional arrogance for the executive's, it would only sharpen the threat to our Constitution.

It is disturbing to consider how—or if—the Congress that I had entered would have responded. The Congress that I led was determined to respond, and it had the tools to do so responsibly. At the very first meeting of our Steering and Policy Committee, I appointed a task force to develop a legislative solution. I regularly reported its progress to the caucus meetings and collected there our members' most novel and imaginative suggestions. With the leadership of the Appropriations Committee and its thirteen subcommittees, we drafted a workable and passable bill. Mike Mansfield and I kept the public informed and pushed together to get nearly identical bills through each chamber.

The result was one of the crowning achievements of my speakership: the Budget and Impoundment Act of 1973. One title of the law carefully restricted the president's powers to impound congressional appropriations and preserved the right of Congress to reverse even those impoundments. Just as important, the remainder of the act gave Congress, for the first time since George Washington, a way to build a comprehensive federal budget from the bottom up rather than cheeseparing one from the top down. What had begun as a political fight and moved to a constitutional confrontation had ended with a victory—a victory not for me, but for the Congress that had proven itself able to act effectively and responsibly.

For all the anti-Congress rhetoric of the White House and all of the doubts of journalists and other political writers, the Congress that I led was usually able to do that. Although deeply divided among ourselves on Vietnam, we were united when the time finally came to bring the curtain down on the entire sorry spectacle. Once the last of our ground forces had withdrawn and our prisoners of war had returned in 1973, Congress erected a legislative barrier against any more waste of American lives or dollars in that cause. In November of that year, we passed over Nixon's veto the War Powers Act, thereby affirming Congress's modern constitutional role and duty in making war. Many in Congress wished that we had done more sooner. Many in the White House wished that we had done less or not at all. It was enough for me that we had done what had to be done to put Vietnam in our past and to keep it from reappearing in our future.

Watergate and Its Aftermath

Future members and students of Congress (at least the more historically conscious of them) may remember my speakership for these things. They will work and live with their consequences. Most likely, though, the public will remember Speaker Carl Albert for the peculiar fact that I was twice the proverbial one heartbeat from the presidency. Both instances came as subplots to the unfolding drama known as Watergate.

Even as investigators were zeroing in on President Nixon and his gang of bright young men, Spiro Agnew suddenly resigned the vice-presidency, trading that high office for his freedom from criminal prosecution. The Twenty-fifth Amendment made me next-in-line until we confirmed my good friend Jerry Ford as vice president. Nixon's subsequent resignation and Ford's elevation to the presidency reopened the vacancy and put me in heartbeat's range again.

Although I almost never have talked about it, a lot of otherwise sensible people tried to get me to skip that heartbeat and grab the presidency outright.

Quite a few tried to convince me that we could stall Ford's confirmation until I had appointed a select committee of known Nixon-haters to impeach and remove the president. Under the order of succession, I would then take his place. A memorandum was prepared for me by Ted Sorenson, one of President Kennedy's most trusted advisors, that outlined everything I would need to know in my first week: where I would take the oath of office, who I should invite to the ceremony, how much my salary would be, the arrangements my wife Mary would have to make with the White House Head Usher and Chief Gardener. There was even a text for my first public speech as president of the United States. "At no time did I seek this awesome burden," I was supposed to begin, "but I cannot shrink from my responsibility."

"Awesome burden?" It was awesome foolishness. The American people would not and should not have stood for any theft of the presidency. As Speaker of the body charged under our Constitution with the sole power of impeachment, my whole responsibility—and this I did not shrink from—was to see that we discharged our constitutional duty fairly and deliberately, guided not by our partisan interest or personal opportunities, but by our obligation to the American people. I am content to let history judge if we did that.

I have made my judgment. I was never prouder of the United States House of Representatives than I was as our Judiciary Committee, led by Peter Rodino of New Jersey, wrestled with Richard Nixon's fate, its members' consciences, and our nation's future.

When it was over, more than one commentator said of the American Constitution: "It worked." Of course it did. It did for the same reason that it always has worked so far. Those who served its institutions understood how those institutions worked and why they did so. As circumstances changed, they had been willing to change those institutions themselves. But it was not change for the sake of change. It was change that maintained the best about the institution while correcting its flaws to preserve what that institution represents.

When Ford became president, some people thought that the Congress and the president would have an easier time getting along. Ford, after all, had served in the House Republican leadership for a long time, and he was a good friend of mine. In fact, when President Nixon asked me for suggestions after Spiro Agnew resigned as vice president, I suggested Ford. But I knew better than to believe that it would be easy. The Congress was still badly divided on many issues, and the wounds that had been created by Nixon would not heal right away.

As it turned out, Ford was more obstinate than Nixon had been. He did not abuse the powers of his office, but he sure used them. During his short presidency, Ford cast more than fifty vetoes. We set a record for overriding presidential vetoes, but most of them were sustained. Ford's plan was pretty obvious to me. He wanted to get elected in his own right in 1976, and so he borrowed a page from Nixon's book: not the one that told how to deceive people, but the one that was headed, "Bash the Congress!" In 1974 and 1975 the economy sunk into its lowest depths since the Great Depression, and Ford had little to brag about. So he tried to blame the nation's woes on congressional Democrats.

My goal was to help get the economy back on track and to establish a record on which a Democrat could run in 1976. We passed the right bills, but it was hard to get the two-thirds vote we needed to override a veto. Even when we lost one of those override votes, though, we still usually won in the end. The public gave us the credit for fighting the recession, and usually Ford compromised down the road on the bills. One thing that I learned about House leadership from Mr. Rayburn was patience. He had the patience of Job, perhaps because he had been there so long. Some of the new members at that time were anything but patient; they wanted us to kick Ford down Pennsylvania Avenue. I knew that would never work. In the end, we elected a Democratic president. As I retired from Congress, I had the joy of seeing the White House returned to my party, in significant part because of the battles I fought with my old friend Jerry Ford.

Those new members were the first wave of the new breed that has become pretty common in the House from what they tell me. I had a lot of respect for them. The members who came to the House during my speakership were as bright and capable as any that I had ever known. They lacked some of the deference that had characterized my peers, and some of them seemed a lot more concerned about getting reelected than about doing the country's business. But every member has to be concerned about elections, and no one can blame them for that. The tough part was balancing their demands against the attitudes of the committee chairs who were used to running things in the House. Old-timers such as George Mahon, Wright Patman, Bill Poage, Edward Hebert, Carl Perkins, Jamie Whitten, and Bill Natcher were the backbone of the House. In 1975 a coalition of new members and more senior liberals managed to oust Patman, Hebert, and Poage from their committee chair seats, using the procedure that we had put in place a few years before. I supported the end of seniority as a hard and fast rule, but I was sorry to see these people get bounced. Patman, especially, was a fine progressive legislator who did not deserve the treatment he got at the hands of the caucus.

As Speaker, I had to consider the implications of all these changes. With the old power structure breaking up and a group of restive members, it was necessary to find new ways of doing business. I was the first Speaker to use ad hoc committees and party task forces to help pass legislation. These techniques were used more extensively by my successors. I hired a press secretary, which Mr. Rayburn and John McCormack would never have considered, and I worked closely with the committees to develop party legislation. I had one foot anchored to the old power structure and the other stepping into the new one. Through it all, one thing never changed; as Speaker, I owed fairness, consideration, and respect to the members of the House.

Final Reflections

In the twilight of my life, I do not often get to Washington. I do keep watch over the House that I have loved so much from a distance. While I do not pretend to be closely acquainted with most of the members who now serve, I do have an impression of what things are like there today. Or more precisely, I have two impressions. The first is that the House of Representatives is still very much the same institution in which I served for more than thirty years. When I read about the legislative struggles inside the House, between the House and the Senate, or between the Congress and the White House, I know that our government is working today as it did during my time, and since its beginning: slowly, awkwardly, inefficiently, yet steadily. When my friends used to report to me about the difficulties that Speaker Foley was having in holding his Democrats together, I found myself smiling for him. I knew what it was like. I bet Newt Gingrich learns to know it too.

The other impression that I have is that the House is a different body in some ways. Obviously, this generation of members does not follow Mr. Rayburn's dictum: they do not go along nor need they in order to get along. This makes it harder for the Speaker to manage legislation. The old committee barons are gone. The most powerful by reputation today hold their power by bargaining with their members, not by commanding them as in the days of old. And there is, I sense, a coarsening of the House, caused by partisan and ideological differences, and an occasional dose of personal meanness. None of this is entirely new, but it seems that the natural frictions of the legislative body are no longer as well lubricated by the courtesy of an earlier day.

The speakership seems to me, therefore, to play a more important role than before, as important as at any time since the great upheavals of the 1850s. The House of Representatives will continue its march into history, led by the speakership. Having watched it up close for nearly fifty years and having served there for six, I know that the speakership has changed notably. Its powers are greater than before, its duties more pressing, its many rewards and its few frustrations both enlarged. Through all of that, the speakership still demands fairness before the members. It demands flexibility in the face of circumstances. It demands steadfastness to the Constitution. It demands love for the House and respect for its ways. It demanded that of forty-five people before me. It will demand that of all who ever succeed me.

10 Rules for Speakers

Tip O'Neill

The office of President of the United States may have more power, and the Supreme Court may have the last word, but I believe the speakership of the Congress of the United States is the greatest office in the land. We have built the freest nation known to humanity: how did it happen? I think our country is a result of our forefathers, who insisted on a government that would function only with the consent of the governed. In our government, the people are paramount. Where do the people first make their voices heard? In the House of Representatives. And where is the focal point of the House of Representatives? In the speakership, of course.

It was my privilege to hold that office for ten years. Perhaps only those who have occupied that chair can fully appreciate the wonders of the office and the working of our democracy. It is true that the presidency is the only office truly voted on by all Americans, and, unquestionably, that office has the most power. The president can certainly affect the lives of more people than any other officer in the federal government. The Supreme Court, by the power of judicial review, makes the final constitutional determination. The Senate fancies itself the greatest deliberative body, but talk dominates action there. None of the other constitutional branches have the intimacy of the House of Representatives, the people's branch. The speakership—and the House of Representatives—are "representative" and that's the beauty of it.

Every two years the American people, divided into microcosms of about a half million people each, select a representative to go to Washington and do their bidding. Every two years! When those representatives gather in one room, the House Chamber, we have a mini-America; every ethnic, racial, religious, and philosophical group imaginable, drawn into a common meeting place to do the public's business.

When I stepped onto the House floor for the first time on January 3, 1953, I found white males sitting in practically every seat. No more. Forty years later the membership included forty-seven women, thirty-eight African Americans, and seventeen Hispanic Americans, as well as five Asian Americans.

As Speaker, looking out from the rostrum, I saw this gathering every day. After a prayer and Pledge of Allegiance to the flag, the Speaker tackles the job of trying to bring order out of what appears to be chaos. Once, Alexander Hamilton took a British visitor to the gallery of the House of Representatives. The visitor looked down at all the hubbub on the floor and asked Hamilton: "What is going on down there?" Hamilton sighed, "Here, sir, the people govern." Isn't that beautiful? It explains it all. When you realize how diverse the group really is and you know how important each of them is (and *think* they are), you wonder how anyone can organize it. Not just organize it, but bring it to a majority. The task seems insurmountable, but somehow it happens, day in and day out. It happens because of the leadership, primarily the speakership.

What kind of person does it take to be Speaker of the House? What kind of person will rise to the top of his or her peers, be trusted enough by them to allow him or (someday) her to change their minds? That is a difficult question, one that trained psychologists might try to answer. I am not sure I know the answer to those deep, psychological mysteries, but I can draw on the lessons of my own experience. That experience taught me that political careers are shaped by people who have influenced your life. To be perfectly truthful, I got through most of my political life on instinct, doing what I thought was right at the time. Lately, reflecting on a lifetime of politics, I could see more clearly that most of what I did had a grounding in my early years through my mentors. So, I cannot say what makes *a* Speaker, I can say what made *this* Speaker.

Thomas P. O'Neill, Sr.

The people who most influenced my life were my father, James Michael Curley, John McCormack, Sam Rayburn, and John F. Kennedy. Among them, my father was number one. From him I learned two great truths: public office is a means to help people, and "all politics is local." He was superintendent of sewers for the city of Cambridge, Massachusetts. People were always coming to our house to ask him for advice or a favor. He would do what he could for people who needed help. During the Depression, people flocked to him to ask if he could get them jobs putting in sidewalks or reconstructing streets. These jobs didn't pay much and were only part-time, but for many families they brought in enough to keep the wolf from the door.

In addition, my father formed organizations to collect food and clothing and to distribute it secretly so that poor people could be helped without being embarrassed. At Christmas and Easter we would prepare food baskets for the needy, which we'd leave at their doorsteps in the dark of night. There was a lot of good will in our neighborhood; in those days people really looked out for one another. I have no doubt that the deep commitment to social programs that I have always had during my public life was rooted in those early experiences. When I fought against Ronald Reagan's attempts to cut social programs, my father was looking over my shoulder, just as if he were there.

He taught me other big lessons, and I've tried to live up to each one of them. The first lesson was loyalty. The second was to remember my responsibilities to my fellow man—I *am* my brother's keeper. The third lesson was to remember, always, whence I came. When people say that I'm like my father, I always take it as a great compliment. Another lesson he instilled in me was a lesson that seemed so natural at the time that I didn't appreciate it until much later. Boston had a reputation for political corruption. But my father, by example, showed me that politics could be grounded in honesty and integrity. In our family, public service was considered a great honor. There are lots of stories (some true and some untrue) about ward politics in Boston. I grew up watching it firsthand, and I know that my father and people like him were as honest as they come.

Compromise was another lesson he stressed. He liked to tell a baseball story to explain the fine art of compromise. He was watching a group of kids play on a Sunday afternoon when the batter hit a line drive over second base and tried to stretch an easy single into a double. After the umpire called him out, all his teammates jumped off the bench to protest. Then the umpire changed his mind and called him safe. Everybody on the other team started to yell at him. Finally, after ten minutes of this yelling and arguing, the umpire sent the batter to first base. When the inning was over, my father went up to the umpire and said, "Son, I've watched baseball my whole life and I've never seen a play like that one. First you called him out, then you called him safe, then you sent him to first base. Why did you do that?" "I'll tell you," said the umpire. "When I saw that we weren't getting anywhere, I asked, 'How many of you think the runner was safe?' Nine guys raised their hands. Then I asked, 'How many of you think he was out?' Nine guys raised their hands. Then I asked, 'How many of you say he was safe when he rounded first base?' All eighteen players raised their hands, so I sent him back to first." "And that," my father would say, "is what compromise is all about—finding areas where both sides can agree." What a lesson for a future Speaker! Later, when I was Speaker, I would sometimes be criticized for not establishing a lot of leadership policy positions. On the things that were important to me and the party, we had positions. But a Speaker who issues too many pronouncements and insists on his positions all the time cannot be successful in bringing people together. I learned that from my father.

In my race for the state House in 1936, my father did everything he could do on my behalf. He went through his files and sent me out to see his many friends and acquaintances. I paid a visit to every one of these people, and then they sent me out to see *their* friends. Everybody I met gave me a warm greeting: "The Governor's boy is at the door." (They called my father "the Governor.") The entire household I was visiting would come downstairs to say hello. They would tell me what my father had done for them. "I worked for the phone company, and your dad got me that job back in 1906 when he was on the city council." Or, "Your dad put me to work for the gas company. He saved my life." I knew my father had helped a lot of people, but I never realized just how many people he had helped until I started making the rounds and hearing the stories for myself. When my son Tommy was campaigning in Lexington for the office of lieutenant governor, a woman came up to him and said, "I'm going to vote for you because your grandfather gave my father a coat during the Depression." It warmed my heart to hear that my father's good name was alive for another generation.

James Michael Curley

The legendary mayor of Boston, James Michael Curley, had a large impact on my political life. From him I learned the practical lessons of how to get things done using the levers of government. After all, you can understand all the principles in the world of politics, but if you can't get it done, they are meaningless. Curley was a man of the people. He gave people jobs, clothes, and food whenever and wherever he could. It was said that he talked to 200 people a day. That meant he was accessible, a valuable lesson for any politician, especially a future Speaker of the House.

Curley opened his home to constituents and would see whomever walked through the door. When I went to Washington, I followed a similar path. My wife Millie and our children remained in Cambridge, and I'd go home every weekend. I was a member of the "Tuesday-Thursday Club"—members who came to Washington on Monday night and returned home on Friday morning. When I was in Boston, following Curley's lead, I opened my office and saw whomever walked in the door. I continued this practice even as a party leader because I thought it was important to be accessible.

Curley gave me some excellent advice on handling constituents. "Over the years," he said, "hundreds and hundreds of people will come to your office and ask you for favors. Some of these favors may be great, and some of them may be small. Some may be important, and some may be trivial. Some will be easy, some will be difficult. But always remember, for the person who comes to you, that favor is the most important thing in the world. If he could take care of it himself, he wouldn't be coming to see you. So treat them all alike and try to help everybody—no matter how big or how small the problem is." When I was a member of Congress, my office had such a good reputation for helping constituents with problems that we constantly received requests from people in other districts who heard about our good reputation. As Speaker, I often helped other members with constituent problems. That helped earn the members' loyalty, too.

Curley gave me one other piece of advice, and I've never forgotten it. He said, "Son, it's nice to be important. But remember—it's more important to be nice." Curley was one of the most loved people in Massachusetts political history. His real strength was his personality. I came to learn that politics is people.

John F. Kennedy

Jack Kennedy influenced my life in politics in many ways. Of course, we had a different upbringing, but our Irish-Catholic heritage was a powerful bond. I got to know him when he ran for Congress in my area while I was in the state House. He didn't exactly distinguish himself in the U.S. House. But after I succeeded him, I saw him grow and mature in the Senate, during the presidential campaign, and in the White House. I was part of the campaign, then one of his strongest supporters and friends when he moved to 1600 Pennsylvania Avenue.

Jack thought that his brother Bobby was a political genius, but Jack himself was very impressive in that regard. After his reelection to the Senate in 1958, when he had already made up his mind to try for the presidency, he came into my office and said, "I understand that Tommy Mullen knows more about our district than anyone else on earth." Tommy was my administrative assistant when I was in Congress, just as he had been at the statehouse. Together, Mullen and Kennedy went over the district precinct by precinct—

where the Irish lived, where the Jews lived, and so on with every ethnic group.

Jack wanted to understand ethnic politics and intended to transfer that information to the national scene for the 1960 presidential campaign. He was acutely aware that no Irish-Catholic had ever been elected president. I had never seen anybody study the voting patterns of ethnic and religious groups in a systematic way before, and I don't think most people realized then or appreciate now that Kennedy was a sophisticated student of politics.

The intensity of his interest also had its funny side. There was one ward in my district with a large French Canadian population. "How did I do in that one?" Jack asked, referring to his Senate race. "You won a thousand and three votes to twelve," Tommy Mullen said. "My God," Kennedy said, "I've never seen a vote like that. How did Tip do in that one?" he asked. "Tip won by nine hundred and ninety-nine votes to sixteen," Tommy said. "The Lefebvres were off us"—referring to a family that was apparently angry at me.

Now Jack had a great memory for the details of politics. Two years later, after Jack was elected, I was at a White House reception. "How are you, Tip?" the president asked. "Say, I've been meaning to ask. What was the vote in that precinct where I won by a thousand and three to twelve?" I replied, "I figured you'd ask. I won by nine hundred and ninety-nine to sixteen." Jack looked me in the eye and said, "Well, Tip, I guess the Lefebvres are still off you!"

This story conveys something of Jack Kennedy's sense of humor and the flavor of ethnic politics in the Massachusetts Democratic party. However, it also teaches a valuable lesson about politics. The ethnic cleavages that concerned Kennedy and me were just one kind of political split in an electorate that was divided in many ways. As a presidential candidate and as president, Kennedy had to adapt himself to a larger and more diverse constituency than he had as a member of the House or as a senator.

When I became a member of the House Democratic leadership, and especially after I became Speaker, I had to make a similar adjustment. My father had taught me that all politics is local, but for every member the "local" had a different meaning. Some districts are divided along racial, ethnic, or religious lines and some by other social or economic forces. As a leader in the House, I learned how important it was to know all about the members' districts so that I could provide more effective leadership. I do believe if you get home often and explain your votes to your constituents, they will understand and allow you to vote nationally. That's what I mean when I say all politics is local.

John W. McCormack

I first met John McCormack in 1948. I was in the state House and he was minority leader in the U.S. House. He sent word he wanted to see me, and when I dropped by, he spent three hours talking politics. The Massachusetts House was controlled by the Republicans and his question to me was: "Have you ever given any thought to making the state House Democratic?"

When I told Mullen about the meeting, he agreed that McCormack made a good point. He pointed out that a majority of the House districts had gone for our Democratic governor, including some districts in which no Democrat had run for the state House seat in years. We got to work, recruiting candidates in those districts. We eventually threw out the Republicans, and I became Speaker. McCormack had seen what none of us had seen.

Many years later, when I was Speaker in Washington, the Republicans would complain sometimes that I was too partisan and too overbearing. I always found this amusing when I thought back on my own experience in the Massachusetts legislature under Republican control. The Democrats had never controlled the General Court (as it is called), and the Republicans saw no reason to do us any favors. We got no office space, not even the leadership, and had no staff. After I became Speaker in Massachusetts I tried to run the House with a strong hand, but I was nicer to the Republicans than they had been to us.

When I finally made it to the Congress of the United States, McCormack was waiting for me. McCormack had no children, and I became a political son to him. As majority leader and later as Speaker, he would be invited to fund-raisers, parties, and receptions every evening. Usually he'd bring me along to these various events, and during my early years in Washington I accompanied him to all kinds of gatherings where I met congressional representatives, senators, generals, admirals, cabinet members, ambassadors, and other prominent people. People began asking, "Who's the big Irishman with McCormack?" At first they thought I was his bodyguard! But soon people came to see me as McCormack's closest friend in Congress—his protégé.

Wherever we went, he introduced me in the same way: "This is Tom O'Neill." (He always called me "Tom.") "Tom was the Speaker of the Massachusetts legislature. He's in Congress now, and I want you to keep your eye on him. Someday, he may become Speaker of the House." McCormack was one of the most powerful people in Washington, and his introductions opened a lot of doors for me. Because of my association with McCormack, not to mention all the people he introduced me to, I was able to get things done a little easier than most of the other junior members of the House.

McCormack hosted a table in the House dining room every morning between 8:30 and the time for the committee meetings to began. And I was always there. Often there were just a few of us, although on occasion there might be a couple dozen. Listening to John was a real education. The talk was mostly business—politics, legislation—and gossip about members of the House. Most days there would also be a few minutes on baseball, because McCormack was a passionate fan.

In addition to being a great talker, he also knew how to listen—and how to pick a fellow's brain. Whenever a visitor came in from Boston, John would invite him to breakfast and ask him all about his business and how it fit into the economy. John was constantly learning, constantly preparing for the next debate. And he was a great debater. When he had the floor, the Republicans had their hands full.

Yet with McCormack, debate was never acrimonious. The worst thing he ever said to an opponent was when he once told a Republican that he "held the member in minimum high regard." McCormack loved people. Perhaps it is a reflection of our Boston-Irish background, but McCormack and I were alike in our love of people. John was never happier than in a room full of people, particularly politicians. I learned from him how important it is for a leader to be accessible to people and to be able to relate to their concerns.

Sam Rayburn

The best thing McCormack did for me was to include me in the inner circle with Sam Rayburn. Rayburn had an after-hours gathering called the "Board of Education," and McCormack frequently invited me to accompany him to listen to Rayburn and his lieutenants talk politics. The boys would have a few pops (except for McCormack, who was a complete teetotaler), and Mr. Sam would hold forth on legislation, the various committee chairs, history, world politics, and sports. Occasionally, a couple of Republicans would be invited in if it would help move along the legislation. Whenever I was a guest, Rayburn usually asked about my experiences in the Massachusetts legislature. He was interested especially in hearing about how badly the Republicans had treated us.

Rayburn also wanted to know about Curley. Curley, of course, had served in the House a few years earlier, and apparently Rayburn had been well aware of his political talents and his great speaking ability. Rayburn also inquired about other Massachusetts politicians, including Maurice Tobin and Jack Kennedy. I wasn't the only one he quizzed; if somebody came in from Chicago, he'd want to hear all about Richard Daley. Through the various guests of the members, old Sam got a rundown on every major politician in the country.

Rayburn had many sayings, and it is amazing how many of them are as true today as they were then. He was a loyal Democrat, but he never forgot that there was a higher allegiance. He used to say, "We're Americans first and Democrats second." And "We're builders, not obstructionists. Any jackass can kick down a barn, but it takes a carpenter to build one."

When I was first elected to the Congress of the United States, I attended, along with the other freshmen, an orientation luncheon in the Speaker's dining room, where Rayburn gave us some good advice, including his most famous line, "If you want to get along, go along." This idea is no longer in fashion, as today's freshmen are more restless and independent. But when I first came to Congress, party discipline meant a great deal. "Learn your job," Rayburn would say. "Don't open your mouth until you know what you're talking about." He also reminded us to pay close attention to our districts: "Your first priority is to get yourself reelected."

Pundits have commented on the "Boston-Austin axis" in the House leadership. Rayburn passed the speakership back and forth with Joseph Martin of Massachusetts and was succeeded by McCormack of Massachusetts. McCormack was succeeded by Carl Albert of Oklahoma, whose district was right across the Red River from Rayburn's, and I succeeded Albert. Then Jim Wright of Fort Worth followed me.

To be perfectly truthful, I don't think these geographic coincidences have been very important in understanding the speakership. Yes, it is important for the leadership to reflect the diversity of the party, and yes, the party historically has divided along geographical lines. But the fact that Rayburn was from Texas instead of Mississippi and that I was from Massachusetts instead of Connecticut didn't make much difference. The key thing was a balanced leadership, and during my career we always needed someone from the South and someone from the Northeast, because that is where most of the Democrats were from.

Getting back to Rayburn, though, the thing that strikes me the most is that Rayburn had learned in Texas the same things that I had learned in Massachusetts. He knew that politics is local, that a politician always worries about elections, and that the Democratic party was supposed to lead the government to do good things for people. His constituents were more conservative than mine, and perhaps he was more conservative than I am. But he was a good Democrat, and I never doubted that. Rayburn also understood that a Speaker must get to know the members so that, as he used to say, he could *feel* what is going on. I always remembered this and tried to keep in close touch with the members. If I didn't know what they were going to do before they did it, I was in trouble.

The next best thing McCormack did for me was to convince Rayburn to put me on the Rules Committee, only the second time a second-termer had gotten on it. One day I was summoned to see Rayburn. When I got to the Speaker's office, Rayburn said, "I know all about you from John McCormack. And I know you understand party loyalty. So I'd like to make you a member of the Rules Committee." I had never dreamed of getting such a prestigious assignment—certainly not during my second term. A sophomore member would normally be too inexperienced, but this is where my four years as Speaker of the Massachusetts legislature made such a difference.

The Speaker made it perfectly clear that he had chosen me for this singular honor for only one reason: I could be counted on to vote with the party. In case I had any doubts about what he meant, he spelled it our for me: "Now I don't give a rat's ass whether or not you like the legislation. If it's a party issue, your obligation is to get it on the floor. Once it gets there, of course, you're on your own and you're free to vote your conscience or your district. But on the Rules Committee, if we need your vote, you'll give it to us even if you hate the bill, and even if it goes against the economy of your area."

The Rules Committee is important because it sets the agenda for the flow of the legislation in the House and ensures that the place runs smoothly and doesn't get bogged down. Almost all congressional legislation goes to the Rules Committee, which decides when and whether to send a bill to the floor. I got to know all the chairs through my position on Rules. After all, they needed me. And I had a general knowledge of every piece of legislation and when it would be brought to the floor. This kind of information made me a valuable source for my colleagues. There's no way to calculate how important this was in my rise to the speakership. Of course, I was eager to share the information, and I believe I was easily approachable. That's my nature and another essential ingredient to success.

During the balance of Rayburn's speakership he came into more frequent conflict with the leadership of the Rules Committee. After about 1937 the southern Democrats in the House had started siding with Republicans on many issues. One of their main goals was to keep civil rights legislation off the

House floor. They would often help Republicans fight against social and economic bills if the Republicans would side with them on civil rights. One of the main arenas for this fight was the Rules Committee. The committee was chaired by Judge Howard Smith of Virginia, an old-line southerner. He and Bill Colmer of Mississippi would often side with the Republicans to kill bills. I always got along well with Smith and often was able to work out compromises, but of course my main loyalty was to the leadership.

After Kennedy was elected president, though, the situation became intolerable. Kennedy told Rayburn that something had to be done about the Rules Committee. Rayburn told Kennedy that he would take care of Smith. Eventually Rayburn decided to add new members to the committee to give the leadership a voting majority. The fight to pack the committee was the last great battle of Rayburn's career. I sided with the leadership, but I kept my lines open to the southerners. I think that this is one reason why I remained acceptable to them.

This fight left a lasting impression of Rayburn in my mind. While the battle against Smith was going on in January 1961, Rayburn looked increasingly gaunt and tired. He died in November of that year, and the House lost its great Speaker. Now my mentor McCormack would be Speaker, and I looked forward to supporting him.

On to the Leadership

McCormack did one more thing for me: he made me head of the Democratic Congressional Campaign Committee, the committee charged with raising funds for Democratic House candidates. That job really propelled me into the political lives of the members. It required that I have a detailed knowledge of every congressional district in America to decide how much money we would put into each race. I had to know the makeup of the district, its political history, and the relative strengths and weaknesses of our candidate and of the opposition. What an education! I worked hard at the job, too. I traveled around the country raising money. The previous chair hadn't done that. In fact, I always found it easier to ask for money for other people than for myself.

Along with my service as head of the campaign committee, two other developments in the late 1960s brought me to the threshold of party leadership. In neither case did I consciously seek personal advancement, but in both cases my role served me well in the Democratic Caucus. The first development was the Vietnam War. At first I supported President Johnson's policy, but by 1967 I had concluded that the war was not in America's best interest. It was difficult for me to break with the president because I am a loyal Democrat and I believe that the president must lead in foreign policy. So I announced my opposition to the war only after careful consideration and was among the first in the House to do so. While my position did not help my relations with the White House, I did find support among House members who shared my reservations about the war but had yet to come out against it. Many of these members later supported me for party leadership.

The second development was House reform. In the late 1960s many new members wanted to change some of the ways we did business on the House floor. One of these procedures was the unrecorded teller vote—in other words, a secret vote. I had concluded that the House needed to open itself up to public accountability. When I was asked to offer a rules change to limit secretly un-recorded voting, I agreed to do it. Later, many of the reformers supported me because I was willing to support change.

And so I was on my way to the leadership of the House. My appointment as whip came next, as a result of my loyalty to McCormack, Albert, and Hale Boggs. When Boggs tragically disappeared in an airplane accident in Alaska, I was ready for election as majority leader. Four years later I was Speaker. I was the only member to serve in all four positions of Campaign Committee head, whip, leader, and Speaker. When these positions were combined with my service as Speaker of the Massachusetts House and my many years of service on the Rules Committee, I felt fully ready for the job of Speaker.

Speaker

I was prepared for the job: Curley had taught me accessibility, my father and Curley had taught me public service meant helping people, Kennedy had showed me the joy of national politics, Rayburn had schooled me in the intricacies of House politics, and McCormack had given me the push to become Massachusetts Speaker, Rules Committee member, and head of the Campaign Committee.

To those I added my own innate sense of humor. How important that facility has been in my career! It has helped me get over many sticky situations for myself and for others. Tom Harkin of Iowa loves to tell the story of how I got him out of a tight spot with organized labor when he was in the House. It seems Tom, who is a strong pro-labor member, found himself committed back home to vote against a labor position. Labor wasn't giving up and kept pressuring him. He came to me for help and I called them all in to my office. I explained that Tom needed understanding. "After all," I said, "he was the first Democrat to occupy that seat since the Depression." I continued, "You know, I've been in Congress now for over twenty years. And in all that time, I have only disagreed with labor twice. Can you believe that? In all that time—labor's only been wrong twice." Well, they all broke up in laughter. They gave Tom a pass.

Having a sense of humor was valuable in being Speaker, but it was more valuable in keeping me sane during the many difficult struggles of my speakership. When I look back on my speakership, three particular periods come to mind.

The first is the Carter administration. The Democrats had sizable voting majorities in both chambers and a newly elected Democratic president. It was my job to consolidate party leadership under the new reforms we had adopted and to press for enactment of the president's program. We got off to a big start. Carter's first major bill was his energy legislation. I created a special ad hoc committee to coordinate House consideration of the bill and gave reporting deadlines to the various committees with jurisdiction. We passed the program virtually intact in six months. By June 1977 I thought that the government, under Democratic leadership, was well on its way.

Unfortunately, President Carter's energy program did not fare as well in the Senate, and it took us two years to get a bill enacted, one that was not much like what the president had proposed originally. Toward the end, it became my job to help stitch together the pieces of a compromise that could pass into law. We finally did it, but it wasn't easy.

The experience of the energy bill was repeated in other areas. Carter's legislative team was inexperienced, and they paid a price for it. Sometimes they made even me mad, although I always liked Carter himself and we got along well. The end result of the administration's mishandling of legislation was a series of floor confrontations on controversial things, such as standby gasoline rationing and hospital cost containment, that tore the Democratic party apart. In fairness to Carter, a lot of the responsibility belonged to the stubborn House Democrats. But regardless of who was to blame, the result was chaos on the floor.

I, too, opposed some of the president's social priorities, and this made it difficult for me as Speaker. Nevertheless, the record shows that more than 80 percent of the Carter legislative program was enacted by the Congress, most of it with my support. Still, the public reaction to legislative conflict, combined with a darkening economic picture and the debacle of the Iran hostage crisis, eventually undermined Carter's support to the point that Teddy Kennedy decided to run against him for the Democratic nomination. This put me in a difficult spot. But I was named to chair the Democratic convention, and, as such, I had to be neutral in the race. Carter ultimately withstood Kennedy's challenge, but he had been greatly weakened and lost that fall to Ronald Reagan.

Reagan's first term is the second distinct period of my speakership. At the outset, I knew that he was riding a crest of popularity that would be hard for the Congress to resist. This was especially true with respect to his tax bill, which took 20 percent out of the revenue base and laid the basis for the enormous federal deficits we saw afterward. We tried to stem the tide, but to no avail. By August 1981, Reagan was able to sign his economic program into law. The effect of the policy changes of the first eight months of 1981 lingered on, and I regretted that we were not able to stop it earlier.

The main change in my role as Speaker was the increasingly public role I played. The Republicans had claimed the Senate in the 1980 elections, and I became the leading elected Democrat for the next six years. As my party's highest elected leader, I had the responsibility to speak out against the mistakes of the Reagan administration and on behalf of my party's policies.

My main adversary was, of course, Reagan. Because of his great public popularity it was necessary for me, in speaking for my party, to address him directly. This led to the clash of the two Irishmen that the press loved so much. Reagan was not my equal as an Irish storyteller, but he had access to a much larger audience. He was very effective on television. The landslide victory he won over Walter Mondale ushered in the last phase of my speakership.

Faced with four more years of Reagan and dealing with a restive caucus, I opened up the circle of party leadership to more members and sought to work through the leadership group. We were able to pass the tax reform bill on terms that were acceptable to a majority of Democrats, and we continued to establish our criticisms of the Reagan program. In foreign policy, we opposed the administration in Central America with profound consequences. When the Congress cut off aid to the Nicaraguan Contras, the administration got itself into the Iran-Contra fiasco that so badly damaged Reagan in his second term.

By the end of 1984 I had decided not to seek another term as Speaker or as a member of the House. At the end of the 99th Congress in 1986, I had completed thirty-four years of service in the House and ten years as Speaker, the longest continuous period of service in that office. The 1986 election brought control of the Senate back to the Democratic party. I honestly believed that our party would win the 1988 presidential election, but I was off by four years. With the election of Bill Clinton as president, I was able to see a united government under Democratic control for the first time since 1980. Many of the policies that my party pursued during the twelve years of Republican administrations had a chance at enactment. The groundwork for these policies was put in place over the past twelve years while we struggled as the party of opposition.

Advice for Speakers

I have some advice to share about the speakership, which draws on my experience.

Accessibility

Accessibility is very important because as a Speaker goes through the day, the temptation is to stay in your rooms and avoid the problems that will come to you as soon as the members spot you on the floor. I always spent time with the members in the cloakroom or on the front row of the chamber. I kept my office door open, literally, and members knew they could drop in anytime. They knew, too, they could come up to the Speaker's rostrum and talk to me. This was easy for me, because, as I have said, I like people. On becoming Speaker, though, even a gregarious person finds it more difficult to see everybody who wants in the door. I relied on my staff for help, but when it came to members, I was always accessible.

Listening

Politicians, by their nature, love to talk. I sure do. But they don't like to listen, particularly to other politicians. Listening is a must for a good Speaker. Good leaders will listen and even ask questions. Sometimes people said that I didn't know enough about the legislation itself. That was because I didn't carry briefing books around with me and stay up at night reading them. But I learned over the years that you can absorb more by listening than by reading because people will always tell you what is important for you to know, and you can ask them the right questions. Listening is also important because it encourages people to go along with you later if they think they've had a hearing. One of the toughest jobs I had as Speaker was getting the ethics bill through the Rules Committee in 1977. Most of the members didn't want to disclose their net worths, and they each had a different reason for not wanting to do so. I called them together for lunch and let them go at me. You never heard such whining. I let them speak and then told them I just had to have the bill. I then went around the table asking for personal commitments. They gave in.

Keeping Your Word

As in life, keeping one's word is a cardinal rule in politics. If a member gives his or her word on a bill and finds he or she must change it, there are ways to do it. First the member must go to the person to whom the word was pledged and explain the new circumstances; they ought never to surprise that person. It will work invariably. This goes for explaining a switch in position to the voters, too. From a leadership perspective, this may mean enforcing a promise, of which I can provide an example. Once the prime minister of Ireland asked me to help start a new international fund to help Ireland and Northern Ireland. I went to President Reagan and told him other countries were agreeable to this and that it was time for us to join in. Reagan agreed. Then I went to Dante Fascell, who headed the House Foreign Affairs Committee. He told me the State Department had just testified against the plan. So, I called the State Department and was told: "You and the president are both for it. With that kind of strength, you don't need the State Department." Oh, no. I knew I needed the State Department *and* Reagan. I called Reagan. "The State Department doesn't think this is the way to go, but you gave me your word on it," I said. "I'm going to take a five-minute special order on the floor of the House and tell the world how you broke your word." He said: "Give me five minutes." Five minutes later, he called back. "O.K., we'll go along. We politicians don't break our word," he said. In this example, my main political adversary felt that it was important to keep his word to me, and I always kept my word to him. During my long political career I had to rely on the word of a member (and keep my own commitments) countless times. Without integrity, a democratic government cannot function.

Timing

Sometimes I think timing is the greatest power of the speakership. The Speaker ultimately decides when a bill will be brought up and when it won't. That means the Speaker can delay consideration of legislation until he or she has the votes to pass it. Elementary. Of course, you can never be absolutely sure of a majority all the time, but the trick then is to determine the moment you can bring up a bill and then work extra hard for the majority at the end of the vote. That involves timing too, because you are placing a member against the expiring clock. It works more often than not. During my speakership, the power that the leadership exercised over the House calendar increased greatly because the Rules Committee was under firm control. This enhanced my standing as Speaker, and the most useful aspect of this power was not in blocking floor legislation, but in timing those bills that we did want to bring to the floor.

Gathering Votes

How does a Speaker get a member to change his or her mind? After all, the members have made their judgments and have heard me say so many times "All politics is local," so why shouldn't they follow what they see as "local"? However, what I meant is that constituents will allow members to vote in the national interest if members will go home and explain their votes.

Of course, sometimes you have to go to great lengths to get a vote. I read that when President Bill Clinton was governor of Arkansas, he personally lobbied his bills through the legislature, even going so far as to follow one legislator into the men's room. That happened to me once when I was Speaker in Massachusetts. Because we needed every vote, I did everything possible to maintain our majority. I once chased Joe Leahy, a Democratic member, for a vote after I learned that he had made a commitment to an outside lobbyist to vote against us. I had locked the doors of the chamber, so the only places he could be were in the reading room and the lavatory. When I couldn't find him in the reading room, I tried the other place. I didn't see anybody there, but it occurred to me that he might be hiding in one of the stalls with his feet up on the toilet. "I know you're in there, Joe," I shouted, "so you better come out because we need you." My hunch was correct, and a red-faced Joe shuffled out and gave us his vote.

Being aggressive is not all there is to it. It is crucial to structure bills so that they can win a majority on the House floor. Sometimes it is necessary to limit or structure the amendments that can be offered as well. This was one thing that the Republicans always complained about. From my point of view, it was simply a matter of ensuring that the House could legislate. We also used task forces to help pass bills. This was a real innovation and proved very helpful on a number of occasions. In short, when you are the party leader and the presiding officer, you've got to do what you can to pass bills. That's what you're there for.

Looking Back

The great temptation is to check on how members vote and then get mad at them for not going along with the leadership. "Don't get mad, get even" is the first instinct. It is far better to try to understand a member's predicament, then file it away. When another vote occurs, return to that member and ask again, reminding him or her of the previous vote. Sometimes the member will feel guilty and will stretch a little to help.

Compromise

"Compromise is the art of politics." That is one of my favorite sayings. I don't mean compromising morals or principles. I mean political compromise where a politician has to defer his or her wish in order to contribute to a majority. If every member kept to his or her first thought about everything, there would be no need for a Congress. Everyone has to compromise at least occasionally to achieve 218 votes in the House and 51 in the Senate (60 to shut off a filibuster). I don't recall a single piece of major legislation in my thirty-four-year career that didn't require significant compromise to pass. One difficulty that I had with Presidents Carter and Reagan and their staffs was that they thought that compromise was not in their best interests. Eventually they did compromise, though; they had to.

Be Proud of Your Office

The term "Speaker" comes from the English Parliament in which the Speaker "spoke" to the king for the House of Commons. I believe our Speaker must be the person who speaks not only *for* the House, but also *to* the nation about the House. The Speaker should be proud of the House, defend it as an institution, and protect its prerogatives (like Speaker Foley filing suit against term limits for members). The House and its members are under attack all the time and we cannot expect the members to defend it. They won't. It's too diverse an institution, too awkward and hard to explain. So they join in the criticism. The Speaker is the one who must save it. It isn't an easy job. Once the father of a newly elected member called me to ask me to put his son on the Ethics Committee: "If you will put him on Ethics, he can become president of the United States." Oh, no, I wasn't going to use my office to help someone succeed by stepping on my members.

In recent years, the House has had its troubles. I don't think any of them were very significant in the grand scheme of things. The ethics process that I helped put in place seemed to work pretty well. The Speaker needs to be tough on ethics violations, and he should not let the House get railroaded by the press.

Lists

The press and, to be perfectly truthful, other members, are always after the Speaker to develop a list of priority legislation. The press just wants something to write about, usually at a recess time. The members of Congress want a list so they can get a pet bill included, going over the head of a committee. Both press and members will criticize the Speaker if he or she doesn't ever get to the bill. So the Speaker should resist the temptation to announce a "must" list of legislation.

With Democrats in the White House, the president's legislative program forms the congressional list. But there is a danger here, too, as I learned under Carter. Presidents want their programs enacted as soon as possible and are often impatient with the legislative process. A loyal Speaker will advise a president of the same party to moderate the pace of legislation to what the Congress can do.

The Press

Keeping the House press corps fed has become a main part of the Speaker's job. Rayburn didn't like the press very much. He had a short press conference just before the House convened and basically just went over the legislative program for the day. This tradition was continued by McCormack and Albert. I expanded the time, sometimes too close to the time the House convened. Think how it would be if the president would meet with the White House press corps for fifteen minutes a day! That's plenty of time for hard questions to be asked.

Of course, I wanted to be prepared and so I had a daily staff meeting just before the press meeting. My staff would brief me on issues that might be asked. I know that my style seems pretty casual, but actually we prepared very carefully for these events because we knew that whatever I said would get wide circulation.

A Speaker can no longer afford to ignore the press the way that Rayburn did. Even if the spotlight is not on the office as it was for me in the 1980s, the Speaker will still be a main focus of press attention. Besides, talking to the press is one of the best ways to communicate with members. So a press strategy is a vital part of the speakership now.

Power

Never forget that the power of the speakership is like all power—temporary. The power has been loaned, not given, and must be used to help members and the country. It is easy for politicians, and especially a Speaker, to conclude that the office they hold is deserved. It is wiser to realize that the people have taken a chance and that their trust must be earned every day.

Conclusion

I am a Massachusetts politician who had the good fortune to rise to the speakership of the United States House of Representatives. Among all of the people who have to this date served as Speaker of the House, I suppose that none was a more partisan politician than I was. I am proud to say that I am a Democrat and that throughout my career I sought to further the policies and interests of my party. But I tried to be fair, and I hope I achieved that.

To me, the United States is the greatest country with the greatest government on earth. The Congress stands for our country and our government, of, by, and for the people. The Speaker is one of only four officials of the government named in the Constitution. (The others are the president, vice president, and chief justice of the Supreme Court.) There was never a day when I took the Speaker's rostrum to gavel the House into session that I did not remember the responsibility that this placed on my shoulders, not only to my party and my constituents, but also to the country and the Constitution. The greatest thing about being Speaker was the opportunity to serve the American people. I am proud I was able to do so.

11 Challenges that Speakers Face

Jim Wright

The speakership provides fully as much challenge as any Speaker is prepared to accept. Ordained by the Constitution as presiding judge and chief voice of the legislative branch of government and third in line of succession to the presidency, the office of Speaker has been what changing times and individual occupants have made of it. Some, such as Henry Clay and Sam Rayburn, have been catalysts of major change. A few, such as Joseph Cannon and Thomas Reed, have thoroughly dominated the House. Others have seen their functions essentially as presiding with fairness and decorum while maintaining as much harmony as possible.

Rayburn was Speaker when I entered the House in 1955. He impressed me enormously. Quite probably I formed my basic concept of a Speaker's function from his example. Rayburn was an effective leader. He saw national needs and made things happen. Under his guidance, the legislative branch fulfilled a role more creative than passive, initiating much of the domestic agenda during the Eisenhower presidency, when one party held the White House and the other led in Congress.

It is possible that from this, and from my personal friendships with Speakers McCormack, Albert, and O'Neill, I had developed an exalted view of the Speaker's role, perhaps even an impossibly demanding conception of what a Speaker should be able to achieve for the country. On the occasion of my first swearing in, set by my wish on January 6, 1987, the 105th anniversary of Speaker Rayburn's birth, I called the office "a treasure more precious than any material possession and an honor more sublime than royalty." To be Speaker, I said, was "the highest responsibility that can come to a lawmaker anywhere in the world."

The Speaker's Role

The challenges that beset a Speaker include both obstacles and opportunities. Some are endemic, embedded in the very nature of our system of government. Others are ephemeral, arising from the times. A Speaker's first responsibility, as with that of any other public official, is to the nation. After that responsibility is fulfilled, he has a specific obligation to uphold the position of the legislative branch in our constitutional balance of powers, to defend the rights and prerogatives of the House in relation to the Senate, and to maintain the authority of the office entrusted to him so that it is passed on to successors with its inherent powers intact.

Beyond all of this, Speakers assume a peculiar responsibility for the well-being of their colleagues, and owe a certain degree of fealty to the political party that elected them Speaker. Against this latter loyalty, every Speaker must balance the overriding duty to promote an atmosphere of peace, comity, and mutual respect among the members. The Speaker must protect the minority from intolerance or abuse by the majority while protecting the majority from the obstructive actions of a minority.

I once defined the ideal House leader as a tripartite personality: "part parish priest, part evangelist, and part prophet." The Speaker's pastoral function challenges him or her to nurture and console, to be a sort of confessor to the flock, helping other members with committee assignments, legislative projects, and, where appropriate, with their reelection efforts.

Like an evangelist, the Speaker must use the pulpit to promote the Congress and its role to the public while selling the legislative program to both the public and the members. By open advocacy and vocal defense of the institution, the Speaker sometimes can make doing the right thing more palatable for the members by making it more generally understood and publicly acceptable.

Above all, I feel that a Speaker worthy of the title must look ahead and see the needs of the future. As with the captain of a ship, the Speaker is responsible; the eyes of one so entrusted must watch both the compass and the waters ahead. Like a sentry on the wall, the Speaker sometimes must sound alarms, calling on the membership to summon vision and courage to act, in the words of that well-known aphorism, not just for the *next election* but for the *next generation*. These challenges are systemic. Others are the products of a given moment in history.

Four Policy Challenges

As I assumed the Speaker's office in January 1987, our government faced four problems of critical proportions: a budget deficit, a trade deficit, a growing social deficit, and a threatened constitutional crisis arising from the Iran-

Contra revelations. The first three had grown menacingly during the years of the Reagan administration, and I worried that they had reached a point at which, absent a serious effort to arrest or at least slow them down, their economic momentum could become irreversible. The fourth, the Iran-Contra scandal, had erupted suddenly on the public consciousness only six weeks prior to my election as Speaker.

These four realities of the historic moment would shape the thrust and direction of my two-and-a-half years as Speaker. To ignore the challenges they represented, to fail to offer leadership in dealing with them, would have been, in my mind, to render not only the office of Speaker irrelevant but the Congress itself inadequate to its constitutional role. Although they were clearly related, each of these problems represented a separate challenge and required a separate strategy.

The Budget Deficit

The budget deficit, unattended, had the potential to doom any serious effort to provide solutions for the trade deficit and the social deficit. The budget deficit was the inevitable result of a colossal misjudgment indulged by President Ronald Reagan in 1981, the Democrats' lack of a cohesive resistance, and the public's gleeful gullibility when winsomely promised something for nothing. No doubt about it, Reagan had sold the nation a bill of goods. We had doubled military expenditures (from $148 billion in 1980 to approximately $300 billion in 1986) while cutting taxes (by $135 billion in the first year).

As a result, we had tripled the national debt. In six years it had skyrocketed from slightly less than $1 trillion to almost $3 trillion as I took the Speaker's chair. In these short months of peace and relative plenty, we had taken on twice as much debt as our predecessor generations accumulated through two whole centuries and thirty-nine presidencies (George Washington's through Jimmy Carter's), a civil war and two world wars, assorted depressions and economic crises, and the costly military conflicts of Korea and Vietnam.

It is ironic that during President Johnson's last year in office, while the Vietnam War was at its height and we were conducting a massive effort to eradicate poverty, Congress actually had produced a slight budget surplus through taxes adequate to sustain all of our government's current activities. Now, in peacetime, and having largely abandoned the war on poverty, we were plunging deeply into debt.

I felt Reagan actually had believed that we could double military spending, drastically reduce taxes for the rich, and still balance the budget by 1983 as he firmly promised to do, simply by cutting out "waste, fraud, and abuse." When the mathematics proved unworkable (by 1987 the total elimination of *all* discretionary domestic expenditures would not have balanced the budget), the president refused to admit error or consent to altering course. It was obvious that if the country were to change direction, Congress would have to take the initiative. To reduce the deficit substantially would require more taxes, among other things, and taxes have always been unpopular. That was the first big challenge that confronted congressional leadership. I considered it unavoidable.

If the essential immorality of indulging whims on a credit card and sending the bills to grandchildren were not enough to concern us, we had only to consider how much this profligacy was beginning to cost the current generation simply for the privilege of owing such unprecedented sums. Interest payments on the debt were the fastest growing item in our federal budget. They would drag $169 billion away from more productive uses in 1987, and this was almost three times the burden they posed in 1980. Siphoning away this much money and making it unavailable for any constructive domestic or military use, the cost of debt service was beginning to hold the national budget in a straitjacket, reducing our options at every turn.

Clearly, this frightening growth in the budget deficits demanded resolute action. I was convinced that it could not be arrested except by a combination of more revenues and cuts in both military and domestic expenditures. No one of these three actions could attain the result. Most members of Congress realized this truth, but to convince them that the public understood and would applaud heroic action on the budgetary front was a major challenge.

Part of the difficulty arose from what many members perceived as a public aversion to the very mention of the forbidden word, "taxes." Walter Mondale, the Democratic presidential nominee in 1984, had told the nation candidly that we needed more taxes if we were ever expected to balance the budget. The only question, Mondale posited, was who would pay the taxes. The Reagan campaign spoke of "Morning in America" and scorned the notion of additional taxes. Reagan won. Members, therefore, were inclined to be as fractious at the very whisper of the word as a flighty young colt confronted by a rattlesnake in its path. And without taxes, I was convinced, we would never balance the budget.

What is a leader to do? I saw the treasury hemorrhaging but I was also aware of my colleagues' nervousness about applying the only tourniquet that would stop the bleeding. I felt that my duty as Speaker was to find a way to demonstrate that Congress could face the crisis, swallow the bitter medicine, and survive. I believed the public would respond to an honest, straightforward appeal for fairly distributed sacrifices now in the interest of the future. Thirty years earlier, as a first-term congressional representative, I had been part of a group that persuaded President Eisenhower that the way to finance the interstate highway program was by pay-as-we-go taxes rather than by adding to the national debt. For three decades, people willingly had paid these taxes, driven the highways, and not grumbled. It was the Speaker's challenge to lead by example, to propose a remedy, and to launch at least a start in that direction. This surely was not the quickest path to popularity, but the path of duty as I saw it.

In my first press conference after the Democratic Caucus nominated me for Speaker in December 1986, I proposed that we freeze tax breaks for people in the upper income brackets at the rates they were paying, and repeal the huge scheduled rate cuts for high income taxpayers contained in the so-called Tax Reform Act of 1986. That suggestion did not seem excessively brave. I was not even actually proposing a hike in taxes but merely opposing additional tax cuts scheduled for the wealthiest Americans. My proposal was a lightning rod, and it drew immediate reaction. Treasury Secretary James Baker called my suggestion "nothing more than a general tax increase" and other administration spokespersons denounced it heartily, but several privately commissioned polls revealed a substantial majority of the people in support of the plan once they understood it. A great many Democratic members were both surprised and relieved at the reaction. The Speaker had mentioned the forbidden word and had not been stricken dumb by lightning.

The specific proposal I mentioned that day was never enacted. But it served its purpose. It broke the ice and tended to demonstrate that Congress could raise revenues for deficit reduction without being crucified. For several years I had been trying to recruit responsible members for service on the Budget Committee. I knew how hard it was to patch together any budget resolution that would pass the House, let alone one with real teeth. Not only did we need to make a genuine reduction in the deficit, we needed to do it in a balanced way while allowing some needed increases in several domestic programs.

Bill Gray of Pennsylvania was chair of the Budget Committee and a gifted ally. Articulate, knowledgeable, and patient, he led the committee with skill and understanding as its members worked and groped their way toward a realistic plan. Several times, Democratic members of the committee asked me to come and sit with them as they talked their way to a logical conclusion.

The resolution that emerged in mid-spring called for $36 billion in actual deficit reduction, half of this in new taxes and half in spending cuts. The $18 billion in reduced expenditures was divided evenly between defense spending and domestic programs. This budget package passed the House by a comfortable margin. Congress still was a long way from achieving the goal, but we had made a beginning. In time I would learn just how hard it was to pass any tax bill with the White House adamantly opposed.

The Trade Deficit

At the beginning of 1987, the trade deficit was only starting to command serious public attention, but it had reached its fingers deeply into American pockets. Six years earlier, in the early 1980s, America was the world's biggest creditor nation. By the time I assumed the speakership, our country had become the world's largest debtor. In the preceding year, Americans spent $175 billion more for goods from other countries than we sold abroad in American made products.

A growing number of American business and labor and academic leaders, alarmed by the trends they saw, had begun to ask for a concerted national effort to stem the tide. Our nation's principal role had reversed precipitately from seller to buyer and from lender to borrower. We were borrowing from other countries not only to finance our purchases from them but to finance our national debt. More and more of our government bonds were held by foreigners. We had begun selling off an increasing share of America's important domestic assets—land, banks, factories, hotels, newspapers. We were like a family that used to own the community bank but discovered suddenly that it no longer did and that it owed more to the bank than any other family in town.

The Democratic Leadership Council held its annual conference in Williamsburg, Virginia, on December 12, 1986. There I addressed the trade issue—the need to improve America's competitive position by enhancing productivity, reviving the level of industrial research, modernizing factories, updating job skills, and tightening reciprocity requirements in many of our trade agreements with other countries. Afterward, I had a long conversation with Lloyd Hand, former White House chief of protocol. Hand made an appointment for me to meet with John Young and other business leaders who in the past year had conducted an intensive study of the trade problem at President Reagan's request and had issued a report that they felt had been generally ignored. At the encouragement of these people, I began to explore the possibility of a national conference on competitiveness to be attended by distinguished specialists from business, labor, and academia.

Eager that our efforts be bipartisan, I talked personally with House Republican leader Bob Michel and Senate Minority Leader Bob Dole, as well as with Senate Majority Leader Robert Byrd. All readily acknowledged the importance of the problem, agreed on the worth of such a meeting and on a broad list of invitees, and assented that invitations to the blue ribbon list go out jointly in our four names. The conference, a solicitation by Congress of the best advice available on the subject of trade, was scheduled for January 21 in the ornate Caucus Room of the Cannon House Office Building. I talked with Treasury Secretary Jim Baker and U.S. Trade Representative Clayton Yuetter, inviting them to join in as well.

A week after the invitations went out to the selected cross section of experts, I discovered how difficult it would be to perfect a truly bipartisan approach to the trade issue. Both Republican leaders Michel and Dole called to tell me they had been under pressure from Reagan administration officials to withdraw from formal sponsorship of the event. The White House apparently felt that we needed no change in our trade policies and resented congressional efforts to take an initiative. I was disappointed but not discouraged. It just meant we would have to work that much harder.

The conference took place as scheduled. It was attended by many Republican as well as Democratic members of each house. The panel of distinguished authorities included corporate executives, union leaders, university presidents, and academic specialists who made a probing analysis of the problems. They gave many constructive suggestions.

So broad was the range of actions suggested—from improved job training for America's work force to a renewal of business incentives for modernizing America's aging industrial plants, from antitrust enforcement to renegotiation of copyright and intellectual property rights agreements—that I knew it would require the active cooperation of at least twelve House committees.

On the next day, January 22, I hosted a luncheon for House committee chairs in the Speaker's private dining room. In the first two weeks of the session, the House, at my urging, already had passed a clean water bill and a highway bill by votes easily big enough to override vetoes, and a spirit of ebullience prevailed. We discussed the agenda for the year, the big bills that would comprise our effort to surmount the three deficits.

We talked of the trade bill, an important centerpiece of the agenda. I promised to respect each committee's turf by assigning separate titles of a composite work to the committees that had jurisdiction over the varied segments. Chairs

Dan Rostenkowski of Ways and Means, John Dingell of Commerce, Jack Brooks of Judiciary, and Kika de la Garza of Agriculture each promised to give top priority to their segments of the trade legislation.

Five days later, following President Reagan's State of the Union message, Senate Majority Leader Byrd and I divided the thirty minutes allotted by the television networks for the Democratic response. By our prearrangement, Byrd addressed foreign and military affairs and I the domestic policy agenda. From the cascade of mail and telephoned response, I knew I had struck a sensitive nerve with the public when I revealed that in the previous year the two top U.S. exports, by tonnage, had been scrap metal, mainly from junked cars, and waste paper.

I explained that the latter, shipped mostly to the Far East, was reprocessed into cardboard boxes to carry television sets, toys, computers, and shoe imports back to America. "That's not acceptable," I had said. "We cannot rebuild prosperity on junk and trash! Our economy should be an engine for the world, not an exhaust pipe." An avalanche of response assured me that the American public was enthusiastically supportive, whether or not the administration chose to cooperate in perfecting solutions.

Still, I was eager for a bipartisan approach to trade. In midafternoon on January 28, I invited leading Democrats and Republicans from twelve House committees to sit together around the tables in the Speaker's dining room and discuss ways to improve our nation's trade balance. We agreed to incorporate the best ideas from our several sources into an omnibus bill and to schedule it for action in the House on April 28.

At the request of Chairs Dingell and Rostenkowski, I appeared personally before their committees in the first part of February to emphasize the importance of the bill. Cabinet officers were invited to testify. Many members of both parties, in spite of a lukewarm attitude by the White House, were enthusiastic. Every committee met its time schedule. We all agreed that the bill's main thrust would be stimulative rather than protectionist, its provisions generic rather than product-specific.

In early March, I got a shocker. Japan's ambassador came by my office to tell me that his country's prime minister Yasuhiro Nakasone would like to be invited to address a joint session of Congress on April 28. This was disconcerting. Requests of this kind normally came from the White House. The April 28 date could hardly be coincidental since I had announced it publicly as the day set for the trade bill vote. I suggested to the ambassador that it would be much more fortuitous, and less potentially embarrassing, for his leader to speak on any other date—a week earlier or a week later perhaps—since on April 28 we would be considering the omnibus trade bill.

"Could you not postpone that bill?" the emissary asked. "No, Mr. Ambassador, I'm afraid we cannot." I called Secretary of State George Shultz's office and suggested that it might save embarrassment all around to invite the prime minister to our country on some other week. I gave assurances that the House would cooperate in issuing the invitation at any other date the White House might desire. I never heard further. Nakasone came to our country during the last week in April, but no request was made for his appearance before Congress. I never knew whether the date of his visit was chosen by him or by our administration, nor what effect it was calculated to have on our trade deliberations.

The bill, H.R. Doc. 3, was almost 900 pages long. Most of it had the active support of both Republicans and Democrats in Congress. It offered a fresh approach to our competitiveness problems. One section authorized funding for new educational programs in science, math, engineering, and foreign language training. Another included a $980 million fund for worker retraining and readjustment to help American laborers who had lost their jobs as a result of foreign imports. Another provision extended help for research and development to stimulate a domestic semiconductor industry. The bill also contained significant initiatives to promote American exports.

This measure passed the House by the preponderant vote of 290 to 137. It represented the most important trade legislation since the 1930s. The Senate held the bill under consideration for more than a year, altering and fine-tuning several of its provisions, and finally passed it largely intact in the summer of 1988. One provision, requiring advance notification of the workers before summarily shutting down an American plant, drew the ire of President Reagan. He vetoed the big bill, protesting that such a requirement had no place in trade legislation. We simply removed that provision, made it into a separate bill, then reenacted both bills simultaneously without changing so much as a comma. President Reagan signed the two bills.

The Social Deficit

The social deficit—a growing backlog of human problems and unmet social needs in our country—presented a different challenge entirely. As hard as I tried to promote consensus on issues of international trade, I knew it would be futile to try to conciliate the position of the congressional majority on social policy with that of the Reagan administration. Too wide a gulf separated us.

Since the Gramm-Latta budget amendments and Hance-Conable tax cuts of 1981 had ridden to passage on the coattails of President Reagan's personal popularity, a lot of poor Americans had fallen through the safety net. For the first time since the 1930s, an army of homeless people had begun to appear on America's streets.

The level of funding had been cut for many vital domestic endeavors. Deficiencies in education and civilian research, arising from several years of underinvestment, had begun to rip holes in our social fabric. One visible factor was the slow deterioration of America's public infrastructure—the roads, bridges, airports, dams, navigable waterways, underground pipes—and the lifeline network of public facilities on which Americans depend. The cities of America, and their problems, were being ignored.

Since 1980, while doubling the amount spent annually on military might and tripling our outflow for interest payments, our government had cut by approximately one-fourth the value of our annual investment in America— the gamut of services such as education, transportation, law enforcement, environmental protection, housing, and public health—those things that tend to make life better for the average citizen.

Something else, new and alien to the American experience, was beginning to appear—the disturbing phenomenon of downward mobility. For the first time since polling entered the American scene, a majority of Americans were saying they did not expect their children to enjoy as good a standard of living as they had enjoyed. It was growing harder, not easier, for the average twenty-year-old to buy a car, the average thirty-year-old couple to buy a home, and for forty-year-olds to lay aside enough to see their kids through college.

As Kevin Phillips would point out in his book, *The Politics of Rich and Poor*, the "two most striking economic groups" emerging on the scene made a vivid contrast—billionaires and the homeless. The gap between rich and poor was widening, thanks in considerable part to the conscious economic policies of the Reagan administration. There would be fewer student loans to improvident youngsters, more breaks for upper income taxpayers.

Our spending priorities during the 1980s, I was convinced, had been skewed badly. A big majority of the Democrats in Congress were eager to begin a reversal of the six-year trend in order to restore some of the necessary social underpinnings. There was evidence that the public supported this objective. Polls showed that 62 percent of the people rated the economy "not so good" or "poor" and 72 percent believed Congress must do more for the homeless, for affordable housing, and for educational opportunities.

As Speaker, I felt a strong obligation to set in motion a reversal of the trends that were moving so rapidly toward mergers and leveraged buyouts, increasing difficulties for wage earners, shrinking opportunities for higher education, crumbling infrastructure, and the concentration of America's wealth into fewer hands. This meant confronting the administration directly on a wide range of domestic priorities. But Majority Leader Tom Foley, Democratic Whip Tony Coelho, Assistant Whip David Bonior, and I agreed that we would have to begin with a few identifiable and achievable objectives.

Getting the Congress and the public to focus on these specific objectives was the challenge. In my State of the Union response in January 1987, I named six action priorities. I had reserved low bill numbers to identify these agenda items. One year later, at the beginning of 1988, I was able to give a televised progress report. The clean water bill, the highway bill, and the trade reform bill were H.R. Docs. 1, 2, and 3. Each was passed on schedule and each prevailed over a presidential veto.

In addition, we passed several other significant measures: the first bill ever to provide help for volunteer groups that offer shelters and meals for the homeless; a fairly major reform of the welfare system; and the first important expansion of Medicare for catastrophic illnesses—a bill that would later be repealed in a fight over funding. We increased amounts for college student aid. We authorized a massive effort to combat drugs, and this bill was crafted and passed with bipartisan support. In 1988, for the first time in more than forty years, Congress passed all thirteen major appropriations bills and delivered them to the president for signing into law before the start of the new fiscal year. The public responded enthusiastically to this activist schedule. Polls showed the American people were giving Congress higher performance ratings than they had in many years.

Of the first three big, overriding challenges, the 100th Congress made good on two of them—the trade deficit and the social deficit. We did less well on the budget. While the House passed a budget resolution cutting the fiscal deficit by an appreciable amount and pushed through a hard-fought reconciliation bill by a margin of one vote to carry out that objective, such a level of deficit reduction, particularly as it involved taxes, could not be sustained in the Senate. Our ultimate performance on the budget was impressive only in the sense that it kept things from getting much worse.

The final agreement, hammered out between House, Senate, and White House negotiators, would reduce the deficit by $33 billion in fiscal 1988 and $42.7 billion in fiscal 1989. New revenues would produce only $9.1 billion of this in the first year (about half what I had hoped for) and $14 billion in the next. As Speaker, I spent a large piece of my political capital in the effort to make the tax burden fall more fairly, only to discover that I had overmatched myself.

Any tax bill, I learned to my dismay, was virtually unattainable without the president's agreement. We simply could not get public opinion focused clearly on the issue of tax fairness and on the unambiguous fact that, without more taxes from somebody, the budget could never be balanced. Without a public mandate, Congress was incapable of rallying the two-thirds vote to override a veto. Leaders of both branches understood this, giving leverage to the president's opposition to upper-income taxes. Having failed to draw that issue sharply enough, I believe my leadership was not quite equal to that challenge.

Iran-Contra

One major challenge remained—to head off the constitutional crisis brewing over the newly revealed Iran-Contra scandal and to settle the bitterly divisive issue of our covert involvement in Central American wars. No controversy since the Vietnam War had rent the country so painfully or produced such sharp polarization among lawmakers. The issue of whether to continue funding military efforts to overthrow the leftist government of Nicaragua was provoking angry confrontations in Congress and between the legislative and executive branches. On three occasions, Congress had voted to discontinue all military assistance to the Contras.

In November 1986 the nation was traumatized by the discovery that a secret group operating out of the White House had contrived, contrary to law, to sell U.S. weapons to Iran. Without notifying anyone in Congress, perpetrators had turned over the proceeds to the military forces trying to overthrow Nicaragua's government. President Reagan vowed that he personally had not known of this, and I wanted desperately to believe him.

This was the most shocking revelation since the Watergate burglary and cover-up. At least four laws—the National Security Act, the Arms Export Control Act, the Department of Defense Appropriations Act, and the Anti-Terrorism Act—had been violated blatantly. These laws specifically forbade undertaking any such covert effort without giving official notice to the intelligence committees or the House and Senate leadership, and these laws prohibited the sale of arms to any terrorist country, specifically naming Iran.

So flagrant was the flouting of law that a hot volcanic lava of anger began boiling inside the Congress. First whispers, then audible demands, for impeachment proceedings growled in private conversations wherever Democratic members met. Fortunately, Congress was out of session when the shocking news broke. But activities in the White House did little to abate the outrage. Soon it was known that Lieutenant Colonel Oliver North was systematically shredding all written evidence relating to the illicit adventure before Congress could reconvene and subpoena the documents. This fanned the flames to a higher intensity.

This situation had explosive potential. Several House committee and subcommittee chairs contacted me during December, each wanting to schedule hearings on some separate facet of the big story that dominated Washington news that month. Without a clear sense of direction, the new Congress could degenerate into a nine-ring circus as committees vied with one another for sensational confrontations with various officials of the executive branch.

The last thing our country needed was an impeachment outcry or a frontal challenge to the president's personal integrity. Like other members of Congress and millions of private citizens, I had agonized through long weeks in 1973 that led to and included the impeachment hearing on President Nixon and culminated in his resignation. I wanted no repeat of that scenario. The country could ill afford it. Determined that all of the pertinent facts must be disclosed in a dignified way, preserving the congressional authority without precipitating a full-scale constitutional crisis, I met with Senate Majority Leader Byrd. He felt exactly as I did.

Together we announced that there would be one congressional hearing on the subject, not several. It would be a joint meeting of select House and Senate committees. Byrd and I would appoint Democratic members; Minority Leaders Michel and Dole would select Republican panelists. Eager to protect the credibility and prestige of the special select committees, I very carefully chose the most respected authorities I could find: Chairs Peter Rodino of Judiciary, Jack Brooks of Government Operations, Dante Fascell of Foreign Affairs, Les Aspin of Armed Services, and Louis Stokes of Intelligence. To signal the importance I attached to this mission, I asked House Majority Leader Foley to serve as my personal representative and appointed Edward P. Boland, principal author of several of the laws that had been violated.

I thought a long while before choosing a chair for the whole group and finally settled on Lee Hamilton of Indiana, ranking member of the Foreign Affairs Committee and former chair of the House Intelligence Committee. I picked Hamilton because of his reputation for objectivity and his judicious, noninflammatory manner. I did not want the hearing to be, or even seem to be, a witch hunt. As much as I disagreed with Reagan on domestic priorities, I did not want anyone on the committee with the private agenda of personally embarrassing the president. To complete my list of appointees, I named Ed Jenkins of Georgia, a good country lawyer. I was not trying to prejudge the committee's findings, but merely trying to moderate their explosive potential for splitting the country apart.

Senator Byrd also chose a responsible panel. He and I agreed that, to the extent of our ability to influence it, the hearing must not smack of partisanship. It would be open to the media and nationally televised. Byrd's chair, Sen. Daniel Inouye (D-Hawaii), was ideally suited by temperament and conviction for his role. His demeanor was calm and rational. He and Hamilton did their best to be impartial and scrupulously fair to Republican colleagues appointed by Dole and Michel and to hold down temptations to inflammatory rhetoric.

Hamilton wanted to agree in advance to an arbitrary date to terminate the proceedings. Otherwise, he argued, they could go indefinitely to the detriment of other business. He also proposed giving limited immunity from prosecution to induce testimony from Colonel North, the individual most involved in handling a number of the details of the covert transaction. At least two of the House panelists privately protested, but a majority agreed to back the chair's decision. As it turns out, this may have compromised the efforts of the special prosecutor, Lawrence E. Walsh. But our overriding concern in the congressional leadership, frankly, was less about embarrassing the administration and sending people to jail than about getting at the truth, maintaining the nation's equilibrium, emphasizing the rule of law, and avoiding a bloody constitutional confrontation.

In addition, I felt that we had to heal the malingering wound that had festered for five years over our country's secret, and sometimes illegal, sponsorship of the gory attempts to overthrow the Nicaraguan government by force of arms. Some 30,000 people had died in Nicaragua along with some 70,000 in El Salvador. Congress itself had been closely divided, vacillating between funding and rebuffing President Reagan's demands for military aid to the Contras.

In July 1987, a Republican former colleague, Tom Loeffler, came by my office to inform me that he had been appointed by the president to help round up votes to revive military funding of the Nicaraguan war. I told Loeffler that in my opinion Congress would again reject that demand. The Iran-Contra revelations had damaged his cause.

Acknowledging that possibility, Loeffler suggested that as Speaker I should join President Reagan in a bipartisan initiative for peace. We would call jointly on the Central American nations to negotiate settlements in Nicaragua and El Salvador based on a ceasefire, political amnesty for those who had been in revolt, and free elections to resolve the issues in dispute by popular will. In other words, ballots instead of bullets, with assurances of U.S. support.

That idea appealed to me. After talking with the White House, Republican House leaders and the bipartisan Senate leadership, I was encouraged. Some of my fellow Democrats were skeptical of the president's intentions, but most felt I should take the risk if there was a chance it could lead to peace. I talked also with Secretary of State Shultz, who was instructed by President Reagan to work with me in the preparation of a joint statement.

Before formally agreeing, however, I wanted to test the waters in Central America. I had personal conversations with Presidents Jose Napoleon Duarte of El Salvador and Oscar Arias of Costa Rica. Both of them rejoiced at the prospect. They believed a united pro-peace front in Washington could lead to a series of negotiated settlements throughout Central America and stop the bloodshed.

Michel and I asked Nicaraguan Ambassador Carlos Tunnermann to meet with us in the Capitol to probe the Nicaraguan government's probable response to an initiative such as we had in mind. "What would it take," I asked, "for your country to get rid of Cuban and Russian military advisors, live in peace with your neighbors, cut off any aid to those who want to overthrow the government of El Salvador, and restore the constitutional freedoms of your people that were suspended in the emergency law?" Tunnermann denied that his country was doing anything to interfere in El Salvador. As for the rest, he vowed that his government would be quite willing to do each of the things I asked if we would simply "stop financing the invasion" of Nicaragua.

The presidents of the five Central American republics would be meeting on August 7 in Guatemala. It was important that President Reagan and I agree on the contents of our statement and issue it before that date. I dictated the first draft. Secretary Shultz suggested minor alterations, which I accepted. The President and I jointly issued the call for a regional ceasefire and peaceful negotiation on August 5, two days before the Guatemala conference.

The result was better than I had dared hope. The Costa Rican ambassador called me from the conference site to report the happy news that all five presidents had entered a formal agreement embodying almost all the elements of the Wright-Reagan plan. The principal architect of the Esquipulas Accords, as the agreement would be known, was President Arias of Costa Rica. For this work, he was awarded the Nobel Peace Prize.

At my initiative, we invited Arias to stop off on his way through Washington in September and address the House. Meanwhile, the Nicaraguan government appointed a peace commission, opened newspapers and radio stations that had been shut down, offered amnesty to those who had made war against the government, and invited them to participate in the political process including free elections, which ultimately would be held in 1990. The same amnesty procedure was going on under Duarte's direction in El Salvador.

At about this point, I discovered that the White House was far from happy with the turn events had taken. While I fully expected our joint statement to stimulate the movement toward peace, President Reagan's advisors apparently anticipated refusal of the Nicaraguan government to comply. From negative comments emanating from the White House, it slowly became clear to me that highly placed people in the administration did not *want* a peaceful settlement in Nicaragua. They actually wanted the talks to break down so they could use the "failure" of the peace efforts as an excuse for renewing the war.

This confronted me with a moral dilemma. At the urging of the administration, I had joined in a bipartisan call for peace. Overjoyed at the initial success of our efforts, I had met at the White House's request with leaders of the Contra Directorate. Most of them, I saw, had faith in the peace effort. I was convinced that most Nicaraguans on both sides were eager for peace. But some bitterness lingered. Someone had to be a go-between, an honest broker who could bring the two sides together.

The only Nicaraguan fully trusted by both sides, I had learned, was Catholic Cardinal Miguel Obando y Bravo. Responsible people in both camps agreed that he was the one to monitor the ceasefire and help arbitrate the differences. As Speaker and co-author of the call for peace, I met with the cardinal, whom I knew personally, on November 13, 1987, and encouraged him to undertake that critical role. He agreed, and Nicaraguan President Daniel Ortega at my personal urging agreed to give the cardinal a free hand. The White House, bitterly resentful of my efforts in helping to keep the peace process on track, began attacking me angrily in the press. The president and Assistant Secretary of State Elliott Abrams considered my endeavors intrusive and presumptuous. Perhaps they were. But having committed myself in good faith to the effort to make peace, I was unwilling to be a party to its deliberate unraveling or to allow that result if I could prevent it.

On two occasions—in December 1987 and February 1988—the president's forces tried to forsake the peace process altogether and revive the war by renewing military aid for the Contras. On both occasions, a majority in Congress voted down the request. At my personal urging, Congress did appropriate funds for humanitarian assistance—food, clothing, shelter, and medical needs—for the Contra forces during the ceasefire.

As a consequence of my unwillingness to abandon the effort I had helped set in motion, I became a target for many personal attacks, both in the conservative press and from some Republican members of Congress. It is ironic that, in bringing peace to Central America, I unconsciously drove a wedge between myself and the congressional minority that ultimately inhibited my capacity to promote consensus on other issues. In retrospect, I firmly believe I did the right thing. One of the unavoidable challenges of the speakership is determining when the end result is worth risking one's own popularity, perhaps even one's moral authority, with a segment of the membership. I do regret my inability to make peace between Democrats and Republicans over the issue.

It was in March 1989, with George Bush now serving as president, that Secretary of State Baker and I, along with others in the congressional leadership, issued a second statement that clearly disavowed the use of force and put all the influence of the United States behind the peace negotiation. This culminated in the free and fair election from which Violetta Chamorro emerged as president of Nicaragua on February 25, 1990. In a broad sense, the fourth goal of my speakership was attained, but its attainment used up almost all that remained of my political capital.

A Challenge on the Floor

In dealing with the major policy challenges facing the country, Speakers will at times encounter critical situations in the legislative process that challenge their judgment and test their resolve. On one occasion a miscount of vote commitments on a crucial bill precipitated a parliamentary crisis, confronting me with a series of critical decisions. Pressured by circumstance, I pursued a forceful course that seriously damaged my relationship with the Republican minority in the House.

The date was October 29, 1987. The issue was the reconciliation bill, embodying hard-won cuts in the deficit. Exactly ten days earlier, the stock market had suddenly plummeted by 508 points, or 22.6 percent—a greater comparative drop than the one in 1929 that had sparked the Great Depression. Economists and market analysts were blaming the deficit. I thought it important to show the American public, and quickly, that Congress was capable of making the tough, controversial choices necessary to reduce the deficit. For this reason, I was determined to pass the reconciliation bill without delay.

There was one hitch. Chairman Rostenkowski and other members of the Ways and Means Committee had worked hard to hammer together a welfare reform bill, itself an object of controversy. They wanted to incorporate the text of that reform into the reconciliation bill to avoid the need for a separate vote. My instinct argued that we could be taking on too big a challenge by wedding the two and inviting a united opposition from the enemies of both. But Majority Whip Coelho and the vote-counting task force insisted, after polling the members, that we had enough solidly committed votes to pass the reconciliation bill with the welfare reform engrafted onto it. Since both were important parts of the leadership agenda, I assented to this strategy.

But the vote count was wrong. Support for joint consideration was softer than we thought. Prominent members of the minority argued persuasively that we were stuffing our welfare reform down the members' throats without any chance to debate—and perhaps amend it—and then vote on it as an important separate issue. When the rule combining the two came to a vote, it was rejected by a tally of 203 to 217. This unexpected event threw matters into sudden disarray. At the worst possible time, Congress was demonstrating what would be interpreted as an inability to come to grips with the deficit. That message, I knew, would be trumpeted to the nation by evening telecasts and morning newspapers. I was unwilling to let matters rest there. We needed to reverse the vote, to demonstrate resolve on the budget issue.

No sooner was the vote announced than Republican leader Michel took the floor to propose that we scrap the reconciliation bill and start anew. He wanted to abandon the long summer's work, go back to the beginning, and try to piece together an entirely different "bipartisan" substitute. Without questioning Michel's sincerity, I knew that such a course, with its attendant delays and uncertainties, would be degenerative of public confidence and disruptive of the legislative agenda. There would have been no way to recoup before mid-November, holding everything else at standstill. I was determined to salvage the reconciliation bill, that very day if at all possible. I thought I saw a way to do it.

We had lost forty-eight Democrats on the vote, most of them over the welfare reform issue. It was obvious that the House wanted to vote separately on the two questions and would support a rule bringing up the deficit-reducing reconciliation bill alone. There was one problem, however. House rules prohibit reconsidering a rule on the same day it is defeated. The only way around that would be to adjourn the House and reconvene for a second legislative day later in the same afternoon, with a new rule to present. This had been done before, but only rarely and in cases of unusual urgency. I thought that the circumstances justified doing so in this instance, and I announced my intention of following that course.

As we reconvened for a second "legislative day" that Thursday, I knew that many Republicans would regard my action as highhanded. The new rule, to consider the revised reconciliation bill with the welfare language deleted, passed by a safe vote of 238 to 182. I thought we were over the hump. What I failed to consider was the disappointment of some who had wanted welfare reform to ride piggyback on the deficit-reduction bill, and the disapproval of others who apparently considered my decision to convene a second legislative day as arbitrary.

When it came to a vote, the big measure teetered between passage and failure. At the expiration of the allotted time, members crowded into the well below the Speaker's rostrum. Some had entered the chamber late and had to be recorded by voice vote. When it appeared that everyone had voted, the count stood at 205 to 205. We were down by one. As was the custom, I asked if any members desired to change their votes.

Someone told me that George Miller of California and Marty Russo of Illinois, having voted no, had changed their minds and were on their way back from the House office building to change their votes. This, as it turned out, was false. But I held the vote open awaiting their return to the chamber. Minutes went by, finally ten minutes, not unprecedented but certainly longer than usual to accommodate members desiring to reverse their votes. Miller and Russo did not return, but Jim Chapman of Texas reentered the chamber and asked to change his vote from "no" to "aye." This reversal flipped the balance and the bill passed by one vote.

Republicans were furious. They felt, and perhaps with justification, that I had stretched the powers of the Speaker to the limit. Almost six years later, on August 5, 1993, another Thursday, I watched the late change of a vote by Rep. Marjorie Margolies-Mezvinsky (D-Penn.) create a dramatic come-from-behind win for President Bill Clinton's deficit-reduction bill. Without her switch it would have gone down, and much of President Clinton's program with it. Déjà vu. I knew the minority would be angry—I hoped not as angry as on that Thursday in 1987.

What does a Speaker owe to the minority? Courtesy, consideration, fair play—certainly all of these. I know that some in the minority felt quite strongly that I strained the rules of comity that day and abused the powers of the majority. I did what I thought was right. In the process, unfortunately, I probably hardened the opposition and made future consensus more difficult.

On other occasions, I went out of my way to cultivate a relationship of mutual respect and trust. Throughout my years on the Public Works Committee and my early years as majority leader, I had worked often with members of the other party to find common ground. On matters such as foreign affairs, national defense, trade reform, environmental concerns, public works, and antidrug legislation, I often joined in bipartisan coalitions and sometimes led them. At times I intervened with the Rules Committee on behalf of Republican requests. At the beginning of each Congress, to satisfy requests of new Republican members, I made a point of accommodating the wishes of Republican leader Michel with regard to committee numbers he needed.

All Speakers face an occasional dilemma in their dual roles as activist and presiding judge. It is the duty of the Speaker to use the rules to get things done. Never, however, should any Speaker deny access and equal protection to the minority party or any of its members. My former colleague, Richard Cheney, later Secretary of Defense in the Bush administration, once joined his wife Lynne in writing a fascinating book titled *Kings of the Hill*. It is about the use and abuse of power in the House of Representatives. From any modern perspective, Republican Speakers Joseph Cannon and Thomas Brackett Reed blatantly denied rights to their political opposition. Reed once said that the only purpose of minority members was to make a quorum and their only right was to draw their pay. While deploring these excesses of power, the Cheneys' book also deplored the failure of timid leaders to use the authority inherent in their positions to break deadlocks, dissolve obstructions, and carry out the programs they were elected to fulfill. How to reconcile the two—legislative effectiveness and fairness to the minority—is a challenge no Speaker escapes.

Standing Up for the House

The Speaker has an obligation to uphold the public reputation of the House. Thus, one of the most difficult challenges all modern Speakers have faced is posed by the news media. All Speakers want their colleagues collectively to get credit for their hard work and the institution for its achievements. These wishes frequently are dashed by reporters, editorialists, pundits, and commentators. Their apparent thirst for scandal, their seeming eagerness to debunk, and their slowness to give credit, their frequent fixation with the trivial and tawdry, their boredom with legislative substance, and their ready assumption of an adversarial relationship against public authority in general and Congress in particular may only seem to be getting worse.

The problem is not new. Contempt for Congress is a well-rehearsed habit. Mark Twain once quipped that America has no native criminal class "except, of course, for Congress." And Speaker Nicholas Longworth ruefully concluded in 1925 that "from the beginning of the Republic it has been the duty of every freeborn voter to look down upon us and the duty of every freeborn humorist to make jokes about us."

Congress is, after all, an easy target, an amorphous and heterogeneous collection of opinionated mortals grappling with extraordinary, and sometimes intractable, problems. When one of its members does something foolish or says something stupid, the world is told gleefully and the whole institution suffers public disfavor.

Throughout my thirty-four years in the House it was common for public opinion polls to reveal that most Americans give a low performance rating to the institution as a whole while evaluating the local representative highly. Few citizens and hardly any journalists speak up to defend Congress. Most members feel Congress gets a bum rap, but there is little personal profit with the voters in correcting the negative misimpressions of the institution. It is easier to separate oneself from Congress in the public view. Some members of Congress even seek to aggrandize their own popularity by cynically joining the chorus of critics. Still, most want the Speaker to stand in the breach.

It has been the goal of every Speaker to improve the public image of Congress. To the degree that any one individual can break through the cacophony of strident attack to speak up for the legislative body, the Speaker has that responsibility. Every Speaker I have known has tried to do this, and each has been repeatedly disappointed. From time to time, waves of public displeasure wash over the Congress, driven by high-profile, sometimes grotesquely overhyped, criticism.

In the past forty years the institution of Congress has been battered from pillar to post by sensational media attacks. Since the 1950s, Congress has been successively whipsawed for nepotism, absenteeism, taking "junkets," Koreagate, and more recently, in 1992, for the highly publicized House banking "scandal" in which members were loosely characterized as "bouncing" checks and even "kiting" checks. The terms were misleading. No check bounced and there was no indication of kiting. Nothing dishonest occurred. Nobody lost any money, least of all the taxpayers. The little private bank was not even federally insured. Nobody got hurt except members themselves, whose collective honor was held up for public scorn.

Perhaps it has always been this way. During one week almost twenty years ago, Congress was characterized in various newspaper editorials as "slothful," "incompetent," "congenitally slow," "lobby-ridden," "structurally incapable of leadership," and as a collection of "jet-set goof-offs." The truth is that Congress is neither much more nor much less than the sum of its 535 parts. It is, as the title implies, *representative* of the public. Composed of mortals, it is fallible. But it can rise on occasion to heights of statesmanship usually unnoted. "Face it, Mr. Speaker," a reporter once insisted, "the praiseworthy is not newsworthy." Congress can and often does behave responsibly. The institution deserves a better perception than it usually enjoys. If that were not so, this experiment in self-government would have perished long ago among the shoals of democracy, as Alexis de Tocqueville prophesied.

As Speaker I tried every stratagem I could imagine to prevail on newspeople to see and report the positive side of Congress. I held daily news conferences. I invited media representatives to join me at working luncheons. I held dinners at my home in McLean, Virginia, where newspeople could visit socially with key House members. I conducted public bill-signing ceremonies. I accepted every request to appear on a radio or television talk show. I took press telephone calls at home, on weekends, and late at night. I wrote courteous personal letters to those whose writings or broadcasts contained factual errors detrimental to the Congress. Once when a staff assistant, without my knowledge, wrote a sarcastic letter to the publisher of the *Los Angeles Times* complaining of inaccuracies in a news story, I even invited the two offended reporters to lunch in the Speaker's private dining room; when the waiter brought out prime steaks for the reporters, he set before me, by my prearrangement with him, a plate of baked crow!

Maybe some of this worked to one degree or another. Frankly, I never felt that any of it did much good in cultivating a favorable public image for the institution I loved and served. A hundred evidences of good work and entreaties of good will could be undone by one thoughtless deed of a colleague magnified by one headline-hungry journalist. I might as well have been trying to teach cats to respect birds.

One incident stands out. It was in January 1989, before the 101st Congress convened. The presidentially appointed pay commission reported a recommendation that federal judges and members of Congress receive cost-of-living salary adjustments. The methodology had been created years before as a "reform" to separate Congress from the task of setting its own pay. After all, it was argued, nobody else in government did so. Congress determined the pay scale of others; why not let others determine theirs?

This made sense superficially but did not work out so well in practice. The reason it did not work, ironically, is that some lawmaker, eager to make points with folks at home, would offer a motion to delete any pay benefit for members of Congress. Some such motions were offered by lawmakers of independent wealth; others by members who secretly hoped colleagues would vote their amendments down. No such luck. Usually a majority, confronted with voting on their own pay and not wanting to appear self-serving, would vote to decline any increase in salary for themselves.

The irony of this was that the public hardly ever knew of their lawmakers' self-abnegating gesture. It would receive scant, if any, publicity, and the membership generally never got any public credit for turning down their own pay raises. In eleven of the previous eighteen years, members had voted in open session to deny themselves the automatic cost-of-living adjustments that Congress was authorizing for practically everyone else in government. (Federal judges, on the identical pay track with members of Congress, had to suffer the same decline in buying power to pay for the purity of their legislative peers. Some judges were retiring prematurely because of this, and a lot of highly qualified lawyers were refusing to accept judicial appointments.)

The presidential pay commission reported that, in terms of constant dollar value, Congress had forced its own members and the judiciary to lose slightly more than one-third the buying power they had enjoyed in 1970. Attempting to rectify the disparity between these two classes and most others in government and business, the commission recommended a 51 percent increase for national lawmakers and judges. Congress had absolutely nothing to do with the commission's decision. I even told members of that panel after their formal proposal was announced that I thought it represented too big a jump at one time. I felt sure the public would have a hard time understanding the commission's reasoning, and experience had taught me not to expect much help from the media in explaining it. But even I was unprepared for the vicious onslaught that ensued.

On the Sunday after the proposal was announced, Senate Majority Leader Mitchell and Minority Leader Dole, answering questions on national television, announced that the Senate would summarily vote down the proposed increase. I made no such announcement. Feeling that my colleagues and the judges deserved some reasonable increase but aware that a 51 percent boost would not fly, I privately polled every Democratic and Republican member of the House, assuring each that his or her individual response would be held in my confidence. I wanted to learn what amount of raise, if any, the majority actually thought fair, and what a majority would be willing to support in a public vote.

Meanwhile, the media lambasted Congress mercilessly for three weeks, accusing members of plotting to avoid a vote on the issue. Several headlines referred to it as an effort to "steal." Since House Republican leader Michel and I had not hastened to denounce the proposed raise publicly, we were singled out and bombarded daily with demands that we promise to kill the "greedy pay grab."

For much of this time Congress was out of session. While I was trying to make personal contact with every member and get a reading on whether we could piece together some fair and reasonable compromise, radio call-in and talk show hosts throughout America importuned their listeners to "contact the Speaker of the House," demanding an end to this "cowardly money grab!" Some broadcasted my home telephone number, and at least one encouraged his listeners to jam my facsimile machine with messages of bitter outrage so that my office had trouble conducting other legitimate business.

Analysis of my private poll showed that most members felt some upward adjustment was fair and needed, but they thought the 51 percent figure excessive. A majority would vote for a 30 percent increase accompanied by the abolition of all speaking and lecture fees. (Members at that time were allowed legally to accept as much as 30 percent of their salary in fees of no more than $2,000 each for public appearances they might make outside their districts.)

But most members, it was clear, would be forced by media hype and resultant public disfavor to reject any increase whatsoever if that vote should arise. Under the rules, there would have been no way to prevent a member from offering such a motion. That, of course, is what happened. Elements in the media enjoyed a brief feeding frenzy at the expense of Congress. Members received nothing whatever at the time except accusations of stealthily plotting to enrich themselves. As Speaker, I was powerless under the circumstances to protect my colleagues and my institution from the largely unjustified criticism.

Up to that point, the Congress had been gaining steadily in public esteem. The fact that we were producing a positive agenda of legislative accomplishments had lifted approval ratings for the institution from about 45 percent to about 68 percent over a three-year period. In the final analysis, the public will support its legislative branch when it perceives that Congress is doing its work, making good on its promises, and seriously addressing the nation's problems.

No amount of cleverness or legislative legerdemain on the part of any Speaker can change that. To expect fair treatment from the media is folly. When all is said and done, two things matter: substance and self-respect. Everything else is window dressing.

12 The Speakership Today

Ronald M. Peters, Jr.

Now that we have now met the contemporary speakership in several of its aspects, what are we to make of this important constitutional office as it presents itself to us today? The findings of the scholars and the perspectives of the three former Speakers provide a substantial basis for interpreting the speakership. This chapter's purpose is to provide a synthesis of the information that they have provided. The speakership is today shaped by four interrelated factors: forces external to the House, the institutional needs of the House, the Speaker's partisan role, and political persona. Let us consider each in turn and then consider how they work together to shape the speakership.

External Forces

The House of Representatives is in many respects an insider's institution. Its rules and traditions are arcane, and it requires the work of a full-time staff of professional parliamentarians to keep track of its precedents. To the uninitiated, the House seems almost occult, its legislative pathways as labyrinthine as are its subterranean passages. Yet the House, as are all American political institutions, is still strongly affected by external forces. The House is affected by world events, social change, and the role of the other institutions with which it interacts in the constitutional system of separated powers.

The effect of world events on the House is best seen in the evolution of the Speaker's role in foreign policy, as presented by Steven Smith and Mark Watts in Chapter 6. Their account stresses the increasing role that Speakers have come to play in foreign policy, culminating with Speaker Wright's significant role in negotiating peace accords in Nicaragua (also discussed in Chapter 11 by Speaker Wright, in Chapter 8 by Roger Davidson, and in Chapter 4 by John Pitney and William Connelly). The changing character of the Speaker's role in foreign policy focuses on two main factors. The first is the global role played by the United States since World War II; the second is the decline of bipartisan foreign policy consensus. The former made the United States a player; the latter ensured that foreign policy would become the subject of political controversy touching the electoral needs of members of the House.

The specific interventions of Speakers in foreign policy issues have been episodic, dependent on events that the Speakers cannot control and personal disposition that presumably they can control. When Carl Albert fought against end-the-war resolutions in the Democratic Caucus, he reacted to external events in a very personal way. When Wright chose to join in the peace process in Nicaragua, he was true to his own personality and instincts. Thus, while world events may force Speakers into the foreign policy arena, the manner in which they respond is subject to considerable discretion. Tip O'Neill's choices in dealing with the crises in Lebanon and Grenada were his to make, and another Speaker might have responded differently. No Speaker could have ignored these world events, however.

The press of world events naturally connects to foreign policy, but other external events can affect the speakership. These might range from natural disasters in the United States or abroad, which may have repercussions in members' districts, to more gradual changes in the character and needs of American society. For example, in her study of the Speaker's leadership of the Democrats in Chapter 3, Barbara Sinclair notes that the changing composition of the Democratic Caucus has altered the circumstances in which Speakers must lead. The southern, conservative-dominated caucus that Albert describes in Chapter 9 slowly gave way to a more homogeneous group as southern Democratic constituencies became increasingly comprised of white and African-American liberals, while southern Republican constituencies became increasingly comprised of conservative whites. These changes in society were extrinsic to the House but affected everything that went on inside it.

The policy agenda is also shaped by such forces. A main factor underpinning the Conservative Coalition was southern Democratic resistance to civil rights legislation. This led the southerners to coalesce with Republicans. After the major civil rights bills of the 1960s were enacted into law, civil rights gave way to other social and economic issues on the national agenda, leading to differing alignments in the Congress. Technological change has also played a major role, both in shaping the way that the House does its business and the business that it addresses. In Chapter 7, Joe Foote describes how recent Speakers have developed strategies to deal with (and, where possible, to shape) media coverage of the House and of political and policy issues. Coping with the media has become an institutionalized aspect of the speakership, and this is unlikely to change. At the same time, economic issues such as the North American Free Trade Agreement (NAFTA), debated by Congress in 1993, cleave the House in unusual ways, turning allies into adversaries. Pro-trade Democrats, led by President Clinton, joined with most Republicans to support the agreement. Speaker Tom Foley, from a port state, sided with the president; majority leader Dick Gephardt (D.-Missouri), and whip David Bonior (D.-Mich.)—both from manufacturing states—opposed Clinton.

Speakers have to fulfill their constitutional role in the system of separated powers. This is especially true when the presidency is in the hands of the opposing party. Then a Speaker becomes a national voice—sometimes the only one—for the majority political party. The media will gravitate to the Speaker, and the Speaker must develop strategies for using the media to the advantage of the institution and to the politics of the majority party. In this era of media dominance, modern Speakers find it necessary to develop a media strategy, even when the majority party also controls the White House. All of the members will be media-sensitive and media-savvy. If Speakers do not use the media to good advantage, they may pay a price in member support. Finally, the media affords an additional avenue of communication to the members. Often members first learn what Speakers are thinking when they hear them say it on television.

The system of separated powers shapes the speakership in other ways. Daniel Palazzolo's account in Chapter 5 of the Speaker's evolving role in the budget process is a good example. The budget process was first put in place under Speaker Albert just so that the Congress could deal more effectively with the budget proposed by the president. Since then it has been typical for the Congress and the White House, as well as the House and the Senate, to squabble over budget priorities. During the Reagan and Bush administrations, these conflicts sometimes paralyzed the budget process and led to a variety of Rube-Goldberg-budget contraptions. The Speaker is expected both to ensure the orderly process of legislation and to guard the political interests of the majority party.

Budget policy is often pushed to the leadership level and sometimes only resolved after negotiations between Congress and the White House in which the Speaker plays a leading role, as in 1982, 1987, and 1990. Speaker O'Neill stood in strong opposition to President Reagan's budget priorities, Speaker Wright pressed for enactment of his own priorities, and Speaker Foley supported the budget proposed by President Clinton. In each case the Speaker's role in the budget process was defined fundamentally in relation to the presidency on the one hand and to the Democratic Caucus on the other hand. In 1987, Speaker Wright forced the Senate and the White House to deal with the House-passed budget on his own terms. In 1990, Speaker Foley engaged in a protracted negotiation with the Senate and White House in which he was forced to agree to some budget provisions that proved unacceptable to House Democrats.

Institutional Needs

In dealing with the president and the Senate on the budget, the Speaker also fulfills an institutional obligation to make the House function as a legislative institution. Here the Speaker's institutional and partisan roles often interact. But this does not always happen. The Speaker has an obligation, as Speaker Albert emphasizes, to deal fairly with members and, as Speaker O'Neill notes, to stand up for the House. The Speaker embodies the House's institutional prestige and constitutional prerogatives. The office is also at the center of the House's legislative mechanisms. If the speakership is ineffective, it is unlikely that the House will be effective. Roger Davidson's account in Chapter 8 of the role that Speakers have played in the process of institutional change illustrates this point. Speakers have played different roles, as resistors or as facilitators of change. But in each case the Speaker acted in accordance with his conception of the House's institutional character and needs. Speaker McCormack's resistance to change eventually undermined his effectiveness; Speaker Albert's willingness to facilitate change was instrumental in enabling the House to cope with the most rapid change in its history.

In a similar way, in Chapter 5 Palazzolo defines four potential roles for Speakers in the budget process: facilitator of process (Albert); manager of conflict (O'Neill with Reagan; Foley with Bush); promoter of party policy (Wright); or supporter of the president's program (O'Neill with Carter; Foley with Clinton). In each case the specific role played by the Speaker varied by political and personal circumstance, but in each case the ultimate aim was to produce a federal budget. This is perhaps most clearly seen in Speaker Albert's strong commitment to the budget process. As he describes it, the enactment and implementation of the Budget and Impoundment Act was not simply a matter of institutional efficiency, but a necessary response by Congress to the reach of an imperial presidency. In facilitating the process, Albert defended the institutional prerogatives of the House.

Sinclair, in Chapter 3, emphasizes new methods of coalition-building that have evolved over the past two decades. Among these methods she stresses strategies of inclusion, recognition of member needs, and use of restrictive rules to shape the legislative process. The Speaker's ability to use the Rules Committee in this way reflects, of course, the dramatically enhanced formal powers of the office in the postreform period. These methods are responses to the House's institutional needs as well as reflections of the Speaker's partisan role. They recognize the increased independence of members (on both sides of the aisle) and the effect that greater member autonomy has had on the legislative process. The greater decentralization of authority made possible by the reforms of the 1970s led to the development of leadership strategies designed to cope with a more fragmented authority structure. The use of these strategies usually presupposes the more cohesive partisan majorities that Sinclair describes. When the majority party and its leadership are internally split, as was the case on NAFTA, the House returns to the state of nature.

Although sometimes put to specifically partisan use, the new techniques of legislative management also can serve the needs of all members. Primary among those needs is reelection. Members prefer to be protected against politically dangerous votes. This can sometimes mean protecting Democrats against Republicans, but sometimes it means protecting incumbents against challengers. Members also want opportunities for policy participation. The decentralized structure of the House lends itself to greater opportunity for members to shape policy, and the rise of the entrepreneurial member has presented a challenge to both Democratic and Republican party leaders. Independent of the partisan implication, however, is an institutional implication: these members want a piece of the action and are less likely to be subservient to an established power structure. The result is a more open legislative system over which the Speaker has the constitutional obligation to preside.

The Speaker's institutional role has a greater implication for the process of selecting Speakers than perhaps any other aspect of the speakership. As Lynne Brown and Robert Peabody note in Chapter 2, the choice of Speaker is typically made years in advance of the actual nomination, and for reasons that are largely institutional. When the majority leadership becomes vacant there is either a contested election (Wright in 1976) or, more commonly, an uncontested anointing of the party whip (Albert in 1962; Boggs in 1971; O'Neill in 1972; Foley in 1986). Often the whip was chosen or selected years before (Albert in 1955; Foley in 1980). Thus, there is a time lag between getting on the ladder and becoming Speaker. Ascent up the ladder is not always automatic, as illustrated by Whip John McFall, who ran last in a field of four candidates for majority leader in 1976. Scholarly and press attention typically has focused on Wright's remarkable upset of Richard Bolling and Philip Burton, but Wright's case is only slightly anomalous; he was a deputy whip at the time. The truly anomalous case is McFall; why did he lose? Brown and Peabody provide an insightful analysis.

The willingness of the Democrats to settle for this system of relatively automatic elevation to the speakership is unusual. It is not matched by the history of House Republicans, Senate Democrats or Republicans, or the leadership of most state legislative institutions. It persists because it serves the institutional and political needs of House Democrats. Their party is diverse and their legislative caucus would be easily fractured by regular leadership contests. Yet there is a more fundamental element at play—the committee system. Contested leadership elections inevitably would pit committee chairs against each other. This would undermine both party discipline and the committee process. Better to remove party leadership selection from the byzantine byways of the committee system.

Partisan Role

There is no denying the partisan character of the speakership today. It is as deeply partisan (although not as entirely authoritarian) as at any time in the past. Every aspect of the speakership that can be explained in other ways can also be explained in simple partisan terms. This does not mean that the speakership is entirely partisan; it does mean that it is inherently partisan. No Speaker thinks of the job in wholly partisan terms (although some come close). Even Speakers O'Neill and Wright, by reputation partisan leaders, testify to the obligation that Speakers bear to be fair. Every Speaker must calculate the partisan implications of every aspect of the job and adapt appropriately. The partisan choice may succumb to the institutional obligation. Speaker O'Neill's management of the budget process, for example, represents to Palazzolo a triumph of politics over procedure. In fact, the politicization of the budget process has led to bizarre procedures since the last Carter budget.

This book confronts the issue of partisanship most directly in the account of the Republican perspective as presented by Pitney and Connelly in Chapter 4. It is plain that Republicans feel that the speakership has become increasingly politicized, especially under Speakers O'Neill and Wright. These two Speakers can (and do) speak for themselves on these issues. Our task is analytic. How does the Speaker's partisan role express itself most significantly today, and what is the implication for the speakership?

If we consider Sinclair's argument on majority party leadership in comparison to that of the views expressed by Pitney and Connelly, several issues emerge. Sinclair, for example, stresses what she calls "coalition building" as an essential leadership strategy. With respect to majority party leadership, this typically means building coalitions among Democrats. The techniques that Democratic leaders have used to build coalitions include such things as task forces on key bills and the use of special rules that shape floor consideration of bills. The Republicans do not object to the former; however, they very much object to the latter. Why?

Legislative parties are free, within the law and House rules, to do what they want to rally party majorities. That is the nature of the game. Restrictive floor rules, however, touch on the very nature of the legislative institution. Sinclair describes what the Democrats are doing, and Pitney and Connelly present the Republican objections to it. The Democrats regard these practices as appropriate under the circumstances; the Republicans do not. Who is right?

On behalf of the Democrats' use of restrictive rules, two arguments are most convincing. One derives from the institutional needs of the House. Absent restrictive rules, floor consideration of bills might become chaotic and lead to legislative paralysis. The other argument derives from partisan considerations. Absent restrictive rules, Republicans will offer mischievous (and often frivolous) amendments that have purely partisan purposes. Why should the Democrats tolerate it? The time-honored right of the minority to offer comprehensive substitutes and the right to seek a vote to recommit are typically not denied by the use of restricted rules.

On the Republican side, two forceful arguments are pressed. First, it is argued that the use of restrictive rules is essentially undemocratic, denying to the minority party the right to participate fully in the legislative process. Second, it is argued, the use of restrictive rules does not serve the public interest; bills could be improved by floor amendments that are not in order under the rule.

The Democrats correctly insist that it is their obligation as the majority party to ensure that bills get passed on the floor of the House; however, they sometimes use the restrictive rules for purely partisan purposes. The Republicans correctly assert that the use of restrictive rules for purely partisan purposes violates the spirit of the Constitution; they cannot deny, however, that they want open rules to promote their own partisan advantage.

So the roots of partisanship go deep into the soil of the House. They mani-
fest themselves in the strategies of party leaders, in the development of media
strategies, in conflicts over the budget and foreign policy, and in debates over
institutional reform. On the Democratic side, partisanship expresses itself in a
tension between the need for policy results and the autonomy of members. On
the Republican side, partisanship expresses itself in a debate between
"accommodationists" and "confrontationists." The most recent incarnation
of this debate between the supporters of Bob Michel and those of Newt Gingrich echoes previous conflicts between Joseph Martin and Charles Halleck, and
between Halleck and Gerald Ford.

Is there a bright light to guide Speakers toward their duty when torn between institutional and partisan obligations? Unfortunately not. Instead, individual Speakers must strike the necessary balance in ways that are satisfactory
to their character and political circumstance. In this, as in all other respects,
the speakership reflects the character of each Speaker.

The Personal Element

In reading the chapters by Speakers Albert, O'Neill, and Wright, one is
struck by how true to their respective personalities their views of the speakership are. Speaker Albert sees the speakership as an office of constitutional
responsibility requiring fidelity to an institutional role. Speaker O'Neill
presents the speakership in terms of the persons who influenced his development as a politician and in terms of the rules of the game that he learned in his
long career. Speaker Wright sees the speakership as an opportunity to shape
public policy and as a set of challenges to the Speaker. All three Speakers are
correct.

For a generation or more political scientists have sought to understand positions of institutional leadership in terms of roles that persons holding them
play. We see ample evidence of this scholarly tendency in this volume, in
which Speakers Albert and Foley are here and there called "facilitators"
whereas Speakers O'Neill and Wright are sometimes called "partisans" or
"policymakers." Speakers, of course, do not think of themselves in this way.
Speaker O'Neill did not decide to be a "conflict resolver," even if that is the
role that he played in the budget process from time to time. Speaker Albert did
not think of himself as a facilitator of change, even as he consciously sought to
facilitate it. Instead, these two Speakers, as Speakers Wright and O'Neill,

thought of themselves as playing only a single role—that of Speaker. Wright never got out of bed saying to himself, "I'm going to be a policy innovator today," but he probably got up every day saying to himself, "I'm the Speaker of the House." Speakers think of themselves as Speakers.

But what does this mean? As students of the speakership, we can parse it in different ways depending on our interests or perspectives. But Speakers do not have the luxury of truncating their own experience; they have to live it whole. Living it themselves, they give it meaning. No gloss on the speakership and no book about it can define it entirely, because every speakership is unique, because every Speaker is unique. So in the end, in order to understand the speakership, we have to consider the choices that Speakers make, the things that Speakers do. For in theorizing about the speakership, the Speakers are both the dependent and independent variables. They are, to a great extent, the architects of their own fate.

Several examples from this book will illustrate. When Speaker Albert decided to oppose efforts to end the Vietnam War, to oppose efforts to end school busing, to support some proposed House reforms and to oppose others—in each of these instances he favored one part of his House constituency and angered another, and the parts were never the same. The decisions that he made were his to make, and he made them consistent with his own character, his understanding of his role as Speaker, and his political situation. No other Speaker would have made exactly the same set of choices. Again, when confronted with the most severe constitutional crisis since the Civil War—the impeachment of Richard Nixon—Albert's responses were dictated by his character and his understanding of the speakership. We know that O'Neill would have proceeded differently; he pushed for a different course of action at the time.

In a similar way, when Speaker O'Neill led the Democrats during the 99th Congress, he made choices that were different from those made by Speaker Wright in the 100th Congress, even though the circumstances were roughly the same. Majority Leader Wright often chafed at strategic choices made by Speaker O'Neill, and Speaker O'Neill may well have questioned decisions made by then-Speaker Wright.

When President Reagan placed American troops in harm's way in Lebanon in 1982, Speaker O'Neill supported him. When, shortly thereafter, the U.S. Marine barracks was bombed and more than 250 soldiers were killed, Speaker O'Neill backed away. Only he could answer the question of why he did this. In

Chapter 6, Smith and Watts argue that the Speaker's role in foreign policy is fundamentally affected by personal choices.

When Speaker Wright resigned his office in 1989, Speaker Foley assumed the office. His approach to leadership was very different from that of his predecessor. Why? Perhaps because Speaker Foley had gone to school on Speaker Wright's experience, but also, perhaps, because Foley and Wright are very different people with different attitudes toward the House and the Speaker's role in leading it.

In these instances and in many others, we see the personal element of the speakership. When the House picks its Speaker, it chooses a person whose values and dispositions will shape the conduct of office. This is why the Democratic leadership ladder becomes increasingly problematical today. The ladder may continue in place for some time to come as Brown and Peabody suggest, but the Democrats (and the House) may pay a price for it. That price is a possible discontinuity between the character and values of its leadership and that of the members, many of whom may not have been in the House when the Speaker stepped on the ladder. Contested election is no guarantee of a good selection, but contemporaneous contested elections may more closely reflect the character of the chamber than contested elections of a decade past.

The leadership ladder has another effect notable in the narratives of the three former Speakers. It has led to a leadership culture woven by interpersonal relationships. Brown and Peabody note the phenomenon of "tapping." Connected to tapping is "socialization," the manner in which leaders learn from each other. The debt that Albert, O'Neill, and Wright express to Sam Rayburn is striking, but not as striking as this fact: Foley was the first Speaker not to have served as a member of Congress with Rayburn since David Henderson left the House in 1903.[1]

The Postreform Speakership

The speakership is not as predictable as a layer cake, nor is it as unfathomable as something out of a food processor. It is more like a marble cake, a blend of identifiable ingredients, the specific form of which depends on circumstance and choices that are made differently by every Speaker brought to the task.[2] We know that the speakership will be shaped by external forces, internal factors, partisan considerations, and personal choices. In Chapter 1 we provided a framework that might guide a Speaker in shaping a speakership or a reader in arraying it for consideration. But the actual shape of any speakership depends on circumstances and the choices that Speakers make, as the experience of the past four Speakers indicates.

The central problem of Albert's speakership was the tension between the established order's senior beneficiaries and the demands of newer members. The trend toward longevity of service in the House peaked in the late 1960s, and during Albert's tenure senior committee chairs still controlled most levers of the legislative process. The newer members wanted a share of the power and, as O'Neill put it, "the boys don't want to give it up." The "boys" were mostly in their sixties and seventies, but that did not diminish their attachment to a system that empowered them.

This generational tension took a specific political form, since the old-guard Democrats were allied in the conservative coalition with the Republicans, while the newer members were far more liberal. Speaker Albert thus sat abreast two divides, one generational and the other ideological. Facing Republican presidents, Albert's task was to nurture the House through a period of institutional change while promoting a legislative agenda around which the Democrats could rally.

This was the structural situation of his speakership. That situation was then shaped by the main political issues of the period: the Vietnam War, school busing, the economy, and Watergate. These external forces gave specific definition to Albert's speakership because they framed the issues that the Congress confronted. Speaker Albert's tasks were to superintend the reform movement, to unify a divided congressional party, to develop a legislative program, and to weather the constitutional crisis.

To this set of tasks he brought a personal constituency grounded in the border South, with strong ties to senior, mostly southern, members, yet with substantial links to northern liberals. If House leaders are supposed to be middlemen, Albert may have been nearly the middle man. His personal commitments were to a bipartisan, Cold War anticommunism and to progressive social and economic legislation. He was thus with the conservatives on national defense issues and with the liberals on social issues.

In seeking to deal with this complex situation, Albert promoted some institutional reforms, facilitated others, and resisted a few. His speakership witnessed the development of many of the techniques of legislative management that would come to characterize the speakership in the postreform House: use of the caucus, task forces, press strategies, policy committees, expanded whip organization, and so forth. His character, personal commitments, and political situation were well-suited to his circumstances in some respects, less well in others. But the speakership that he created was a product of the underlying character of the office, the circumstances, and his choices.

Speaker O'Neill's tenure spanned ten years and a variety of political circumstances. During the Carter administration, O'Neill's central challenge was to rally a divided Democratic Caucus behind the legislative proposals of a president who was more conservative than was he. By 1977 the intramural squabbles over House reform were largely at rest, and O'Neill did not have to devote major attention to questions of institutional change. Furthermore, with the party's legislative agenda set largely by the administration, it was not necessary for the Speaker to develop a legislative program for the House.

This did not lead to easy going for Speaker O'Neill. Indeed, in some respects O'Neill found the Carter years more challenging than the Reagan years; at least in the latter situation, the enemy was clear. During the Carter presidency, O'Neill had to rally the House to support policies that he sometimes opposed himself. He had to ask members to cast difficult votes on behalf of an administration that sometimes seemed indifferent to the members' electoral needs. In some highly publicized instances the House rebelled against the administration and the leadership, and O'Neill was left to put the best face on defeat.

The distance from policy that he had maintained throughout his legislative career served him well in this situation. As a leadership staff member put it once, "Tip often sounds like a beleaguered janitor." Speaker O'Neill had a remarkable capacity to appear both powerful and powerless as the need served him. When it was a question of his institutional power, he loomed to his full height and girth both institutionally and personally. When it was a question of assuming responsibility for legislative defeats, he was able to deflate himself rapidly. Either the administration did not handle the situation correctly or the members just would not go along.

During the Reagan administration, Speaker O'Neill faced greater challenges and greater opportunities. On the one hand, the Reagan program threatened his most fundamental beliefs as well as the well-being of his beloved Democratic party; on the other hand, he became the nation's leading Democrat, and spoke for and symbolized the national party. While presiding over the further development of the leadership machinery, O'Neill made himself an icon, drawing to him both the passionate support and fervid opposition that icons attract. The Speaker won several substantial legislative victories, helped perpetuate a budget stalemate that will endure for some time to come, and became the best known Speaker in American history.

Any Democratic Speaker would have faced the same circumstances and the same challenges; but Speaker O'Neill's personality and political situation shaped the speakership that he created. His anchor in the Democratic Caucus was among northeastern liberals and younger members from around the country. Unlike Speaker Albert, who was near to the middle of the party's ideological and geographic basis, O'Neill was firmly in the northeast and on the left. O'Neill had been around long enough to have decent relations with the senior committee chairs, and fewer of them were from the South. His tendency, as was Albert's, was to defer to the committees except on rare occasion. Since the committee system was by now more democratic and participatory, deferring to the committees often meant a lack of policy control. This explains the evolution of the new techniques of coalition-building at the floor stage that Sinclair describes.

If Speaker O'Neill was a "man of the House," as his autobiography suggests, he was first, last, and always a partisan Democrat. This is how the Republicans saw him and this is how he described himself. The main legacy of his speakership is tied to his partisan character in two ways. As is noted in several places in this book, the 1980s witnessed an increase in the partisan division in the House. Speaker O'Neill did not cause that increased partisanship, but his political persona contributed to it. The main policy result of this partisan division is the dramatic increase in the federal deficit. Speaker O'Neill bears no more (and probably less) responsibility for this than does President Ronald Reagan, but the deficit remains and continues to grow. These institutional and policy consequences arose from the weave of the O'Neill speakership as O'Neill himself created it.

As Speaker Wright notes in his chapter, the deficit situation was among the four main challenges that he confronted as Speaker. The simple fact that he states his situation in these policy terms is striking. Both Speaker Albert and Speaker O'Neill understand their speakerships in relationship to the main policy issues of their day, but neither defines their speakership in relationship to them. Instead, Albert stresses issues of institutional reform and O'Neill offers lessons on how to be Speaker. Albert defines the Speaker's responsibilities in terms of the institutional needs of the House; O'Neill defines the Speaker's responsibilities in terms of the rules of the political game. Neither stakes the speakership on policy outcomes.

This difference in attitude toward the job, which is presented in a straightforward manner by the three Speakers, reflects in an equally straightforward way the manner in which they are depicted by the studies presented in this book. Among the three, Speaker Wright is consistently characterized as the policy-oriented Speaker. It should be noted, however, that in describing the central challenges of his speakership in terms of public policy, Wright takes for granted the structural situation that he inherited. Speaker Albert struggled with House reform, while Speaker O'Neill developed the new techniques of leadership (assisted by Majority Leader Wright). The machinery was oiled and ready to go and Wright was ready to use it.

Still, Wright's speakership cannot be understood simply as he describes it, in policy terms. The House that Wright was chosen (without intra-party opposition) to lead as Speaker in 1987 was different from the House that he was elected (in a bitterly contested intra-party contest) to serve as majority leader in 1976. The coalition that had elected Wright was a natural political coalition comprised of members who preferred a moderate Democrat from Texas to either of the two more liberal candidates in the race. The coalition that nominated Wright for Speaker in the 1986 Democratic Caucus was a very different beast. There were no opposing candidates, and the foundation of that uncontested election did not simply rest on precedent, ideological congruence, or geographic loyalty. It rested on the ten years of unrelenting effort that Wright had invested on behalf of members, including hundreds of campaign trips and countless legislative favors. As Brown and Peabody note, it also included numerous campaign contributions from his leadership PAC. By the time he declared his candidacy for Speaker (in 1985, after Speaker O'Neill announced his intention to retire), Wright was able to claim the support of the majority of Democrats because he had earned it the old-fashioned way.

Wright had won the speakership by doing things for members; as Speaker, he came to ask them to do things for him. He wanted his Democrats to join him in making hard policy choices, in enacting his policy preferences. In striking out on this leadership path, he challenged the Democrats and he threatened the Republicans. He walked head up into a partisan divide that had been a decade in the making. One of the central facets of Wright's speakership was the intense partisanship of the House. In his single-minded drive to affect public policy, Wright fanned the fires of partisan division in ways that eventually undermined his support among those Democrats whose support had initially rested on a foundation of political favors rather than personal commitment.

In the 100th Congress, Speaker Wright had things his way. The rules of the House and the leadership machinery were used to enact party legislation even in the face of an opposed administration. The speakership that Wright created then was the most powerful since the days of Uncle Joe Cannon; there is no doubt about it. He demonstrated that a Speaker who is willing to use the full powers of the office can drive the legislative process and pull the Senate and the administration along. On many important items of legislation Wright forged conditions that brought bipartisan support; Republicans were afraid to oppose popular bills. In part as a result, almost every member of that Congress seeking reelection in 1988 was returned by the voters. Wright had served the interests of all incumbents by driving a successful legislative agenda.

But along the way, something happened. Gingrich and other conservative Republicans perceived the danger of a consolidated Wright speakership, and they launched personal attacks on him. Some Democrats chafed under his firm exercise of power. Members who were more closely aligned with other Democratic leaders had no particular reason to prefer Wright's leadership. Marginal supporters such as these would quickly jump ship if threatened politically by the Speaker's leadership. This is precisely what had happened to Speaker Cannon in 1910, and the voters had kicked the Republicans from power in 1912.

History records that Speaker Wright resigned in the summer of 1989 amid a House Ethics Committee investigation of some of his personal affairs. No one doubts that the charges against him were in part politically motivated; Gingrich has admitted it. In writing about his speakership in this book and in another recently published work, Speaker Wright has made it clear that he believes that the animus against him derived significantly from his role in the Iran-Contra investigation and the related Nicaraguan peace negotiations.[3] In his view, his opponents were driven more by concern over his use of the powers of his office for policy aims with which they disagreed than over any perceived abuse of office or violations of ethical principles.

Our task is not to sit in judgment of these matters, but instead to take Speaker Wright's point of view seriously. For it is our contention that Speaker Wright created his speakership. If his ultimate downfall is to be explained in terms of partisan opposition to his policy role, we must ask these questions: is there a limit to the capacity of the modern speakership to affect public policy through the use of the full powers of that office? And if so, did Wright find it?

In answer to these questions we may hazard the following observations. First, Speaker Wright might well have continued in the speakership (and the aggressive use of it) had he not been vulnerable (rightly or wrongly) on the ethics charges. His situation is not similar to Cannon's, whose power was undermined solely because of his use of it. Second, the kind of party governance to which Wright put the powers of his speakership is exactly the kind of thing that many reformers have long sought in the american political system. One knew who was responsible; it was Wright. Third, this suggests that Wright might have continued in his speakership for as long, and just as long, as he had solid support among his fellow Democrats. Fourth, the Democrats are likely to be unified only when the electoral needs of Democratic members are served by it. Yet this is unlikely to be commonly the case because of the character of the political system (with its geographically defined districts) and the character of the Democratic party (with its diverse constituencies). Witness the NAFTA vote. As a consequence, we may conclude that the use of the powers of the speakership to shape public policy must be episodic rather than consistent. The speakership as Wright created it could work for a period of time, but to have been lasting, Wright would have had to modify it, using its full powers more selectively. As Wright himself put it, "Striving for conciliation, I had reaped polarization." [4] Wright's successor, Speaker Foley, created a different speakership based on the more selective use of the powers of the office. Should it surprise us that some Democrats complained that he was sometimes not assertive enough?

Conclusion

On November 8, 1994, a tidal wave hit Washington, D.C. For the first time since the 1952 elections, the nation's voters sent a Republican majority to the U.S. House of Representatives. Washed away in the wake was Speaker Foley, who became the first sitting Speaker to lose a reelection bid since 1860. How will the Republicans run the House, and what sort of Republican speakership might emerge? The questions tantalize political scientists who have awaited for almost two generations for a new variable to control. They fascinate pundits, whose perspective on the House Republicans has been shaped by ideological propensities (both of the pundits and of the Republicans) rather than on their institutional habits. Yet the Republicans' management of the House will be shaped by both factors.

In Chapter 4 Pitney and Connelly speculate about a potential Republican speakership, a development that seemed improbable at best just a year ago. Elsewhere, I have considered what a Republican speakership might be like.[5] Pitney and Connelly conclude that the Republicans' long period in the minority would lead to a more equitable management of the House. I concluded that the Republicans' historical tendency was toward even more centralized party governance than the Democrats have demonstrated in recent years. Which path will Speaker Gingrich and his GOP majority take? The answer to this question cannot now be known, but some of the indicators can be identified. The Republicans, for example, have long complained that committee ratios were unfairly stacked against them. Will they now offer exact proportional representation to the Democrats on all committees? Republicans have been livid about the Democrats' use of restrictive rules to push bills through the House. Will the Republicans now rely on open rules more often? Republicans have often felt that House resources, such as committee staff, have not been equitably divided. Will they treat the Democrats better than the Democrats treated them? These choices will demonstrate the Republicans' true attitude toward partisan control of the House.

With respect to the speakership itself, Gingrich offers an intriguing combination of qualities. He has won the speakership through ideological commitment and vicious partisan attack. The nemesis of Democratic Speakers now sits in the Speaker's chair. Will the Democrats treat him as he treated them? Will Speaker Gingrich choose to confront the Clinton administration with his own legislative program, or will he seek compromise with the president? Will Gingrich be able to harness his Republican majority to pass legislation reflecting the ideological convictions of the conservative majority within the Republican conference in the House? Or will moderate Republicans hold the balance of power in a House that is still closely divided? And how will this Republican Speaker shape his personal relationship with a president to whom he is so strongly ideologically opposed?

Speaker Gingrich will have to take his bearings with one eye on his legislative majority and the other on the White House. As Speaker, he will discover what all of his predecessors have come to realize—that the speakership and the presidency are linked by forces that neither can wholly control.

The speakership is in many respects more finite than the presidency. The presidency is a highly personal office anchored in little but the president's electoral constituency and the press of events. The speakership, by contrast, is anchored in the institutional life of the House of Representatives. This feature of the speakership, that it is an office of institutional power—makes it more, but not completely, explicable. As it continues on its path through American history, we can be sure that it will continue to resemble in many ways the office as we find it today; but we can be just as sure that it will be in many ways different. In the future, other Speakers may write of their experience. We hope that many will, because their insights will be better than ours. When they do, we will understand the office as they describe it, as they have experienced it, and as they have shaped it. We will have in hand the categories that must be applied, but only they will have applied them. We will say then, just as we must say now, that this is the office of Speaker of the U.S. House of Representatives, and these are the persons who have served it. It is what they, and not we, have made it.

Notes

1. Speaker Cannon was defeated for reelection to the House in 1912 but was elected again in 1914 and served as a member until 1923. Rayburn was elected in 1912 and joined the House in 1913.

2. The culinary metaphor is borrowed from the rich vocabulary of Federalism. See Harold Seidman and Robert Gilmour, *Politics, Position and Power* (New York: Oxford University Press, 1986), 197.

3. Jim Wright, *Worth It All* (Washington, D.C.: Brassey's, 1993), x.

4. Ibid., 258.

5. Ronald M. Peters, Jr., *The American Speakership: The Office in Historical Perspective* (Baltimore: Johns Hopkins University Press, 1990), 290ff.

Index

Halberstam, David, 141
Halleck, Charles, 38n17, 65, 142, 187
Hamilton, Alexander, 63, 203
Hamilton, Lee, 167, 173, 234, 235
Hand, Lloyd, 227
Hansen, Julia Butler, 162, 189
Hansen Committee, 162-163, 166, 191
Hardeman, D. B., 141
Harkin, Tom, 213-214
Hebert, Edward, 199
Hefner, Bill, 92-93
Hollings, Ernest, 91
House of Representatives, U.S.: Albert's view of, 178, 200-201; competition within, 34-35; criticism of, 171-173; energy policy dispute, 166-169; ethics code, 169; leadership in, 29-30; pressures for change in, 158-159; reform years, 157, 213; impact of rules on, 53-54; Post Office scandal in, 76; southern representatives in, 179, 181-183; views of, 1-2; Wright's view of, 241-246. *See also* Speakers; Speakership
Hoyer, Steny, 30, 43
Humphrey, Hubert, 127

Inouye, Daniel, 235
Iran: hostage rescue in, 128-129
Iran-Contra scandal, 119, 129; Wright's view of, 233-238

Jefferson, Thomas, 115
Jenkins, Ed, 29, 235
Johnson, Lyndon B., 9, 126; foreign policy, 112
Jones, Jim, 93

Kennedy, John F., 10, 19, 140, 187; and the media, 141; as influence on O'Neill, 203, 206-207, 213
Kennedy, Ted, 215
Kennelly, Barbara, 43
Knowland, William, 125-126

LaFalce, John, 68
Latta, Delbert, 93
Leahy, Joe, 218
Lebanon: peace-keeping force in, 113-114, 255
LeBoutillier, John, 69, 83n41
Legislative Reorganization Act of 1970, 142, 162, 189-190
Lewis, John, 43
Loeffler, Tom, 235

Long, Gillis, 24
Longworth, Nicholas, 5, 64, 242
Lott, Trent, 70, 72
Lungren, Dan, 72

MacArthur, Douglas, 65
McCloskey, Frank, 71
McCormack, John, 19, 22, 32, 37n11, 65, 184, 185; Albert's view of, 187-189; and foreign policy, 112, 127; and the media, 141-142; as influence on O'Neill, 203, 208-209, 211, 213; during reform era, 160, 161, 164, 189
McFall, John, 26-27, 34, 166, 252
Machiavelli, Niccolò, 16
McIntyre, Rick, 71
Mack, John, 73
MacKay, Buddy, 97
McMillan, John, 163, 164, 182
Macon, Nathaniel, 4
Madden, Ray, 160
Madison, James, 63, 115
Mahon, George, 199
Mansfield, Mike, 143, 144, 195, 196
Margolies-Mezvinsky, Marjorie, 240
Marino, Ralph, 79
Martin, Dave, 165
Martin, John Bartlow, 145
Martin, Joseph W., Jr., 9, 10, 38n17, 65, 111, 139, 187; as Speaker, 64-65
Martin, Lynn, 75
Matthews, Chris, 149
Mayaguez incident, 134n48
Media. *See* News media
Michel, Robert, 10, 36, 61, 68, 71, 72-73, 74, 75, 76, 78, 228, 234, 236, 239, 245
Miller, George, 240
Mills, Wilbur, 163
Minow, Newton, 145
Mitchell, George, 244
Mitchell, Lee, 145
Moffett, Toby, 168
Mondale, Walter, 225
Monroney, A. S. Mike, 160
Mrazek, Robert, 83n41
Muhlenberg, Frederick A. C., 3
Mullen, Tommy, 206-207, 208
Multiple referrals, 41, 45, 169-170
Mutual Security Act of 1956, 111

NAFTA (North American Free Trade Agreement), 249
Nakasone, Yasuhiro, 229-230

Natcher, William, 61, 199

News media: Albert's relationship with, 143-146; McCormack's relationship with, 141-142; O'Neill's relationship with, 122, 124, 146-150; Rayburn's relationship with, 136-141; and Speakers, 12-13, 33, 49, 57-58, 121-125, 135-136, 153-155, 220, 248; Wright's relationship with, 122, 124, 150-152, 243

Nicaragua: U.S. involvement in, 73-74, 114, 119-120, 233-238

Nixon, Richard, 127-128, 140, 142, 144, 161; Albert's view of, 194-196; and Watergate scandal, 197, 198

North, Oliver, 234

North American Free Trade Agreement (NAFTA), 249

Obando y Bravo, Miguel, 120, 237

O'Brien, Tom, 180

O'Connor, John J., 22

O'Neill, Millie, 205

O'Neill, Thomas P., Sr., 203-205, 213

O'Neill, Thomas P. "Tip," Jr., 10, 12, 15, 19, 22, 24, 31-32, 162, 163, 166, 257; and budget process, 86, 87, 90-95, 249, 252; and Carter, 128-129, 214-215; Cheney's view of, 61-62; Curley as influence on, 205-206, 213; and ethics code, 169; father as influence on, 203-205; and foreign policy, 107, 112-114; Kennedy as influence on, 206-207, 213; leadership style, 32, 33, 35; McCormack as influence on, 208-209, 211, 213; and the media, 13, 122, 124, 146-150, 220; path to speakership, 212-213; Rayburn as influence on, 209-212, 213; relationship with House Republicans, 67-71; relationship with Reagan, 69, 72, 117, 215; on Rules Committee, 211-212; as Speaker, 10, 14, 27, 32, 83n41, 166-168, 174, 213-216, 254, 255, 258-259, 260

Ortega, Daniel, 120

PACS. See Political action committees

Palazzolo, Daniel, 249, 250, 252

Park, Tongsun, 26

Party leadership: patterns of succession, 18-28

Patman, Wright, 199, 200

Patterson, Jerry, 167

Peabody, Robert L., 6, 34, 251, 252, 256, 260

Penny, Tim, 78

Perkins, Carl, 199

Perot, H. Ross, 77

Persian Gulf war: Foley's position on, 115

Peters, Ronald M., Jr., 163, 171

Phillips, Kevin, 231

Pitney, John J., Jr., 9, 247, 252, 253, 262

Poage, Bill, 182, 199

Political action committees (PACs), 30

Polk, James K., 4

Presidents: relationships with Speakers, 115-117, 125-129

Prewitt, Kenneth, 25

Priest, Percy, 184

Randall, Samuel J., 4

Rayburn, Sam, 9, 18-19, 22, 32, 178; Albert's view of, 183, 185-186; relationship with Eisenhower, 111-112, 117, 125-126, 133n42; and foreign policy, 111-112; and the media, 136-141; as influence on O'Neill, 203, 209-212, 213; relationship with Republicans, 64; as Speaker, 5, 10, 13, 159, 174; Wright's view of, 222

Reagan, Ronald, 9, 32, 150; budget process under, 92-95, 97; foreign policy, 113-114, 129; and the media, 42; and O'Neill, 69-70, 72, 117, 215, 217

Reed, Thomas Brackett, 4, 107, 241

Republicans' relationship with Speaker, 61-63; during Foley's tenure, 75-77; before O'Neill, 63-67; conflict with O'Neill, 67-71; under Republican majority, 77-81; during Wright's tenure, 71-75, 238-241

Rhodes, John, 66, 67

Richards, James, 111

Richardson, Bill, 43

Robinson, John, 3

Rodino, Peter, 198, 234

Rohde, David, 29

Roosevelt, Franklin, 179

Rostenkowski, Dan, 11, 24, 37n11, 162, 229, 239

Rota, Robert, 76

Rules Committee, 45, 48, 186-187; O'Neill as member of, 211-212; as partisan issue, 68, 253

Rumsfeld, Donald, 161

Russo, Marty, 240

Sandinistas, 119-120

Senate: as viewed by the Speaker, 13-14

Shultz, George, 120, 230

Sinclair, Barbara, 28, 29, 135-136, 248,

251, 253
Sisk, B. F., 161
Smith, Howard W., 64, 186-187, 212
Smith, Steven, 247
Solomon, Gerald, 77-78
Sorenson, Ted, 198
Speakership: Albert's view of, 190, 200-
201; character of, 6-14; and committee system, 11-12, 41; Democratic era, 5; evolution of, 2-6; external influences on, 12-14;
feudal era, 4-5; framework for understanding, 14-17; future of, 36, 58-59, 77-81,
103, 262-264; leadership strategies, 8-9;
O'Neill's view of, 202-203; parliamentary
era, 3-4, 5; partisan era, 4, 5; impact of
partisanship on, 125-129, 252-254; and
party program, 10-11; paths to, 30-32,
251-252; powers of, 169-171, 192, 217-218,
221; in reform era, 159-166; impact of
Republican majority on, 59, 77-81, 175,
262-263; views of, 254-256
Speakers of the House: agenda-setting
role of, 55-58; average tenure of, 6-7, 18;
and budget process, 86-87, 103, 249-
250; floor leaders as, 19; assembling floor
majorities, 52-55; and foreign policy,
107-110, 117-121, 129-131, 247-248; goals
of, 15-16; and institutional change, 157-
158, 174-175, 250; leadership strategies, 46-
49; leadership styles, 32-33, 35-36; and
the legislative process, 42-46, 49-52, 251;
and the media, 12-13, 33, 49, 57-58,
121-125, 135-136, 153-155, 220, 248;
O'Neill's advice for, 216-221; as party
leaders, 40-41; relationships with presidents, 115-117, 125-129; responsibilities
of, 7-8, 41-42; succession patterns, 18-28,
33-34
Spivak, Lawrence, 136
Steering and Policy Committee, 44-45, 92
Stevenson, Andrew, 4
Stockman, David, 69, 93
Stokes, Louis, 234
Sununu, John, 99

Taft, Robert A., 126
Tapping, 23-25, 256

Tauke, Tom, 61
Teague, Olin, 163
Tobin, Maurice, 210
Trade deficit: Wright's view of, 227-230
Truman, Harry, 65, 194
Tunnermann, Carlos, 236
Twain, Mark, 242

Udall, Morris, 8, 37n11, 161, 168, 188

Vietnam War: Speakers' positions on,
112-113, 127, 212-213
Voorhis, Jerry, 195

Walker, Robert, 69, 70, 76, 148
Walsh, Lawrence E., 235
War Powers Act, 197
Washington, George, 3
Watergate scandal, 197-200
Watts, Mark, 247
Weber, Vin, 64, 69, 70-71
Whip, 38n20; importance of, 27-28; 1989
election for, 34-35; role of, 43-44
Whitten, Jamie, 61, 199
Wicker, Tom, 142
Wilson, Woodrow, 11, 180
Wright, Jim, 7, 12, 15, 19, 22, 27, 29, 31,
32, 39n32, 65, 167, 169, 210; on budget deficit, 224-227; and budget process, 86, 87,
95-97, 249, 250; and Central American issues, 72, 118-121, 235-238, 247; view of
Congress, 241-246; election as Speaker, 26-
27, 30, 34; ethics charges against, 74-75,
171; and foreign policy, 114; on Iran-Contra scandal, 233-238; and the media, 13,
122, 124, 150-152, 243; and multiple referrals, 170-171; relationship with Reagan,
72, 117; relationship with House Republicans, 71-75, 238-241; on social ineq-
uities, 230-233; as Speaker, 10, 52, 55-56,
58, 59, 254, 255, 259-262; on Speaker's
role, 222-223; on trade deficit, 227-230

Yates, Sidney, 61
Young, John, 227
Yuetter, Clayton, 228